Rampage Shootings and Gun Control

While the causes of rampage violence have been analysed thoroughly in diverse academic disciplines, we hardly know anything about the factors that affect their consequences for public policy. This book addresses rampage shootings in Western Europe and their conditional impact on politicization and policy change in the area of gun control.

The author sets out to unravel the factors that facilitate or impede the access of gun control to the political agenda in the wake of rampage shootings and analyses why some political debates lead to profound shifts of the policy status quo, while others peter out without any legislative reactions. In so doing, the book not only contributes to the theoretical literature on crisis-induced policy making, but also provides a wealth of case-study evidence on rampage shootings as empirical phenomena. In particular, the extent to which gun control gets politicized as a policy failure can either result from a bottom-up process (event severity and media pressure) or from a top-down logic (issue ownership and the electoral cycle). Including 12 case studies on the rampage shootings which have triggered a debate over the appropriateness of the affected countries' gun policies, it illustrates that the way political processes unfold after rampage shootings depends strongly on specific causal configurations and draws comparisons between the cases covered in the book and the way rampage shootings are typically dealt with in the United States.

This text will be of key interest to scholars and students of public policy, policy analysis, European Politics and more broadly of comparative politics, criminology, psychology, and sociology.

Steffen Hurka is a post-doctoral researcher at the Geschwister-Scholl-Institute of Political Science at the Ludwig-Maximilians-University Munich, Germany.

Routledge Research in Comparative Politics

61 Party Organization and Electoral Volatility in Central and Eastern Europe
Enhancing Voter Loyalty
Sergiu Gherghina

62 Politics of Religion and Nationalism
Federalism, Consociationalism and Seccession
Edited by Ferran Requejo and Klaus-Jürgen Nagel

63 Deficits and Debt in Industrialized Democracies
Edited by Gene Park and Eisaku Ide

64 Citizenship and Democracy in an Era of Crisis
Edited by Thomas Poguntke, Sigrid Roßteutscher, Rüdiger Schmitt-Beck and Sonja Zmerli

65 Drivers of Integration and Regionalism in Europe and Asia
Comparative Perspectives
Edited by Louis Brennan and Philomena Murray

66 Generations, Political Participation and Social Change in Western Europe
Maria T. Grasso

67 The Politics of Think Tanks in Europe
Jesper Dahl Kelstrup

68 The Statecraft of Consensus Democracies in a Turbulent World
A Comparative Study of Austria, Belgium, Luxembourg, the Netherlands and Switzerland
José M. Magone

69 Policy Change under New Democratic Capitalism
Edited by Hideko Magara

70 Rampage Shootings and Gun Control
Politicization and Policy Change in Western Europe
Steffen Hurka

71 Growth, Crisis, Democracy
The Political Economy of Social Coalitions and Policy Regime Change
Edited by Hideko Magara and Bruno Amable

Rampage Shootings and Gun Control

Politicization and Policy Change in Western Europe

Steffen Hurka

LONDON AND NEW YORK

First published 2017
by Routledge
2 Park Square, Milton Park, Abingdon, Oxon OX14 4RN

and by Routledge
711 Third Avenue, New York, NY 10017

Routledge is an imprint of the Taylor & Francis Group, an informa business

© 2017 Steffen Hurka

The right of Steffen Hurka to be identified as author of this work has been asserted by him in accordance with sections 77 and 78 of the Copyright, Designs and Patents Act 1988.

All rights reserved. No part of this book may be reprinted or reproduced or utilized in any form or by any electronic, mechanical, or other means, now known or hereafter invented, including photocopying and recording, or in any information storage or retrieval system, without permission in writing from the publishers.

Trademark notice: Product or corporate names may be trademarks or registered trademarks, and are used only for identification and explanation without intent to infringe.

British Library Cataloguing in Publication Data
A catalogue record for this book is available from the British Library

Library of Congress Cataloging in Publication Data
Names: Hurka, Steffen, author.
Title: Rampage shootings and gun control : politicization and policy change in Western Europe / Steffen Hurka.
Description: Abingdon, Oxon ; New York, NY : Routledge, 2017. | Series: Routledge research in comparative politics | Includes bibliographical references and index.
Identifiers: LCCN 2016055029| ISBN 9781138630437 (hardback) | ISBN 9781315209425 (ebook)Subjects: LCSH: Gun control–Europe, Western. | Violent crimes–Europe, Western.
Classification: LCC HV7439.E85 H87 2017 | DDC 363.33094–dc23
LC record available at https://lccn.loc.gov/2016055029

ISBN: 978-1-138-63043-7 (hbk)
ISBN: 978-1-315-20942-5 (ebk)

Typeset in Times New Roman
by Wearset Ltd, Boldon, Tyne and Wear

Printed and bound in Great Britain by
TJ International Ltd, Padstow, Cornwall

For my wife Tanja

Contents

Lists of figures	ix
List of tables	x
Acknowledgements	xi

1 Introduction   1

2 Rampage shootings, politicization and policy change   8

2.1 *Rampage shootings as potential focusing events 8*
2.2 *Conceptualizing politicization 11*
2.3 *Conceptualizing policy change 12*

3 The impact of focusing events on public policy   16

3.1 *Theoretical frameworks on the political process 17*
3.2 *The politics of gun policy 22*
3.3 *Typologies of crises and disasters 24*
3.4 *Rampage shootings in the academic literature 26*
3.5 *Beyond rampage shootings: findings on event-related policy change 31*
3.6 *Research gap and research promise 34*

4 Theorizing conditions for politicization, policy change and stability   41

4.1 *Theoretical expectations on the politicization of gun control 41*
4.2 *Theoretical expectations on policy change and stability 48*
4.3 *Summary of the theoretical expectations 55*

viii *Contents*

5 How to study the political impact of rampage shootings 59

5.1 *Scope conditions 59*
5.2 *Case identification procedure 63*
5.3 *Pool of cases and some background information 65*
5.4 *The methodology of (fs)QCA 67*
5.5 *QCA: a primer on terminology and technique 69*
5.6 *The varying applicability of QCA in the present research
      context 74*

6 Paths to the (non-)politicization of gun control 79

6.1 *Operationalization, measurement and descriptive
      information 80*
6.2 *Set calibration 82*
6.3 *Analysis of necessity 85*
6.4 *Analysis of sufficiency 92*
6.5 *Summary of the findings on politicization 103*

7 When laws bite the bullet (and when they do not) 108

7.1 *Great Britain 109*
7.2 *Germany 115*
7.3 *Finland 128*
7.4 *France 136*
7.5 *Austria 139*
7.6 *Switzerland 143*
7.7 *Belgium 147*
7.8 *Comparative assessment 151*

8 Conclusion 169

Appendix A: non-selected cases 177
Appendix B: robustness checks for the analysis of politicization 178
Index 183

Figures

4.1	Party positions on gun control	46
4.2	Summary of theoretical expectations	55
5.1	Media attention towards gun laws in Germany	63
6.1	Direct set calibrations	86
6.2	Summary of the findings on (non)-politicization	103

Tables

5.1	Overview of cases	66
5.2	Logic of necessity	70
5.3	Logic of sufficiency	71
6.1	Raw data matrix for the comparison of politicization patterns	82
6.2	Sets used in the fsQCA on politicization	85
6.3	Analysis of necessity: absence of politicization	87
6.4	Analysis of necessity: politicization	90
6.5	Analysis of necessity: disjunctions of individual conditions	91
6.6	Truth table: absence of politicization	93
6.7	Analysis of sufficiency: absence of politicization	96
6.8	Truth table: politicization	99
6.9	Analysis of sufficiency: politicization	100
7.1	Summary of the case studies	152
A.1	Non-selected cases	177
A.2	Results for varying 0.5-thresholds in the DEATH set	179
A.3	Results for varying 0.5-thresholds in the MEDIA set	180
A.4	Results for varying 0.5-thresholds in the GREEN set	181
A.5	Results for varying 0.5-thresholds in the ELECTIONS set	182

Acknowledgements

The completion of this book would not have been possible without the support of many people. First of all, I thank my parents for enabling me to study and pursue an academic career. Over my entire life, their unconditional support has kept me going and I cannot thank them enough for everything. The same applies to my wife Tanja, who endured my complaints and whining about the horrible job of writing a doctoral thesis with never-ending patience. Although both she and my parents have never read a single word I wrote ('why can't you just write it in German!'), they never turned a deaf ear to my concerns. It is impossible to put the importance of their support into words. I also thank my supervisor Professor Christoph Knill not only for his comments and ideas, but also for the excellent working environment he and the University of Konstanz have provided me with. Considering the difficult job market for political scientists, the working conditions I was able to enjoy may not be taken for granted. During the completion of this book, I was financed by the ERC Advanced Grant 'MORAPOL – Comparative Analysis of Moral Policy Change' (Grant No. 249388). In the project, I was lucky to have wonderful colleagues who gave me helpful and constructive input during the entire research process and I would like to thank them very much for that. I also thank the faculty at the University of Konstanz, in particular my other supervisors, Professor Breunig and Professor Leuffen for their useful comments on earlier drafts of this book. Another big 'Thank you' goes to the two reviewers of my book proposal for their positive assessments of the book project. Finally, I would like to thank the editorial staff at Routledge, in particular Andrew Taylor and Sophie Iddamalgoda, who did an outstanding job during the editing process.

Steffen Hurka
Munich, November 2016

1 Introduction

On 27 September 2001, Friedrich Leibacher entered the regional parliament of Zug (Switzerland) and opened fire on local politicians, killing 14 and wounding 14 others severely. While the rampage shooting sent shockwaves across Swiss society, it did not have any direct repercussions for the country's gun laws, despite the fact that the perpetrator had been a licensed gun owner. A few years later, on 11 May 2006, Hans van Themsche bought a rifle in the Belgian town Antwerp, left the store and shot a woman of Malian descent and her child to death on the street. As a result of the event, the Belgian gun laws immediately came under political scrutiny and were overhauled significantly within a short period of time. In both cases, the perpetrators had acquired their murder weapons by legal means. Yet, although both events signified very similar policy failures, their political processing could have hardly been more different. This book sets out to provide a better understanding of the conditions under which rampage shootings lead to the politicization of gun control and the factors that facilitate and obstruct the reform process. The motivation for this endeavour originates from several observations.

First, while the causes of rampage shootings have received considerable attention in the disciplines of psychology (e.g. Verlinden *et al.* 2000), criminology (e.g. Levin and Madfis 2009), and sociology (e.g. Harding *et al.* 2002), the political consequences of these events have hardly been analysed systematically from a comparative political science perspective. Given the fact that rampage shootings have resulted in very different policy responses over the course of the past decades, this scientific neglect appears quite surprising. While some countries instituted drastic restrictions on civilian gun ownership in the wake of rampage shootings, reform initiatives petered out without any political consequences in other cases. As Parker (2011: 8) notes:

> The precise relationship between mass shooting incidents and particular legal responses is far from clear. In many cases, these incidents have acted as a driver to strengthen gun laws, but because legislative responses are ultimately political, and thus negotiated, outcomes vary widely.

This variance in terms of political fallout represents a veritable research puzzle, which has not yet been addressed, despite its indisputable societal relevance.

2 Introduction

Thus, what is still lacking is a systematic comparative approach that is designed to identify the conditions under which rampage shootings become subject to politicization and lead to policy change. In the European context, some instructive case studies on the most devastating events have provided us with some valuable insights into the political dynamics that have followed individual massacres (e.g. Karp 2003; Peters and Watson 1996; Thomson *et al.* 1998). However, these case studies have invariably put the empirical focus on positive cases, i.e. cases with political consequences. As a result, the scarce knowledge we have to date is based on the most influential, and thereby hardly representative, cases.

Second, this latter argument is further aggravated by the overwhelming geographical focus of the remaining academic literature on the United States, and in particular on the school shooting at the Columbine High School of Littleton, Colorado (Altheide 2009; Birkland and Lawrence 2009; Fleming 2012; Haider-Markel and Joslyn 2001; Lawrence 2001; Lawrence and Birkland 2004). The problem caused by this narrow empirical focus is obvious. Based on the fact that the USA is an extreme outlier with regard to gun policy arrangements on many accounts, the findings that can be gained by studying this particular case can also hardly be generalized to a wider population of countries. The exceptional status of the US is not only based on its very special legal, cultural and institutional background, but also on the disproportional occurrence of severe rampage shootings in the country and a generally elevated problem pressure due to high homicide rates. Therefore, it is impossible to make more general statements on the political processing of rampage shootings solely based on empirical evidence from the United States. In order to arrive at such statements, it is imperative to employ a comparative research design that incorporates empirical evidence from a multitude of different institutional settings. This approach is clearly justified given the fact that while the United States suffers the most under repeated rampage violence, existing research demonstrates that mass shootings are anything but an exceptionally American phenomenon (Lankford 2016).

One of the reasons for the existence of the research gap lies in the difficulty to incorporate events like rampage shootings into a coherent theoretical framework of policy change due to their often-random occurrence. Given this difficult endeavour, it might often appear easier to conceptualize such events as 'random errors', which evade scientific consideration because of their unpredictability. Throughout this book, I argue that this is not the way we should approach the phenomenon of external shocks in general and rampage shootings in particular. Past studies have shown that potential focusing events can have substantial transformative power and that their occurrence can have dramatic consequences for public policies (Birkland 2006; Kingdon 1984). One rather recent example for such an event is the nuclear disaster which occurred in Fukushima (Japan) in 2011. The catastrophe led the German government to phase out the production of nuclear energy, whereas other countries showed no political reaction at all. Thus, even though the occurrence of such potential focusing events is more or

Introduction 3

less random, this does not mean that the political reactions they evoke are random as well. Instead, it seems sensible to suspect that the way potential focusing events are processed and ultimately cause (or do not cause) policy change depends on the configurations and interplay of different contextual conditions. The acquisition of a better understanding of the mechanisms linking an event to the politicization of its implied policy failure to actual reforms is one of the continuing challenges of policy change research. However, the puzzle of why similar events lead to very different political outcomes is not only relevant from an academic point of view. It is also a matter that regularly pops up in the public debate and therefore bears substantial societal relevance. As Schildkraut and Cox Hernandez (2014: 371) note, 'understanding how legislatures respond to incidents of mass shootings, both on and off school campuses, is important in the continual understanding of how people perceive and understand these random acts of violence'.

Building on these considerations, this book pursues an empirical, a theoretical and a methodological objective: First, as the first systematic and internationally comparative analysis of the political processing of rampage shootings, the book assembles a wealth of empirical evidence on 17 events which have occurred in different geographical and temporal settings. So far, no study has gone beyond an analysis of more than two cases and therefore, the envisioned contribution of data is unique and hopefully helpful for future studies on crisis-induced policy change. Second, with regard to its theoretical aspirations, the book seeks to contribute to a better understanding of how political systems process potential focusing events politically. Existing theoretical frameworks handle these types of events quite differently and fail to come up with convincing causal mechanisms which can explain why some shocks are taken up by a political system and why others are not. Accordingly, the book analyses the relevance of several conditions that have the potential to serve as causal links between a focusing event, the politicization of the implied policy failure and the occurrence of policy change. The core argument of the book is that those conditions do not function in isolation from one another and that both politicization and policy change can result from different causal paths. In contrast to many other empirical applications in the social sciences, however, this book does not treat such patterns of equifinality as a fundamental obstacle complicating the acquisition of scientific knowledge, but as an empirical reality, which should be taken seriously. A good and systematic inquiry into equifinal processes enables more precise statements about the world than overly simplified models which sacrifice precision for parsimony by default. Based on this argument, the final contribution of the book is a methodological one. Specifically, the study seeks to explore the suitability of fuzzy set Qualitative Comparative Analysis (fsQCA) (Ragin 1987, 2000; Schneider and Wagemann 2012) for the analysis of the political processes unfolding after potential focusing events. Unlike most QCA applications, the book defines individual events, instead of countries, as the unit of analysis and examines their variant political impacts in a comparative manner. The book shows that while fsQCA is a very

4 *Introduction*

useful methodological tool if the theoretical concepts under examination can be translated convincingly into set-theoretic language, the application of the method is more difficult if we cannot rely on solid, quantitative data in order to calibrate the required sets. Consequently, the book combines fsQCA with comparative case studies in order to answer two research questions: First, why do some rampage shootings immediately lead to controversial political debates over the affected country's gun control arrangements, while other rampage shootings are completely ignored by policy makers? Second, why do some events that get politicized lead to rapid policy reforms, while the momentum for policy change fades quickly in other instances? Building on the scarce literature available, the book develops a set of theoretical expectations on the factors driving both politicization and policy change after potential focusing events in general and rampage shootings in particular. While the research puzzle on varying patterns of politicization is addressed by the use of fsQCA, the second research puzzle on policy change is addressed by 12 case studies on the politicized events in order to identify the combinations of factors that facilitate or impede the reform process.

At this point, it should be emphasized that the book does not seek to resolve the debate on the effectiveness of gun control measures in preventing crime committed with firearms. The debate on this issue is led by both sides with strong convictions (e.g. Donohue and Ayres 2009; Lott 2003, 2010) and I will not take sides here. Changes in gun control measures are outcomes the study seeks to explain, not the independent variable. Finally, it is essential to clarify that the book is not about policy change in the firearm policy subsystem in general. This would require a theoretical and empirical approach that is fundamentally different from the one adopted by this book. Instead, the book is about the political reactions towards a specific type of potential focusing event and the comparative analysis of the political reactions evoked by these empirical phenomena for a specific policy area. Accordingly, the book takes the shootings as a given and analyses their outcomes in terms of ensuing politicization dynamics and policy change in the area of gun control in a comparative manner. This is a direct consequence from choosing shootings as cases and not countries or governments. In other words, nothing in the book suggests that countries cannot change their gun policies in the absence of a rampage shooting. In fact, there are examples of countries which have changed their firearm regimes in response to international agreements, like the European Union's Firearm Directive.[1] Other than that, however, firearm-related policy change rarely occurs without an external stimulus, and this stimulus often comes in the form of a rampage shooting.

The book is structured as follows: Chapter 2 delineates the key concepts used throughout the book. This concerns the definition of rampage shootings as instances of potential focusing events, a specification of how this book conceives of politicization, and a conceptualization of the ambiguous term policy change. After those conceptual clarifications, the current state of the art in policy change research is discussed in Chapter 3 with a particular emphasis on the role of

Introduction 5

potential focusing events as catalysts for policy change dynamics. This is accomplished in two parts. In the first part, the central theoretical frameworks that have been put forward over the past decades are addressed and put into perspective concerning the research question. The second part presents the most relevant empirical studies available, elucidates their relative strengths and weaknesses and distils their implications for the present inquiry. Chapter 4 develops a set of theoretical expectations on the causal mechanisms which potentially constitute empirical linkages between the occurrence of a rampage shooting, the subsequent politicization of gun control, policy change and stability. Those theoretical expectations structure the empirical section of the book. Chapter 5 first presents the rationale behind the case selection, then defines scope conditions and provides some descriptive information on the resulting pool of cases. In addition, this chapter contains a brief introduction to the terminology and epistemology of (fs)QCA, which will function as the method of comparison in the first section of the empirical analysis on politicization. Chapter 6 presents the results of the fsQCA on the causal paths that link the occurrence of a rampage shooting to the politicization of gun control. Based on the findings for the first research question, Chapter 7 presents case studies on the 12 cases that led to the politicization of gun control in order to address the second research puzzle on policy change. The empirical analyses yield a range of intriguing new insights into the political processing of rampage shootings. In a nutshell, the first analysis demonstrates that the politicization of gun control after a rampage shooting can result from two equifinal processes. If the gun control issue is represented by a partisan cleavage in the affected country's party system, the party that owns the issue will try to provoke a political debate. However, it will be demonstrated that, contrary to conventional wisdom, this only holds true if elections are *not* imminent. If elections are close, even political actors who have a reputation of favouring policy change will be cautious to try and exploit the crisis politically. The other path towards politicization results from a conjunction of high event severity and high media attention. If an event is severe in objective terms and simultaneously portrayed as such by the media, policy makers cannot escape a political debate over gun control, regardless of the proximity of elections and the cleavage structure of the party system. As far as the second research question on policy change is concerned, the case studies demonstrate that a multitude of factors can obstruct and facilitate the reform process, depending on their configuration. In particular, the empirical evidence demonstrates that in order to arrive at a good understanding of the various political processes triggered by rampage shootings, we must evaluate the role of political and societal actors in their special institutional environment. Specifically, it is found that while both political and socio-cultural institutions can facilitate and impede policy change dynamics after rampage shootings based on their configuration, the extent to which reform opponents act as a cohesive group and varying levels of societal mobilization critically qualify the influence of these institutional factors. Accordingly, policy change and stability after rampage shootings results from the complex interplay of both structural factors and more proximate and

6 Introduction

time-variant conditions. In the concluding chapter of the book, I discuss the broader theoretical implications of those findings for research on the progress of public policies in general and identify a range of pathways for future research in the field.

Note

1 Council Directive 91/477/EEC of 18 June 1991 on control of the acquisition and possession of weapons.

References

Altheide, D. L. (2009). The Columbine Shootings and the Discourse of Fear. *American Behavioral Scientist* 52(10), 1354–1370.

Birkland, T. A. (2006). *Lessons of Disaster: Policy Change after Catastrophic Events.* Washington, D.C.: Georgetown University Press.

Birkland, T. A. and Lawrence, R. G. (2009). Media Framing and Policy Change After Columbine. *American Behavioral Scientist* 52(10), 1405–1425.

Donohue, J. and Ayres, I. (2009). More Guns, Less Crime Fails Again: The Latest Evidence from 1977–2006. *Econ Journal Watch* 6(2), 218–238.

Fleming, A. K. (2012). *Gun Policy in the United States and Canada: The Impact of Mass Murders and Assassinations on Gun Policy.* New York: Continuum International Publishing Group.

Haider-Markel, D. P. and Joslyn, M. R. (2001). Gun Policy, Opinion, Tragedy, and Blame Attribution: The Conditional Influence of Issue Frames. *Journal of Politics* 63(2), 520–543.

Harding, D. J., Fox, C. and Mehta, J. D. (2002). Studying Rare Events Through Qualitative Case Studies: Lessons from a Study of Rampage School Shootings. *Sociological Methods & Research* 31(2), 174–217.

Karp, A. (2003). Dunblane and the International Politics of Gun Control. In S. S. Nagel (ed.), *Policymaking and Peace – A Multinational Anthology* (pp. 193–211). Lanham: Lexington Books.

Kingdon, J. W. (1984). *Agendas, Alternatives, and Public Policies.* Boston: Little, Brown.

Lankford, A. (2016). Public Mass Shooters and Firearms: A Cross-National Study of 171 Countries. *Violence and Victims* 31(2), 187–199.

Lawrence, R. G. (2001). Defining Events: Problem Definition in the Media Arena. In R. P. Hart and B. Sparrow (eds), *Politics, Discourse, and American Society: New Agendas* (pp. 91–110). New York: Rowman & Littlefield.

Lawrence, R. G. and Birkland, T. A. (2004). Guns, Hollywood, and School Safety: Defining the School-Shooting Problem Across Public Arenas. *Social Science Quarterly* 85(5), 1193–1207.

Levin, J. and Madfis, E. (2009). Mass Murder at School and Cumulative Strain: A Sequential Model. *American Behavioral Scientist* 52(9), 1227–1245.

Lott, J. R. (2003). *The Bias Against Guns: Why Almost Everything You've Heard About Gun Control is Wrong.* Washington, D.C.: Regnery.

Lott, J. R. (2010). *More Guns, Less Crime – Understanding Crime and Gun Control Laws* (3rd edn). Chicago: University of Chicago Press.

Parker, S. (2011). Balancing Act: Regulation of Civilian Firearm Possession. In Small Arms Survey (ed.), *Small Arms Survey 2011: States of Security*. Cambridge: Cambridge University Press.

Peters, R. and Watson, C. (1996). A Breakthrough in Gun Control in Australia after the Port Arthur Massacre. *Injury Prevention* 2(4), 253–254.

Ragin, C. C. (1987). *The Comparative Method: Moving Beyond Qualitative and Quantitative Strategies*. Berkeley: University of California Press.

Ragin, C. C. (2000). *Fuzzy-Set Social Science*. Chicago: University of Chicago Press.

Schildkraut, J. and Cox Hernandez, T. (2014). Laws that Bit the Bullet: A Review of Legislative Responses to School Shootings. *American Journal of Criminal Justice* 39(2), 358–374.

Schneider, C. Q. and Wagemann, C. (2012). *Set-Theoretic Methods for the Social Sciences: A Guide to Qualitative Comparative Analysis*. Cambridge: Cambridge University Press.

Thomson, S., Stancich, L. and Dickson, L. (1998). Gun Control and Snowdrop. *Parliamentary Affairs* 51(3), 329–344.

Verlinden, S., Hersen, M. and Thomas, J. (2000). Risk Factors in School Shootings. *Clinical Psychology Review* 20(1), 3–56.

2 Rampage shootings, politicization and policy change

The provision of clearly specified concepts is a critically important task that strongly determines the quality and rigor of any research project (Sartori 1970). Moreover, the precision by which the central concepts are specified crucially determines the connectivity of the study to the overall stock of knowledge. This is particularly true for the social sciences where conceptual meanings are often contested and blurry. Therefore, in order to be clear about the scope and precise nature of the analytical inquiry, it is essential to clarify what exactly this book is about. Accordingly, this chapter has three objectives. First, it clarifies the term rampage shooting and conceptualizes this class of events as empirical instances of potential focusing events. Second, the chapter specifies the way politicization is used as an analytical concept and distinguishes its meaning from the concept of (governmental) agenda setting. Finally, the chapter introduces the concept of policy change and spells out the attributes that give the concept meaning.

2.1 Rampage shootings as potential focusing events

The public policy literature is not short of conceptualizations that try to grasp events whose occurrence is beyond the control of political actors. While the important role of such events is generally uncontested within the discipline, there is no agreement on a common terminology. Instead, public policy scholars have coined different terms like focusing events (Birkland 1997; Kingdon 1984), external events or perturbations (Sabatier 1988; Sabatier and Jenkins-Smith 1993), or critical junctures (Pierson 2000). Nohrstedt and Weible (2010: 5) correctly argue that this diverse vocabulary is one source of the lack of systematic knowledge on the political consequences of such events and suggest that it might be beneficial to distinguish the terms with regard to the extent to which they imply a political or societal reaction. More specifically, they argue that the terms critical juncture and focusing event imply a certain increase in political attention, while external shocks, events and perturbations merely capture the impetus, but do not necessarily imply a political reaction. On first sight, this argumentation appears reasonable and suggests that for the present inquiry, the latter three concepts would generally appear more useful, since variant increases in political

Conceptual clarifications 9

attention are an outcome the study seeks to explain and should therefore not be included in the definition of the unit of analysis.

However, the way scholars of the Advocacy Coalition Framework (ACF) have defined external events (or perturbations) is not compatible with the way this book conceives of external stimuli for political action. According to the ACF, external (system) events include changes in socio-economic conditions, changes in public opinion, changes in the systemic governing coalition, and policy decisions and impacts from other subsystems (Sabatier 1998: 102). Within the ACF, such external events have been identified as very important drivers of major policy change (Sabatier 1988: 148). However, the broad political developments which fall under the category of an external event are not exogenously given, but represent possible results of previous triggering events. For example, an event can lead to changes in socio-economic conditions (e.g. the financial crisis), or to changes in public opinion (e.g. the Fukushima catastrophe and the German take on nuclear energy), or to changes in the systemic governing coalition (see Boin *et al.* (2009) for a plethora of examples). Thus, what Sabatier described as an external event in the original conception of the ACF is the process by which the political system reacts to the event, not so much the event itself. In a revision of the ACF, Sabatier and Weible therefore added the concept of 'internal shocks' to the framework's vocabulary (Sabatier and Weible 2007: 204). Internal shocks originate within the policy subsystem and are conceptually very close to focusing events. Such shocks are argued to 'confirm policy core beliefs in the minority advocacy coalition(s) and increase doubt within the dominant coalition' (Sabatier and Weible 2007: 205).[1] Sabatier and Weible suggest that both external and internal shocks 'redistribute critical political resources' (Sabatier and Weible 2007: 204), but that the difference between the two types of shocks is that 'an internal shock directly questions policy core beliefs of the dominant coalition, while the relevance of those beliefs is less clear in the case of an external shock' (Sabatier and Weible 2007: 205). Despite these conceptual improvements, however, I consider Birkland's concept of 'potential focusing events' most useful in order to classify the types of events this book deals with. According to Birkland (1997: 22), a potential focusing event can be defined as

> an event that is sudden, relatively rare, can be reasonably defined as harmful or revealing the possibility of potentially greater future harms, inflicts harms or suggests potential harms that are or could be concentrated on a definable geographical area or community of interest, and that is known to policy makers and the public virtually simultaneously.

This definition is broad enough to cover different types of events, but it is also narrow enough not to cover anything that happens. Most importantly, however, the term does not imply a political reaction and thereby turns our attention to the fact that similar events can have dramatically different consequences. In this context, the adjective 'potential' is critically important, as it opens the possibility

10   *Conceptual clarifications*

that events which share many important characteristics can focus attention on an implied policy failure in one context and be ignored in another. Therefore, the book will refer to rampage shootings as potential focusing events before politicization and as focusing events when the political debate has started. Yet, which characteristics does an event have to combine in order to qualify as a rampage shooting?

Much of the criminological and psychological literature on homicidal behaviour deals with school shootings as one very particular sub-type of rampage shootings (Muschert 2007). This book does not narrow the focus down to school shootings, but also considers multiple-victim shootings which occur outside educational institutions. This is mainly because also those latter events have led to intense societal debates on the national approach towards guns.[2] Accordingly, by their suddenness, harmfulness and rarity, all rampage shootings imply the potential to impact upon the political discourse and lead to policy change. According to Newman *et al.* (2004: 14f.), rampage shootings are defined

> by the fact that they involve attacks on multiple parties, selected almost at random. The shooters may have a specific target to begin with, but they let loose with a fusillade that hits others, and it is not unusual for the perpetrator to be unaware of who has been shot until long after the fact. These explosions are attacks on whole institutions – schools, teenage pecking orders, or communities.

This definition appears useful for the purposes of this book, although some parts of it are less important than others. For example, the requirement of an almost random selection of victims is probably very meaningful for a psychological inquiry, but rather unimportant for this exercise in political science. Whether or not the victims are selected at random or on purpose arguably does not make a major difference for the identification of a policy failure. The latter part of the definition is more important for our purpose, as it spells out the public dimension of rampage shootings and accordingly, their potential for political conflict. Since rampage shootings are generally conceived of as acts that threaten public security, they automatically generate a sense of vulnerability among the overall population and thereby create incentives for 'crisis exploitation' (Boin *et al.* 2009).

In addition to these considerations, Newman's definition must be enhanced with some more detail in order to render it useful for the present inquiry. While the manner by which the victims are selected is arguably of lesser importance for the political treatment of a rampage shooting, the way the perpetrator had obtained his weapons should critically determine the event's potential for politicization. In order to make sure that this potential for politicization is held constant across all cases, the legality of the used firearm(s) is introduced as an additional attribute of rampage shootings. Specifically, the rampage shooting must have been carried out with a firearm acquired by legal means either by the perpetrator himself[3] or by people in his immediate environment. This definition

Conceptual clarifications 11

excludes events that were carried out exclusively with firearms acquired on the black market, because such events can hardly be framed as instances of a policy failure relating to the regulation of civilian gun possession, but are typically conceived of as a matter of law enforcement. It is not essential that the perpetrator has obtained the weapon himself, but at least somebody in his direct social environment must have granted him easy access to the gun, either on purpose or by accident. Such events can reasonably be portrayed as results of dysfunctional firearm regulations and are therefore relevant for the analysis.

In addition to this requirement of a legally acquired firearm as the murder weapon, the empirical inquiry further only considers rampage shootings that have occurred in public areas or public buildings and have resulted in at least two fatalities (excluding the perpetrator). Those scope conditions will be discussed in some greater detail in Chapter 5, but it should be pointed out here that while the former attribute makes sure that the event has a public dimension (and therefore signifies a public problem), the latter qualification primarily rests on research pragmatic grounds. To sum up, this book is *concerned with events in which a perpetrator makes use of one or several legally acquired firearms in order to inflict physical harm on a group of people either in a public area or a public building, resulting in at least two fatalities (excluding the perpetrator).* Such events can be understood as potential focusing events and accordingly, the study should be read as a contribution to this line of inquiry.

2.2 Conceptualizing politicization

One central goal of this book is to explain the varying extents to which rampage shootings become subject to efforts of politicization. Why do some sufficiently similar events function as an impetus for political actors to highlight a certain policy failure and suggest a corresponding policy solution, while other events are simply ignored? In order to address this first research question of the book analytically, it is essential to first clearly specify the concept of politicization, and additionally distinguish it as precisely as possible from the concept of governmental agenda setting.

The essence of the politicization concept has been captured neatly by Brändström and Kuipers (2003: 280f.):

> Actors that struggle to 'name' failures and assign blame set in motion a 'politicization process'. Actions and events in public policy become politicized when influential actors in the political arena succeed in framing them as blameworthy violations of crucial public values.

Thus, politicization occurs if one or several important political actors challenge the status quo in a given policy area by highlighting a deficiency in the existing policy arrangements. Yet, while the mere identification of an undesirable social condition by political actors is one necessary component of politicization, the concept entails a second component: the suggestion of a policy solution that can

12 *Conceptual clarifications*

help to remedy the policy failure. Very often, actors from across the political spectrum agree that a certain condition is undesirable, but this does not necessarily imply the emergence of a political conflict. In the context of the present inquiry, most political actors typically agree that the perpetrator should not have been able to acquire his weapons and in general, it is hard to deny that a policy failure has occurred. If all actors draw the same lesson from the event, namely that it was an unfortunate and isolated incident that cannot be prevented by any means, politicization does not occur despite the broad agreement that the policy has failed. However, if one group of actors puts forward a policy solution that is supposed to help to prevent similar events in the future, we have a political conflict and politicization has occurred.

Thus, it is important to distinguish the politicization process from the setting of the governmental agenda. As the considerations above suggest, the politicization of policy failures is clearly not a prerogative of governments. On the contrary, all political actors participate in the process of 'meaning-making'. Accordingly, the question of whether or not a rampage shooting leads to a national political debate over gun control cannot be fully controlled by those actors in power. While the further political processing of the event in terms of real legislative change is of course critically determined by the responsiveness of governments, the initial spark that ignites the political search for meaning can come from various sources and the book follows the goal of identifying those sources and their interaction.

2.3 Conceptualizing policy change

A few clarifying paragraphs are also necessary in order to specify the concept of policy change as it is used in this book. As Capano (2009: 14) notes:

> It really makes a substantial difference if policy change is defined in terms of the transformation of the definition of the issues in question, or as the structure and content of the policy agenda, or in terms of the content of the policy program, or as the outcome of implementation of policy.

This book is interested in the third type of policy change Capano mentions: the extent to which countries adapt their firearm policies in the wake of rampage shootings. This refers exclusively to regulatory changes expressed in legally binding laws and regulations (Knill *et al.* 2012).[4] Accordingly, policy change has occurred whenever a country alters the legal framework for gun ownership as a direct response to a rampage shooting.

Another peculiarity of the concept policy change as it is used in this study should be made explicit. The neutral term 'change' does not imply any direct information about the direction of this change. Theoretically, change can imply either a shift towards a more permissive design of an existing regulation or a shift towards a more restrictive policy. However, with regard to changes in firearm policies after rampage shootings, the former type of change is extremely

Conceptual clarifications 13

unlikely in most parts of the world. It seems relatively safe to say that the US is the only country in the world in which more permissive gun laws are seriously debated as a viable response to gun violence (Lott 2010; Spitzer 2012). In the rest of the world, such extreme positions are empirically simply not relevant and the political conflict after rampage shootings typically unfolds between advocates of the status quo and advocates of a more restrictive approach towards guns (Hurka and Nebel 2013). With regard to the regulation of private gun ownership, moves towards liberalization have been almost entirely absent in the past decades around the globe and a clear pattern of convergence towards a prohibitive model can be identified (Hurka 2015). Accordingly, in the context of this study, the term policy change should be understood as a concept which implies an increase in the intensity and strictness of existing regulations, and not as a concept which implies the weakening of existing regulatory arrangements. As outlined above, the latter is empirically not relevant outside of the United States and therefore, the direction of policy change is not of further analytical interest here. However, its speed and scope will be scrutinized comparatively.

In order to make sure that the policy changes can clearly be attributed to a rampage shooting, the focus is put on policy changes that occur in the short run. For the purposes of this book, it is therefore considered useful to conceptualize policy change as a change of the existing laws and regulations concerning firearms within the first year after a rampage shooting. In the English language, such types of policy change are often pejoratively labelled as 'knee-jerk legislation', a term that implies the connotation of an unconscious and emotional ad-hoc policy response to some external stimulus.[5] In all of the instances of policy change discussed in this book, the link between the occurrence of the event and the political reaction is direct and the reader will find that the instances in which policy change occurred can clearly be traced back to the occurrence of the rampage shooting. Thus, while the possibility that change may have occurred without the respective event can never be ruled out completely, it is arguably very low for the events scrutinized in this book. Throughout the book, we will find that pressure for policy change sometimes accumulates over longer periods of time and the occurrence of a focusing event serves as a catalyst for rapid policy change to occur. To sum up, for the purposes of this book, policy change is conceptualized as *the intensification of existing laws and regulations on firearms within one year after the occurrence of a rampage shooting.*

Notes

1 This hypothesis clearly bears relevance within the scope of this inquiry and is related to arguments on the cohesiveness of status quo coalition in the wake of rampage shootings (Hurka and Nebel 2013). The line of argumentation will be taken up in section 4.2.3.
2 The events in Mauterndorf (Austria, 1997), Zug (Switzerland 2001) and Nanterre (France 2002) are cases in point. Consult Chapter 7 for more information on these cases.

14 *Conceptual clarifications*

3 Whenever I refer to perpetrators in this book, I do so in the male form. This is not meant in any discriminatory way, but simply reflects the fact that rampage shootings are usually perpetrated by men (Lankford 2013). In fact, of all the cases discussed in this book, only one was committed by a woman (the shooting in Lörrach, Germany, 2010).
4 As an additional restriction, I refer to policy change and stability only on the *national level*. In some countries, like the US and Australia, sub-national entities enjoy enormous leverage with regard to their approach to regulate guns. For this reason, those countries are not included in the analysis (for a more detailed discussion of this scope condition, see section 5.1.2).
5 In the German language, the term 'Anlassgesetzgebung' better captures the essence of the concept, as it clearly refers to a triggering event as the cause of the policy change. However, it carries the same negative connotation as the term 'knee-jerk legislation'.

References

Birkland, T. A. (1997). *After Disaster – Agenda Setting, Public Policy, and Focusing Events*. Washington, D.C.: Georgetown University Press.

Boin, A., 't Hart, P. and McConnell, A. (2009). Crisis Exploitation: Political and Policy Impacts of Framing Contests. *Journal of European Public Policy* 16(1), 81–106.

Brändström, A. and Kuipers, S. (2003). From 'Normal Incidents' to Political Crises: Understanding the Selective Politicization of Policy Failures. *Government and Opposition* 38(3), 279–305.

Capano, G. (2009). Understanding Policy Change as an Epistemological and Theoretical Problem. *Journal of Comparative Policy Analysis: Research and Practice* 11(1), 7–31.

Hurka, S. (2015). Handguns: On Target towards Authority? In C. Knill, C. Adam and S. Hurka (eds), *On the Road to Permissiveness? Change and Convergence of Moral Regulation in Europe*. Oxford: Oxford University Press.

Hurka, S. and Nebel, K. (2013). Framing and Policy Change after Shooting Rampages: A Comparative Analysis of Discourse Networks. *Journal of European Public Policy* 20(3), 390–406.

Kingdon, J. W. (1984). *Agendas, Alternatives, and Public Policies*. Boston: Little, Brown.

Knill, C., Schulze, K. and Tosun, J. (2012). Regulatory Policy Outputs and Impacts: Exploring a Complex Relationship. *Regulation & Governance* 6(4), 427–444.

Lankford, A. (2013). A Comparative Analysis of Suicide Terrorists and Rampage, Workplace, and School Shooters in the United States From 1990 to 2010. *Homicide Studies* 17(3), 255–274.

Lott, J. R. (2010). *More Guns, Less Crime – Understanding Crime and Gun Control Laws* (3rd edn). Chicago: University of Chicago Press.

Muschert, G. W. (2007). Research in School Shootings. *Sociology Compass* 1(1), 60–80.

Newman, K., Fox, C., Harding, D. J., Mehta, J. D. and Roth, W. (2004). *Rampage: The Social Roots of School Shootings*. New York: Basic Books.

Nohrstedt, D. and Weible, C. M. (2010). The Logic of Policy Change after Crisis: Proximity and Subsystem Interaction. *Risk, Hazards & Crisis in Public Policy* 1(2), 1–32.

Pierson, P. (2000). Increasing Returns, Path Dependence, and the Study of Politics. *The American Political Science Review* 94(2), 251–267.

Sabatier, P. A. (1988). An Advocacy Coalition Framework of Policy Change and the Role of Policy-Oriented Learning Therein. *Policy Sciences* 21(2–3), 129–168.

Sabatier, P. A. (1998). The Advocacy Coalition Framework: Revisions and Relevance for Europe. *Journal of European Public Policy* 5(1), 98–130.

Sabatier, P. A. and Jenkins-Smith, H. C. (1993). *Policy Change and Learning: An Advocacy Coalition Approach*. Boulder, CO: Westview Press.

Sabatier, P. A. and Weible, C. M. (2007). The Advocacy Coalition Framework: Innovations and Clarifications. In P. A. Sabatier (ed.), *Theories of the Policy Process* (2nd edn, pp. 189–220). Boulder, CO: Westview Press.

Sartori, G. (1970). Concept Misformation in Comparative Politics. *The American Political Science Review* 64(4), 1033–1053.

Spitzer, R. J. (2012). *The Politics of Gun Control* (5th edn). Boulder, CO: Paradigm.

3 The impact of focusing events on public policy

This chapter provides an overview of the existing theoretical and empirical literature relevant for this study. It proceeds from an overview of the theoretical literature to concrete empirical applications and is divided into three parts. The first part reviews the most relevant theoretical literature. In so doing, the section discusses the promises and pitfalls of the major existing theoretical frameworks on the political process. Building on a brief introduction to incrementalism as the 'baseline model of politics', this review includes a discussion of the multiple streams approach (Kingdon 1984), the garbage can model (Cohen *et al.* 1972), Birkland's (2006) model of event-related policy change, and the punctuated equilibrium framework (Baumgartner and Jones 1993). The discussion puts a particular focus on the distinct ways those frameworks conceptualize and model the policy impact of potential focusing events.

In the second part of the chapter, the reader is introduced to the politics of gun policy and existing typologies of crises and disasters. The discussion reveals that while the characteristics of the gun issue should lead us to expect high levels of political conflict after potential focusing events, a purely deductive approach to the comparative study of those phenomena is complicated by the ambiguity of existing crisis typologies. Accordingly, an inductive approach is found to be the more promising path to the comparative analysis of potential focusing events.

In the third part of the chapter, the reader is introduced to the existing empirical literature on rampage shootings and similar events. The section has several purposes. First, it familiarizes the reader with the literature on the causes of rampage shootings in order to illustrate the fact that the phenomenon is complex and offers political actors the possibility of framing the event in their favour. Second, this part of the chapter reveals that while a plethora of factors contribute to the occurrence of rampage shootings, none of them is by itself sufficient (e.g. consumption of violent media content, social rejection, etc.). In addition, none of those factors taken alone is necessary for the occurrence of a rampage shooting, with one major exception: the easy availability of firearms. In other words, the perpetrators' comparably easy (and often legal) access to guns is a central constitutive element of rampage shootings. Given this observation, a comparative evaluation of the variant political consequences of those events in the area of gun control is argued to be in order. However, as the empirical literature on the

Focusing events and public policy 17

political consequences of rampage shootings demonstrates, this strand of literature has not yielded any systematic results, yet. In fact, by far the most extensive literature on the consequences of rampage shootings has developed in the areas of communication and sociology. While patterns of media attention and framing are the main dependent variables in the former discipline, the impact of the events on local communities are at the centre of attention in the latter. Only few studies have actually dealt with rampage shootings as an empirical phenomenon from a political science perspective and the few studies that do hardly ever adopt a comparative approach. Moreover, they focus exclusively on the United States, which implies the problem that their findings cannot be generalized to a broader population of countries. Thus, while the literature on the causes and consequences helps to justify the empirical focus of the book, it does not yield any good starting points for theory building. Therefore, the focus on the third part of the empirical literature review is put on the body of literature that deals with the policy impacts of other types of potential focusing events. This review demonstrates, in a nutshell, that the extent to which an event hits on an existing partisan cleavage should be critically important for the explanation of politicization processes. Moreover, existing studies have identified variables such as the proximity of elections, the relative severity of the event and efforts of societal mobilization as important variables which come into play in post-crisis policy making.

3.1 Theoretical frameworks on the political process

In order to get a sense of how political science has been trying to describe and analyse patterns of politicization and policy change, this section introduces the major theoretical frameworks on those questions. While there have been several attempts to explain why policies sometimes change dramatically within a short period of time, such a review should nonetheless start with the baseline model of policy making: incrementalism.

3.1.1 Incrementalism: the baseline model of politics

In most areas of public policy and at most points in time, governing can be considered the art of 'muddling through' (Lindblom 1959, 1979). According to this logic of incrementalism, policies proceed evolutionarily and in small steps rather than in revolutionary overthrows of existing arrangements. Sometimes, policy makers even merely engage in a search for the next best alternative ('satisficing'), instead of trying to find the best policy approach available (Simon 1955). Theorists of incrementalism base those claims on the assumption that decisions of human beings are boundedly rational, i.e. constrained by limited amounts of information, cognitive capacity and time. Moreover, incremental policymaking is the result of the fact that more often than not, policymaking are required to forge compromises in complex legal environments. Accordingly, most policy decisions only change the status quo to a minimal extent and thus, incrementalism can be regarded as the baseline model of policy change.[1]

18 *Focusing events and public policy*

As far as gun policy is concerned, the notion of incrementalism adequately captures many policy developments which have occurred in the past (Hurka and Nebel 2013; Vizzard 1995). In most parts of the world, the issue of gun control hardly ever makes it to the political agenda and the policy debates are usually confined to small circles of experts.[2] One of the main reason for this pattern is the fact that without an external stimulus, political actors usually have little to gain from politicizing the issue, because the transaction costs outweigh any potential electoral benefits and the eventual policy outcomes are uncertain. This even holds for political actors who are cohesively in opposition to the regulatory status quo. However, the costs of politicizing gun control can be lowered tremendously by the occurrence of rampage shooting, which provides change advocates with the public attention they usually lack. Thus, potential focusing events like rampage shootings can break the default model of incrementalism and lead to major political reforms via a massive impact on the political agenda. Accordingly, while incrementalism is the regular mode of policymaking rather than the exception, a range of important theoretical frameworks all speak to the puzzle of why the baseline model of incrementalist policy making is not always tenable when confronted with empirical reality.

3.1.2 Multiple streams, punctuated equilibria and event-related policy change

In the 1970s and 1980s, several scholars claimed that while being rare, large-scale transformations of the political agenda and the occurrence of major policy change are not as elusive as the incrementalist school of thought had predicted. In his multiple streams approach (MSA), for instance, Kingdon (1984) attributes changes in the public agenda to the coupling of three more or less independent factors: problems, policies and politics. In the problem stream, the attention devoted to a certain societal condition and its perception as a policy problem varies over time. In the policy stream, solutions to policy problems are developed. Finally, the politics stream is composed of time-variant power and interest constellations among the political actors. According to the logic of the MSA, major alterations of the policy agenda are possible if the streams are coupled and a 'window of opportunity' opens, which can be exploited by policy entrepreneurs who have been waiting for their chance to push their cause. Windows of opportunity can open, for instance, as a result of new political majorities after elections or in a cyclical manner during budgeting processes. In those scenarios, the opening of the policy window can be anticipated by the involved stakeholders to a certain extent. In other scenarios, however, the policy window opens due to chance in the wake of a 'focusing event like a crisis or disaster that comes along to call attention to the problem, a powerful symbol that catches on, or the personal experience of a policy maker' (Kingdon 2003: 94f.). In the context of the present inquiry, in particular the first type of focusing event Kingdon mentions is relevant. If such a focusing event occurs, policy entrepreneurs get the opportunity to exploit the crisis and the accompanying increase in

Focusing events and public policy 19

public attention by coupling the streams and opening the window for reform (see also Mintrom and Norman 2009).

The central argument of the MSA is built on the garbage can model originally introduced by Cohen *et al*. (1972). This model had originally been put forward as an attempt to understand the way organizations prioritize and solve problems and was later adapted by Kingdon to the area of federal government. In the garbage can model's logic, solutions lie in wait for problems they can be attached to and whether or not this actually occurs is for the most part due to chance. Thus, the MSA and the garbage can model place a strong emphasis on contingency. Every now and then, political actors enjoy the opportunity to champion their favourite solutions, simply because a random external development suggests the potential existence of an adequate problem. In the area of gun control, the benefits of such a theoretical approach are obvious. If we assume that political actors have their favoured solutions to the eradication of rampage shootings, the occurrence of such an event provides them with an opportunity to place them onto the political agenda. However, the precise policy failure indicated by external shocks in general, and rampage shootings in particular, is not necessarily determinable objectively and as a result, often a matter of contestation. As Kingdon (1984: 109f.) himself puts it: 'Problems are not simply the conditions or external events themselves; there is also a perceptual, interpretive element.' As will be argued in the chapter on theoretical expectations, there is good reason to assume that the amount of problem definitions which can be attached to a given potential focusing event should be related to the scope of the ensuing political reaction. In this context, framing contests assume a central role (Boin *et al*. 2009; Hurka and Nebel 2013).

Both the MSA and the garbage can model have mainly been criticized for their built-in tendency to produce tautological statements. As Mucciaroni (1992: 463) notes: 'To say that something gets on the agenda when a problem is recognized, people believe something should be done about it, and political conditions are favourable to give it serious consideration comes close to stating a truism.' Another major point of critique of the aforementioned theoretical frameworks relates to the models' unfortunate implication that both agenda and policy change become almost impossible to predict *ex ante*. More often than not, we do not know when a crisis hits the system, and accordingly, the models' predictive power is very limited. However, despite those justified concerns, the critiques put forward against the MSA and the garbage can model should not be read as calls to give up on research examining variant impacts of potential focusing events on the political agenda and on policy change. They imply, however, that we must pay careful attention to the way we set up the corresponding research designs.[3]

Thus, the impossibility of anticipating potential focusing events should not be interpreted as a major obstacle to conducting comparative research on those events. Specifically, just because potential focusing events are often impossible to predict does not imply that the political processes they generate are random once they have occurred. In other words, if we understand potential focusing

20 Focusing events and public policy

events as the unit of analysis, there is no reason why the comparative evaluation of their effects should not be considered a viable research enterprise. In order to avoid making tautological statements, however, it is critically important to make sure that both events with positive and negative outcomes are considered simultaneously and in a comparative fashion. This latter argument has been defended most strongly by Thomas Birkland in his work on agenda setting and policy change in the wake of disasters (Birkland 1997, 1998, 2006; Birkland and DeYoung 2013).

Other than the MSA and the garbage can model, Birkland's model goes beyond the explanation of agenda setting and also includes decision-making. Building on May (1992), Birkland argues that potential focusing events often indicate policy failures and thereby provide the basis for policy-oriented learning. However, the general model is built on the observation that a mere increase in attention to a certain policy issue does not imply anything about the prospects of policy change. As Birkland (2006: 180) notes, 'increased attention is a necessary, but not sufficient, condition for event-related policy change.' As outlined above, this basic assumption is clearly very important in the context of this book.

Furthermore, the model emphasizes the crucial role of group mobilization in the wake of potential focusing events. In fact, Birkland's model even implies that group mobilization should be considered a necessary condition for real policy learning and change after a potential focusing event, although the author later acknowledges that 'reality is not quite so neat' (Birkland 2006: 171). In the empirical reality, Birkland even finds that group mobilization does not even always occur after a potential focusing event, which is to a certain extent attributable to the fact that Birkland mainly addresses very technical areas of public policy. Nevertheless, the general claim that broad societal mobilization contributes to politicization and policy change in the wake of potential focusing events should certainly be considered an important element of an integrated theory of event-related policy making.

Another theoretical framework that is closely related to the MSA has built on a model developed in evolutionary biology (Eldredge and Gould 1972) in order to understand disruptive policy dynamics. The punctuated equilibrium framework (PEF) suggests that just like the evolution of species, policy making is an erratic process, characterized by long periods of stasis and punctuated by radical deviations from the status quo (Baumgartner and Jones 1993). While the periods of incrementalism are influenced by negative feedback from the environment, sudden shifts to positive feedback on a given policy issue can destabilize the so-called policy monopoly and lead to substantial policy change. Such change can either follow from a change in the policy image or from the opening of new institutional venues. Baumgartner and Jones (1993) use the example of US nuclear policy in order to demonstrate the empirical validity of their argument. However, recent research suggests that patterns of punctuated equilibria are much more common, also in other countries and institutional settings (Baumgartner et al. 2009).

Focusing events and public policy 21

While the PEF is capable of describing many patterns of policy output in established democracies, its explanatory potential is somewhat underdeveloped (Prindle 2012). Most importantly, and this is a common problem of all theoretical frameworks, the distinction between an incremental policy change and a major policy change is often hard to make in an non-arbitrary way, especially if the policy output in question can hardly be measured on an interval scale.[4] Policy changes after rampage shootings are a case in point. While proponents of stricter gun control have called the tightening of storage regulations after the school shooting in Winnenden (Germany) a purely symbolic act, gun owners interpreted it a drastic measure that dramatically limits their personal freedom and even challenged the provisions in the German constitutional court. Thus, how do we know a policy punctuation when we see one? This question can hardly be answered independently from the specific empirical context in which the PEF and all other theoretical frameworks discussed above are applied.

In the realm of gun control, even large-scale increases in public attention have often yielded only minimal, incremental adjustments of the regulatory status quo. Sometimes, increases in public attention even petered out without any legislative reaction. Accordingly, increases in attention do not imply policy change. As Schildkraut and Cox Hernandez (2014) impressively demonstrate, sharp increases in public attention towards the issue of gun control have often led nowhere in terms of legislative change. This implies that while the general argument of the PEF that public (and political) attention towards a given policy issue is clearly not normally distributed over time is certainly valid and useful for the analysis of agenda-setting dynamics, its explanatory potential for policy change dynamics is limited.

3.1.3 Main lessons from the theoretical literature

While incrementalism can be considered the baseline model of politics, it is the non-incremental episodes that have attracted the most scholarly attention over the past few decades. In this context, all major theoretical frameworks on politicization and policy change have acknowledged the crucial role played by potential focusing events for the political process. What is still lacking, however, is a more thorough examination of the precise causal mechanisms at work (John 2003). While it is safe to argue that external shocks matter, the interesting question is: what shocks matter for which outcomes under what circumstances?

Unfortunately, none of the existing theoretical frameworks provides a good (or better testable) answer to this question. While all theoretical frameworks place a certain emphasis on external shocks, attributing political change to some external shock can often be considered 'the easy way out'. As Nohrstedt and Weible (2010: 5) correctly observe: 'One obvious risk of broadly conceptualizing external shocks is the tendency for scholars to link policy change to arbitrarily chosen exogenous phenomena.' Accordingly, since it is always easy to identify a politically relevant focusing event in retrospect, scholars often fall prey to the temptation of ignoring the vast amount of similar events that do not

22 *Focusing events and public policy*

fit their explanation. The result of this neglect is confirmation bias that arises from sampling on the dependent variable (Geddes 1990). More recently, Emmenegger (2010: 1) has taken up this discussion in his call to take 'non-events' seriously in comparative research, i.e. 'critical junctures during which actors do not alter the policy path although the counterfactual case of policy change was a likely possibility'. Such a perspective has the potential to provide us with a much better understanding of the factors that facilitate the political process by contrasting them with the constellations that impede it.

With the exception of Birkland's model of event-related policy change, none of the theoretical frameworks introduced above is a genuine framework of crisis-induced policy making. Instead, the approaches rather represent broad heuristics for conceptualizing the political process in general. Accordingly, the frameworks serve as analytical guides for the basic categories of factors which arguably dominate politics in (democratic) political systems: actors and institutions. All of the theoretical approaches discussed above place varying emphasis on those two drivers of the political process. While the MSA is more strongly centred on the role of political actors, in particular policy entrepreneurs, the PEF places a stronger emphasis on institutional arguments. However, it hardly makes any sense to interpret the two as rival explanations for policy change. Instead, the political process should be interpreted as a product of the interaction of actors in a certain institutional environment.[5] Accordingly, the chapter on theoretical expectations will take into account both actors and institutions when theorizing the conditional impact of potential focusing events on politicization and policy change. Thus, politics in the wake of these events is by no means an automatic process that always proceeds along the same, predictable lines. Instead, just as the entire political process is often characterized as a compilation of black boxes, so the political reactions to potential focusing events can depend on a multitude of factors, which hardly ever work in isolation from one another.

In the next section of this chapter, we climb down the ladder of abstraction one step and take a look at the policy area examined in the empirical context of this book. What distinctive features characterize the politics of gun control and are there any good typologies on crises and disasters that facilitate the development of theoretical expectations on the precise causal mechanisms that drive policy making in the wake of potential focusing events?

3.2 The politics of gun policy

In order to approach the question of why similar types of events have varying impacts, it is useful to first think about the distinctive features of the affected policy area. Over the past decades, there has been a steady supply of typologies designed to facilitate this task. In the classic (and still most influential) typology provided by Lowi (1972), we would certainly classify gun policy as a regulatory policy, as it involves the definition of rules and sanctions for a given individual conduct. While Lowi points out that levels of conflict should be highest in re-distributive policies, it has also been argued that regulatory policies are more controversial than re-distributive policies, because in the latter, 'the individual citizen feels the hand of government less directly' (Spitzer 2012: 4). To a certain extent, the level of political conflict a regulatory policy generates varies across countries and it is therefore difficult to rank-order policies according to their potential for conflict in a consistent manner across space and time. In general, however, it has been acknowledged in the literature that regulatory policies which directly affect individual social behaviour tend to be more controversial than regulatory policies which affect individual economic behaviour, because the values associated with the former are more fundamental than the values associated with the latter. Such policies have been discussed under the headings of social regulatory policy or morality policy respectively (Bruce and Wilcox 1998; Knill *et al.* 2015; Spitzer 2012; Tatalovich and Daynes 2011). Essentially, however, both labels address one and the same policy type and the differences between the two are negligible.

The values commonly associated with classic morality policies such as abortion or euthanasia are primarily derived from religious convictions and relate to the sanctity of life and the notion of sin. Such morality policies can alternatively be understood as 'manifest' morality policies (Knill 2013), whose defining feature is a conflict of fundamental values or first principles (Mooney and Schuldt 2008) and a negligible role of functionalist or instrumental reasoning. Unlike in those manifest morality policies, however, functionalist arguments are certainly a considerable part of the debate in the area of gun policy. Such policies can be understood as 'latent' morality policies (Knill 2013), whose potential for moral contestation generally looms under the surface but can erupt on an irregular basis as the result of some moral shock. The values at stake in the area of gun control are not directly derived from religious faith. Instead, the value conflict relates to the relationship between the state and the individual. How strongly may a state interfere with individual liberties? How can a state reconcile the policy goals of maximizing individual freedom with the need to provide collective security? While such questions do not touch upon transcendental convictions, they nevertheless require a decision between competing, albeit secular, values.

Another useful approach to classify public policies has been provided by Wilson (1973). Unlike the previously discussed typologies, Wilson unambiguously classifies policies according to the extent to which associated costs and benefits are concentrated or diffuse. Four ideal types emerge, but one of them is arguably most relevant for the classification of gun policy. Within the area of gun policy, the costs are usually quite concentrated on those who own (or want to own) guns. On the other hand, the benefits associated with gun control are rather diffuse, affecting society at large and not only closely defined sub-groups of the population. Such policies generate what Wilson calls 'entrepreneurial politics'.[6] Since costs accrue narrowly, dominant interest groups emerge and guard the payers' interests. Due to the fact that the benefits are not as tangible and clearly defined as the costs, the beneficiaries of the policy find it difficult to organize. Every once in a while, however, a policy entrepreneur manages to

24 *Focusing events and public policy*

mobilize beneficiaries by rallying broad public support. Occasionally, such situations occur as the result of a crisis that suddenly boosts public attention to the issue. Thus, entrepreneurial politics leads to policy change if a policy entrepreneur manages to portray his goal as 'incontrovertibly good' and thereby make 'the groups being opposed seem utterly self-serving' (Wilson 1973: 335).

In the area of gun policy, such patterns emerge on a regular basis. While financial endowments may vary, gun owners tend to be very well organized in most countries in the world and invariably outperform proponents of gun control in this respect. When a rampage shooting occurs, however, the latter can more easily be mobilized due to heightened public and political attention to the gun issue. Such mobilization does not always occur and the extent to which it occurs is certainly not random. In any case, social mobilization is a crucial component of any theoretical framework that seeks to explain the politicization of policy failures and related policy changes in the wake of external shocks.[7]

As an interim finding, two conclusions can be drawn. First, the literature on policy classifications suggests that due to its (social) regulatory nature, gun control should entail relatively intense political conflicts. Second, the politics of gun policy is based on a varying concentration of costs and benefits, which implies that the involved actors' ability to organize is asymmetric. In such an environment of entrepreneurial politics, the disadvantaged side of the debate relies heavily upon exogenous events which help to legitimatize its policy goals. Yet, does the existing literature offer any good advice on how we should structure our thinking about such exogenous events?

3.3 Typologies of crises and disasters

In order to address the research questions posed by this book, it might not only be useful to think in analytical categories as far as the policy area under study is concerned, but also with regard to the study's unit of analysis. How have different types of events been categorized in the literature and can we derive any clear-cut theoretical expectations from those typologies?

In comparative public policy research, attempts of grasping different types of crises have rarely been undertaken. An exception is the contribution of Nohrstedt and Weible (2010), who classify crises according to their geographical and policy proximity. In principle and in the research tradition of the ACF, the authors put forward the argument that the extent to which we observe policy change in a given policy subsystem after an external event is determined by characteristics of the event (policy proximity and geographical proximity) and the level of conflict in the affected policy subsystem (unitary, collaborative, adversarial). Policy-proximate events directly and clearly affect a certain policy subsystem, whereas policy-distant events only remotely touch upon a subsystem. Geographical proximity in turn simply relates to the event's locality, implying that the closer the event, the higher the consequences. Events which are proximate both in terms of policy and geographical distance are termed 'immediate crises' and are hypothesized to be most consequential in terms of the policy

Focusing events and public policy 25

response they evoke. Due to their strong proximity to the gun policy subsystem and the fact that they are usually treated as national tragedies that strongly affect the local community, rampage shootings can certainly be characterized as such immediate crises. However, the varying policy responses suggest that even very similar types of events can have dramatically different consequences. The hypotheses presented by Nohrstedt and Weible (2010: 23f.) hardly facilitate the investigation of this puzzle because they are arguably almost impossible to falsify. The authors suggest several possible subsystem reactions for every level of conflict and eventually, one of those reactions will necessarily occur (stalemate, minor change, or major change). It remains unclear which factors make one reaction more likely than the other.

In addition to their geographical and policy proximity, crises and disasters can also be distinguished with regard to the extent to which they allow for framing contests (Boin *et al.* 2009). While the causes of some events are difficult to deny and often beyond the direct control of human beings (e.g. plane crashes or natural disasters), blame attribution is often much more complex if human actions are involved. It has also been noted that certain policy areas are more prone to external events that highlight human misconduct. This is particularly true for regulatory policies in general and morality policies in particular (Hurka and Nebel 2013). Clearly, a rampage shooting can be framed in various ways. The blame may be put on the individual or on society. It may be put on politicians who failed to act or on the media who glorify violence. The event may be interpreted as the tip of the iceberg or as an idiosyncratic event lacking comparable antecedents. Its causes may be ascribed to a wide range of reasons including violent video games, social exclusion, political extremism or gun fanaticism. In any case, rampage shootings should be understood as complex events whose causes are rarely obvious on first sight and more often than not, multiple causes can be brought to bear in order to explain their occurrence.

In order to structure thinking about different types of crises and to put forward coping strategies for policy practitioners, the crisis management literature has developed typologies of crises which emphasize different aspects such as man-made vs. natural causation, predictable vs. unpredictable crises, or corporate vs. public crises (for an overview see Gundel (2005)). Gundel himself suggests distinguishing disastrous events on two dimensions: predictability and influenceability. While predictability in principle refers to the extent to which an event's timing and location could have been anticipated from the outset, influenceability refers to the extent to which the event's negative effects can be remedied 'within a reasonable timeframe or at best anticipate the event by prevention' (Gundel 2005: 109). Since Gundel introduces the proactive element of prevention on the influenceability dimension, it is questionable whether the two dimensions are really different from one another. However, the more important problem with such a distinction rests with the fact that the extent to which an event is predictable and influenceable is often contested. The lines between the types of crises Gundel suggests (conventional, unexpected, intractable and fundamental) are blurred. A rampage shooting, for instance, could be a conventional crisis in some

26 *Focusing events and public policy*

countries (i.e. the United States), while it is an unexpected one in many others. Some rampage shootings may even be considered fundamental crises due to their mere scope (consider the Utøya massacre in 2011). Thus, a rampage shooting could be any type of crisis mentioned above depending on the precise circumstances. As a result of those ambiguities, while classifications of crises developed in the crisis management literature may have their merits for practitioners who look for optimal coping strategies once an event has occurred, they are only of limited use for political science research interested in the varying policy impacts of specific types of crisis events.

To sum up, existing typologies of crises hardly facilitate theory building on their respective effects for public policies. Some typologies are blurry which makes it hard to classify certain events unambiguously. Other typologies are more clear-cut, but their empirical implications are not. The problem which affects both sorts of typologies is the fact that external shocks never come with an operation manual, but are often subject to interpretation. Obviously, the main lesson we can draw from those unsatisfactory facts is that an inductive approach of examining the effects of rampage shootings may be more fruitful than a strictly deductive one. Thus, in order to structure thinking about rampage shootings as crisis events, it seems appropriate to look into the literature which has addressed both the causes and the consequences of this particular type of event.

3.4 Rampage shootings in the academic literature

Why do rampage shootings occur and how do they exert their effects? This section of the book discusses the relevant academic literature on those two questions. In so doing, the research gaps the empirical part of the book seeks to fill are identified. The first part focuses on the causes of rampage shootings and the second part focuses on their consequences. Even though this book is concerned with the explanation of varying political consequences of rampage shootings, it is considered important not to ignore the body of literature on the events' causes. This is due to the fact that causes and consequences are intertwined and the perception of the former often implies the scope of the latter. In order to understand how societies and political systems react to an event, we should first acquire a sound understanding of the various causes of those events. But also perceived causes matter. The attribution of 'causal stories' (Stone 1989) plays an important role in the aftermath of rampage shootings and ensuing framing contests (Hurka and Nebel 2013).[8] In this sense, the discussion of causes is important because it demonstrates the complexity of rampage shootings. Very often, several causes can be attributed to the occurrence of such events, but as the discussion shows, the perpetrators' affection towards firearms and their often legal access to them remains one of the most pervasive characteristics.

Focusing events and public policy 27

3.4.1 Causes of rampage shootings

The question of why rampage shootings occur has mainly been addressed within the US context. Within this literature, one of the most common causes which have often been attributed to the occurrence of rampage shootings in general and school shootings in particular is some form of prior social rejection of the perpetrator (Leary *et al.* 2003; Levin and Madfis 2009; Newman and Fox 2009; Newman *et al.* 2004). People who commit rampage shootings often do so as a reaction to some perceived injustice. This is true of most school shooters (Leary *et al.* 2003), but also of other killers like Friedrich Leibacher, who targeted Swiss local politicians because he felt treated unjustly (consult section 7.6.1 of the book for more information on this particular case). In some instances, rampage shooters target specific populations which they deem responsible for their personal problems. In school shootings, these populations are often either other students or teachers. In other cases, politicians are the victims. Still other shooters have specifically targeted women, like Marc Lépine, the shooter responsible for the shooting at the *École Polytechnique* in Montréal (Canada) in 1989 or Tim Kretschmer, the school shooter of Winnenden, Germany (2009). Thus, the perpetrator's perception of being subject to social injustice has been identified as one of the most common motivations behind rampage shootings.

In addition to these societal origins, other risk factors are more closely related to specific characteristics of the perpetrator himself. For instance, an important cause which is often cited in the context of rampage shootings is the perpetrator's defective mental condition (e.g. Harter *et al.* 2003). Sometimes, the shooter had suffered from some mental disorders which evoked both homicidal and suicidal tendencies. In some instances, those mental conditions had been known before the shooting, in others they had not. Accordingly, scholars who argue for a prominent role of mental health in the causation of rampage shootings typically call for better prevention programs and more resources in the health sector.

Another individual-level risk factor often assumes a major role in the public debate following rampage shootings: the excessive consumption of violent media content, either in the form of music, movies, or video games (Anderson 2004; Böckler *et al.* 2011; Kiilakoski and Oksanen 2011; Muschert and Sumiala 2012; Ybarra *et al.* 2008). However, the empirical validity of this link has also been questioned by some scholars on empirical grounds (Ferguson 2008; Savage 2004), implying that no scientific consensus has emerged over the actual relationship between the consumption of violence in the media and an increase in the consumer's tendency towards violent behaviour. In any case, it can be reasonably concluded that the exposure to violent media content, just like all other factors mentioned above, is neither a sufficient nor a necessary condition for a person to carry out a rampage shooting. The factors are not sufficient because many people suffer from social rejection, have mental disorders or consume violent media content and do not carry out rampage shootings.[9] The factors are also not individually necessary because many perpetrators have carried out rampage shootings although it could later not be established that they

28 *Focusing events and public policy*

had been particularly exposed to any single one of the causes cited above. The case studies presented in Chapter 7 include a brief discussion of the particular circumstances leading up to the respective rampage shooting in order to substantiate this claim.

Just like social rejection, the existence of a mental condition, or the consumption of violent media content, the easy availability of firearms is not a sufficient condition for the occurrence of rampage shootings. However, in contrast to the other causes, there is good reason to believe that it is a necessary one (Muschert 2007: 68f.). First of all, however, it should be pointed out that acts of firearm violence are not evenly distributed across the globe (Lankford 2016) and several scholars have demonstrated that rates of firearm availability correlate with rates of firearm homicide (see Hepburn and Hemenway (2004) for a comprehensive review of this literature). In countries with virtual bans on civilian firearm ownership like Japan, guns are rarely used in crime whereas the number of gun homicides in countries with more permissive firearm laws is much higher (Krug *et al.* 1998: 216). However, this relationship on the aggregate level does not imply that singular events of high magnitude cannot occur in states with strict gun control. In fact, history has shown that also states with comparably strict rules for private gun possession, like Great Britain and Germany, have experienced rampage shootings.[10] Thus, while the legal acquisition of firearms is more difficult in those countries and higher obstacles must be overcome, it is far from impossible. Nonetheless, the rate of occurrence of rampage shootings in Western Europe is nowhere near the rate of the United States, where the easy accessibility of firearms has been demonstrated to be one of the most pervasive features accompanying the occurrence of rampage violence (Newman and Fox 2009; Verlinden *et al.* 2000: 43). Thus, the extent to which potential perpetrators are able to acquire firearms legally in a given country is strongly related to the degree of firearm-related violence this country experiences.

To sum up, it is commonplace that the occurrence of rampage shootings evades simple explanations. Very often, multiple causes can be brought to bear in order to explain one and the same event, which implies that it may often be interactions of individual causes which bring about the shooting. To a certain extent, the focus on individual causes and the neglect of plausible interactions has hampered scientific development (Muschert 2007). It has been observed, however, that while there are no sufficient causes of rampage shootings (if there were, it would arguably be much easier to address them politically), there is one necessary condition (almost) all rampage shootings have in common: the perpetrator's access to guns. The complex causation of rampage shootings implies that these events typically leave much room for interpretation and thereby for strategic framing. Highlighting certain causes and downplaying others can serve as a political strategy either to protect the status quo or to promote policy change (Hurka and Nebel 2013). However, while the aspect of framing is one important part of research on the political consequences of rampage shootings, it is by far not the only one, as the following discussion will show.

Focusing events and public policy 29

3.4.2 Consequences of rampage shootings

When it comes to understanding and explaining the societal and political consequences of rampage shootings, much remains to be done. In social science, research on the effects of rampage shootings is 'greatly underemphasized' (Muschert 2007: 71), especially when compared to research on their causes. Several studies on rampage shootings in general, and on school shootings in particular, have focused on micro-level consequences like students' fear of victimization (e.g. Addington 2003). While studies on the broader social and political dynamics triggered by rampage shootings are comparably rare, some of them exist and will be discussed in the following paragraphs.

In the public arena, a common characteristic of rampage shootings is the disproportionate increase of public attention they generate. As Muschert and Ragnedda (2011: 345) have observed, 'the rarity of such events may not justify the attention they receive, despite their horrible consequences'. In the sociological literature, such reactions have generally been referred to as 'moral panics' (Burns and Crawford 1999; Cohen 1972), which are often the result of extensive media coverage. Not surprisingly, by far the most pronounced research program with regard to the consequences of rampage shootings has emerged on the analysis of this media coverage and emphasized the critical importance of framing efforts for individual event perception (Birkland and Lawrence 2009; Burns and Crawford 1999; Chyi and McCombs 2004; Frymer 2009; Harding *et al.* 2002; Hawdon *et al.* 2012; Lawrence 2001; Lawrence and Birkland 2004; Muschert and Carr 2006; Muschert and Sumiala 2012; Park *et al.* 2012; Schildkraut and Muschert 2014). The overwhelming majority of this literature focuses upon school shootings as one particularly gruesome sub-type of rampage shootings and almost all of the literature is geographically focused on the US. Within this literature, some have stressed the relevance of different event frames for varying levels of community solidarity (Hawdon *et al.* 2012), others have focused on ramifications of framing contests for the political process (Birkland and Lawrence 2009; Hurka and Nebel 2013; Lawrence and Birkland 2004). The media have also been identified as driving forces behind the emergence of moral panics, in particular after school shootings (Burns and Crawford 1999). All of these contributions generally acknowledge that the media are critical actors when it comes to the definition of the problem signified by the event. More specifically, it has been observed that the media frequently switch frames during the reporting of an incident, moving from a description from the situation 'on the ground' towards the implications of the shooting for society as a whole (Muschert 2009; Muschert and Carr 2006). Thus, by speculating on the causes of the shooting, the media contribute to the setting of the political agenda.

The above-mentioned studies indicate that communication scholars have made substantial progress in understanding the media dynamics triggered by rampage shootings. Until recently, however, there has been virtually no research on the policy consequences of rampage shootings. In the past few years, scholars in the US have begun to compare local reactions to school shootings in particular

30 *Focusing events and public policy*

with regard to the introduction of new security arrangements and prevention programs (Addington 2009; Fox and Savage 2009; Muschert and Peguero 2010). In a recent study, Schildkraut and Cox Hernandez (2014) discuss several failed attempts to introduce additional gun control measures in the wake of some high-profile mass shootings in the US, both on the national and state-level. They argue that shifts in public opinion resulting from the events have often contributed to the introduction of new legislation, but the authors cannot explain why almost all of those bills have eventually failed to become law. Addressing this question, Anthony Fleming (2012) compared the varying legislative reactions to mass shootings in the United States and Canada. Fleming (2012: 133f.) argues that the reluctance of US politicians to enact comprehensive gun control in the United States primarily stems from the activities of interest groups (in particular the National Rifle Association) and the high hurdles imposed by the political institutions of the United States. But also the interplay between the ideological orientation of the party in power and institutional factors is found to be important. In the United States, the only meaningful alteration of the national legal framework in the area of gun policy has taken place during a time of unified government controlled by Democrats in 1993 (Fleming 2012: 134). In the Canadian setting, Fleming argues that both the overwhelming pressure of social movements and the change-friendly parliamentary system have contributed to the more pronounced legislative reactions in Canada. Thus, although Fleming does not explicitly discuss his results this way, they clearly point to the relevance of complex causal processes unfolding in the wake of rampage shootings. Instead of trying to discover the one decisive factor driving politicization, policy change and stability after potential focusing events, it seems more promising to examine the impact of different causal configurations.

The scarce comparative literature on varying policy impacts of rampage shootings for policy arrangements in the area of gun control suffers from one central problem: it over-emphasizes positive cases and under-emphasizes negative ones. Two examples illustrate this point. In an application of the MSA to gun politics in California, Godwin and Schroedel (1998) describe the policy window which opened in the wake of the Stockton massacre in 1989. While the authors' argument that the massacre was critically important in bringing about an assault weapons ban in California is certainly valid, the authors fail to deliver an explanation as to why the similarly horrible incident at San Diego in 1984 had not led to policy change. Thus, while there is good reason to believe that random large-scale events can have a meaningful impact on public policy, this impact is not absolute and must be conditional on other factors. Also studies applying the PEF suffer from this problem. Despite its intuitive appeal in the area of gun policy, the PEF has only been applied in the US context by True and Utter (2002). The authors argue that the development of gun control in the United States can be interpreted in terms of punctuated equilibria. In particular, the two policy changes in 1968 and 1993 were strongly influenced by events, which directed both public and political attention towards gun policy (the assassination of John F. Kennedy and the failed assassination of Ronald Reagan).

Focusing events and public policy 31

Those events provided the ground for a re-definition of the gun control issue. As in many other studies on the policy effects of external events, however, also the authors of this study fail to come up with an explanation as to why so many other comparable events did not result in a re-definition of the gun control issue. Once again, this demonstrates that one of the major shortcomings of the existing literature on external shocks in general, and rampage shootings in particular, is the overwhelming focus on positive cases and the accompanying neglect of negative ones.

Thus, the literature on the effects of rampage shootings has two shortcomings. First, it predominantly focuses upon societal and not on political consequences. Second, the literature is strongly biased towards the United States of America. Both shortcomings are addressed by the research design of this book. Yet, while the scarcity of research on the consequences of rampage shootings helps to justify the empirical focus of this study, the few existing studies hardly facilitate theory building. Therefore, it appears promising to extend the discussion from the narrow focus on rampage shootings to the policy consequences of potential focusing events in general.

3.5 Beyond rampage shootings: findings on event-related policy change

Several empirical studies have taken up the challenge of tracing the impact of disasters or crises on the political agenda and explaining ultimate policy consequences. Those empirical investigations have taken place in a wide range of policy areas, including nuclear energy policy (Nohrstedt 2005, 2008, 2010), tobacco policy (Wood 2006), education policy (Jensen 2011), judicial policy and police reform (Maesschalck 2002; Walgrave and Varone 2008), defence policy (Brändström and Kuipers 2003) or financial policy (Williams 2009). Also natural disasters (Albright 2011; Farley *et al.* 2007), food scandals (Lodge 2011), dog attacks (Lodge and Hood 2002) and even explosions in firework factories (de Vries 2004) have been examined as events driving the politicization of otherwise dormant policy issues and ensuing policy change. Since the existing literature on the particular phenomenon of rampage shootings is not very well developed, as the previous section has shown, it might be promising to explore the empirical and theoretical contributions of studies which assess the political processing of similar types of events.

The main theoretical contribution offered by Williams (2009) relates to the common misunderstanding that exogenous shocks automatically change the rules of the game in affected policy subsystems. As the author observes, while the impetus for political action often originates outside of a given policy subsystem, the way this impetus is ultimately processed is heavily influenced by endogenous, established patterns of interaction within this subsystem. 'To understand policy change we should integrate factors associated with normal politics and the exogenous events to try to predict likely patterns of response' (Williams 2009: 32). This argument implies that comparative political science must resist

32   *Focusing events and public policy*

the urge to ascribe inflated explanatory power to the simple occurrence of exogenous shocks. Instead, the precise causal mechanisms that link the occurrence of such shocks to eventual policy impacts should be of stronger analytical interest. In sum, the study by Williams therefore suggests that exogenous shocks should not be understood as causes of policy change in their own right, but rather as windows of opportunity which can either be exploited or not. The finding that the mere occurrence of an exogenous shock does not directly imply any political consequences is also one contribution by the empirical studies of Daniel Nohrstedt.

In three studies on the impacts of nuclear disasters on energy policy in Sweden, Nohrstedt (2005, 2008, 2010) applies the Advocacy Coalition Framework (ACF) in order to understand processes of policy-oriented learning in the wake of crisis episodes. In addition to the theoretical contribution mentioned previously, another particularly important contribution of these studies is their joint emphasis on the importance of partisan cleavages for politicization and policy change. If a focusing event affects an existing divide in the party system, the shock will have more profound policy implications than if such partisan cleavages are absent. When transferred to this study, it can be said that while opinions on gun control are probably not the most central characteristic that delineates parties in most countries in the world, such divisions may often become visible as a result of an external shock. As will be discussed in the theoretical section of this book, a cleavage on the issue of gun control can be expected between conservative, liberal and rural parties on the one hand and progressive, in particular green, parties on the other hand.

In an application of the punctuated equilibrium framework (PEF) in the area of education policy in Denmark, Jensen (2011) also emphasizes the role of political parties for the political processing of focusing events, but rather points to their ability to block reform efforts if they are averse to change and enjoy a pivotal position by occupying the relevant cabinet portfolio and the median legislator in parliament. In such situations, even devastating focusing events can go by without any meaningful alterations of the status quo, because the pivotal party can act as a policy dictator. Thus, while the existence of a relevant partisan cleavage may be critically important for the extent to which an event gets politicized, decision making is critically affected by the distribution of power among the parties. Despite the parsimony of Jensen's theoretical argument, however, it must be noted that it is probably a little bit too simplistic. As subsequent sections of this study will show, the ideological orientations and power positions of political parties are important elements of an explanation of the political processes following focusing events, but certainly not the only one.

The public outrage over the case of the child molester Marc Dutroux and its effects on public policy in Belgium are at the centre of attention in the studies of Maesschalck (2002) and Walgrave and Varone (2008). Combining the MSA and the PEF, Maesschalck concludes that scandals should be understood in the particular context in which they occur. In particular, experiences from prior events are found to be important for the way an external shock is processed, but also individual policy entrepreneurs are ascribed much power in bringing about policy change in the wake of a crisis. In a similar application of the PEF on the same case, Walgrave and Varone (2008) come to a conclusion similar to that of the studies presented before: parties make a critical difference both for the speed and scope of reform efforts after an external shock. The main theoretical conclusion the authors draw is therefore that the role of political parties should be a more integral part of the PEF, which had been developed in the US context. In Europe, however, political parties exert a much more decisive influence on public policies than in the United States, where individual politicians assume a much greater role.

Another aspect that has received some attention in studies on crisis-induced policy making is the relative severity of comparable events. In their empirical study on two policy failures in the military, Brändström and Kuipers (2003) show, however, that the severity of an event is not always easy to determine objectively. Instead, political actors engage in framing and construct an event's severity based on the question of whether the event violates some core societal values. If actors are successful in their framing efforts, political and policy consequences become more likely. In a similar vein, also Boin *et al.* (2009) come to the conclusion that the way an event is framed by the involved political actors has important implications for the way it is processed politically. In her study on political reactions to explosions in fireworks factories, de Vries (2004) even concludes that the most typical outcome of an external shock is policy stability, because the involved political actors will find it easy to attribute blame to outside circumstances they cannot influence. Of course, this latter finding is also particularly relevant in the context of rampage shootings, when change-averse policy makers try to frame the event as an isolated and unfortunate tragedy which cannot be prevented by policy measures.

Analogically, Lodge (2011) shows that, to a certain extent, argumentation patterns are linked to the type of regulatory response in the wake of a crisis, in his empirical context food safety regulations. Specifically, the manner by which political debates are commonly structured in a country (e.g. hierarchy vs. individualism) can have ramifications for the scope and type of the ensuing regulatory response. In a similar vein, Lodge and Hood (2002) show that regulatory responses to similar types of external shocks depend to a significant extent on the design of entrenched institutions and that the conventional wisdom of default 'Pavlovian politics' as a reaction to external stimuli is demonstrably false. On the contrary, the authors argue that institutions 'function less as weathervanes than as filters or distorting lenses for outside pressures' (Lodge and Hood 2002: 3). As such, they are important intervening variables which can either amplify or decrease the scope of the ensuing political reaction. Furthermore, the authors' empirical evidence on political reactions to individual dog attacks in Great Britain and Germany suggests that the objective severity of an event is not necessarily the single best indicator for the political reaction we should expect. Instead, also events of rather minor magnitude can have strong implications for public policy, especially if they are accompanied by an extreme increase in media attention.

34 *Focusing events and public policy*

In sum, the existing literature on the policy impacts of exogenous shocks includes several important messages: first, the analytical emphasis of comparative research should be shifted more strongly to the identification of the causal mechanisms that link external shocks to the politicization of policy failures and to subsequent policy change. In order to learn something about the varying policy impacts of such events, we must open the black box. Second, much of the empirical research suggests that this box probably contains the 'usual suspects' in the form of political actors (in particular political parties) and political institutions. However, this perspective is probably insufficient to account for all of the variation we observe in crisis-induced policy making and must be complemented by a more systematic focus on the strategic use of competing interpretative frames. Most importantly, the inconclusive findings of the cited empirical studies suggest that we need to evaluate complex interactions of individual factors in order to arrive at a better understanding of the political processes triggered by potential focusing events.

3.6 Research gap and research promise

This literature review has summarized both the current state-of-the-art of research on crisis-induced policy change and the major theoretical approaches on politicization, policy change and stability. What main lessons can we draw from this review?

First, the discussion of the theoretical literature clearly suggests that while incrementalism still appears to be the regular mode of political decision-making, it is often the episodes of radical change which are the most interesting from an analytical point of view. However, as all major theoretical frameworks underscore, there is a clear need to integrate the analysis of stability and change, instead of focusing only on one at the expense of the other. Since most existing theoretical frameworks do not directly speak to the political processing of focusing events, all of them acknowledge that such events can have major policy ramifications. However, their comparative analysis requires the inclusion of potential and real focusing events in order to avoid the trap of confirmation bias. The literature review has argued that much of the existing literature on external shocks suffers from exactly this problem. Therefore, instead of merely advancing the blunt argument that external shocks matter, we should move towards the identification of the precise circumstances under which they exert an influence on public policy and the circumstances under which they are absorbed. While the theoretical frameworks place varying emphasis on actors and institutions, it seems reasonable that both play a role and that their configuration at the time of the respective event should be assessed.

Second, the existing empirical literature on rampage shootings suffers from two major shortcomings. The first shortcoming relates to the literature's strong focus on the identification of the causes of rampage shootings, and its simultaneous neglect of the event's (political) consequences. While we have learned a lot about the factors which increase the risk of violent behaviour, we do not know

Focusing events and public policy 35

very much about why such violent behaviour is dealt with differently within different institutional settings. As a second shortcoming, the scarce literature on the effects of rampage shootings displays an extreme geographical bias towards the United States, which has the unfortunate implication that the generalizability of the findings is arguably rather low. Of course, this problem has its roots in the status of the US as an extreme outlier case as far as the regulation of firearms is concerned. Accordingly, a comparative approach is in order and such an approach is delivered by this book.

Third, the ambiguity of existing typologies of public policies, crises and disasters complicate the derivation of clear-cut and testable empirical implications. While crisis typologies are often indeterminate and make the unambiguous allocation of rampage shootings difficult, policy typologies only suggest expectations on levels of conflict and the actors involved, but hardly allow for the derivation of (falsifiable) hypotheses on policy change and stability. As a result, the purpose of analysing rampage shootings (and probably external shocks in general) in a comparative fashion is arguably better served by an inductive, instead of a strictly deductive approach. This does not imply, however, that the analysis of rampage shootings should be entirely explorative. Instead, it is possible to develop some reasonably broad theoretical expectations on the factors that drive politicization and policy change in the wake of rampage shootings and refine them along the way. This task will be carried out in the following chapter.

Finally, despite the scarcity of the existing literature, some factors have been identified repeatedly as important drivers of politicization and policy change after the occurrence of potential focusing events. The following chapter will attempt to organize these distinct types of factors into a theoretical grid that guides the empirical analysis. It will be argued that both politicization and policy change can be conceived of as outcomes shaped by the interplay of several contextual conditions. In the following chapter, the theoretical arguments underlying this claim will be specified in greater detail.

Notes

1 In later works, however, Lindblom acknowledged that incrementalism is a matter of degree and non-incremental policy making exists (Lindblom 1979).
2 It goes without saying that the major exception to this rule is the United States of America, where gun control has traditionally been a highly controversial topic and debates have been led on a broad societal basis (Spitzer 2012).
3 This problem has also influenced empirical applications of the MSA in the area of gun control, as section 3.4.2 demonstrates.
4 Presumably for this reason, many comparative applications of the PEF still focus strongly on changes in public budgets. More recently, however, also other indicators of political attention have been scrutinized systematically (Baumgartner *et al.* 2009).
5 This idea of boundedly rational actors, who interact under certain institutional rules of the game is anything but new. In fact, it is the central constitutive element of Fritz W. Scharpf's 'actor-centred institutionalism' (Scharpf 1997).
6 On a side note, Wilson used to be a strong opponent of gun control in the United States (Wilson 2007).

36 *Focusing events and public policy*

7 This observation clearly coincides with the arguments put forward by Birkland (1998).
8 The phenomenon that people attribute very diverse causes to one and the same rampage shooting has been described as the 'Rashomon effect' by Muschert (2007: 61).
9 It has been found, however, that the combination of the individual factors increases the risk (Bondü *et al.* 2011: 24; Verlinden *et al.* 2000).
10 The laws governing gun licensing in Northern Ireland are different from the laws in Great Britain. Since the events discussed in this book took place in Scotland and England respectively, the term Great Britain is used instead of United Kingdom.

References

Addington, L. A. (2003). Students' Fear after Columbine: Findings from a Randomized Experiment. *Journal of Quantitative Criminology* 19(4), 367–387.
Addington, L. A. (2009). Cops and Cameras: Public School Security as a Policy Response to Columbine. *American Behavioral Scientist* 52(10), 1426–1446.
Albright, E. A. (2011). Policy Change and Learning in Response to Extreme Flood Events in Hungary: An Advocacy Coalition Approach. *Policy Studies Journal* 39(3), 485–511.
Anderson, C. A. (2004). An Update on the Effects of Playing Violent Video Games. *Journal of Adolescence* 27(1), 113–122.
Baumgartner, F. and Jones, B. D. (1993). *Agendas and Instability in American Politics.* Chicago: University of Chicago Press.
Baumgartner, F. R., Breunig, C., Green-Pedersen, C., Jones, B. D., Mortensen, P. B., Nuytemans, M. and Walgrave, S. (2009). Punctuated Equilibrium in Comparative Perspective. *American Journal of Political Science* 53(3), 603–620.
Birkland, T. A. (1997). *After Disaster – Agenda Setting, Public Policy, and Focusing Events.* Washington, D.C.: Georgetown University Press.
Birkland, T. A. (1998). Focusing Events, Mobilization, and Agenda Setting. *Journal of Public Policy* 18(1), 53–74.
Birkland, T. A. (2006). *Lessons of Disaster: Policy Change after Catastrophic Events.* Washington, D.C.: Georgetown University Press.
Birkland, T. A. and DeYoung, S. E. (2013). Focusing Events and Policy Windows. In J. Eduardo Araral, S. Fritzen, M. Howlett, M. Ramesh and X. Wu (eds), *Routledge Handbook of Public Policy* (pp. 175–188). London: Routledge.
Birkland, T. A. and Lawrence, R. G. (2009). Media Framing and Policy Change After Columbine. *American Behavioral Scientist* 52(10), 1405–1425.
Böckler, N., Seeger, T. and Heitmeyer, W. (2011). School Shooting: A Double Loss of Control. In W. Heitmeyer, H.-G. Haupt, S. Malthaner and A. Kirschner (eds), *Control of Violence: Historical and International Perspectives on Violence in Modern Societies* (pp. 261–294). New York: Springer.
Boin, A., t'Hart, P. and McConnell, A. (2009). Crisis Exploitation: Political and Policy Impacts of Framing Contests. *Journal of European Public Policy* 16(1), 81–106.
Bondü, R., Cornell, D. G. and Scheithauer, H. (2011). Student Homicidal Violence in Schools: An International Problem. *New Directions for Youth Development* 2011(129), 13–30.
Brändström, A. and Kuipers, S. (2003). From 'Normal Incidents' to Political Crises: Understanding the Selective Politicization of Policy Failures. *Government and Opposition* 38(3), 279–305.

Focusing events and public policy 37

Bruce, J. M. and Wilcox, C. (1998). Introduction. In J. M. Bruce and C. Wilcox (eds), *The Changing Politics of Gun Control* (pp. 1–16). Lanham: Rowman & Littlefield.

Burns, R. and Crawford, C. (1999). School Shootings, the Media, and Public Fear: Ingredients for a Moral Panic. *Crime, Law and Social Change* 32(2), 147–168.

Chyi, H. I. and McCombs, M. (2004). Media Salience and the Process of Framing: Coverage of the Columbine School Shootings. *Journalism & Mass Communication Quarterly* 81(1), 22–35.

Cohen, M. D., March, J. G. and Olsen, J. P. (1972). A Garbage Can Model of Organizational Choice. *Administrative Science Quarterly* 17(1), 1–25.

Cohen, S. (1972). *Folk Devils and Moral Panics: The Creation of the Mods and Rockers.* London: MacGibbon and Kee.

de Vries, M. S. (2004). Framing Crises: Response Patterns to Explosions in Fireworks Factories. *Administration & Society* 36(5), 594–614.

Eldredge, N. and Gould, S. J. (1972). Punctuated Equilibria: An Alternative to Phyletic Gradualism. In T. J. M. Schopf (ed.), *Models in Paleobiology* (pp. 82–115). San Francisco: Freeman, Cooper and Company.

Emmenegger, P. (2010). Non-Events in Macro-Comparative Social Research: Why We Should Care and How We Can Analyze Them. *COMPASSS Working Paper Series 2010–60.*

Farley, J., Baker, D., Batker, D., Koliba, C., Matteson, R., Mills, R. and Pittman, J. (2007). Opening the Policy Window for Ecological Economics: Katrina as a Focusing Event. *Ecological Economics* 63(2–3), 344–354.

Ferguson, C. J. (2008). The School Shooting/Violent Video Game Link: Causal Relationship or Moral Panic? *Journal of Investigative Psychology and Offender Profiling* 5(1–2), 25–37.

Fleming, A. K. (2012). *Gun Policy in the United States and Canada: The Impact of Mass Murders and Assassinations on Gun Policy.* New York: Continuum International Publishing Group.

Fox, J. A. and Savage, J. (2009). Mass Murder Goes to College: An Examination of Changes on College Campuses Following Virginia Tech. *American Behavioral Scientist* 52(10), 1465–1485.

Frymer, B. (2009). The Media Spectacle of Columbine: Alienated Youth as an Object of Fear. *American Behavioral Scientist* 52(10), 1387–1404.

Geddes, B. (1990). How the Cases You Choose Affect the Answers You Get: Selection Bias in Comparative Politics. *Political Analysis* 2(1), 131–150.

Godwin, M. L. and Schroedel, J. R. (1998). Gun Control Politics in California. In J. M. Bruce and C. Wilcox (eds), *The Changing Politics of Gun Control* (pp. 88–110). Lanham: Rowman & Littlefield.

Gundel, S. (2005). Towards a New Typology of Crises. *Journal of Contingencies and Crisis Management* 13(3), 106–115.

Harding, D. J., Fox, C. and Mehta, J. D. (2002). Studying Rare Events through Qualitative Case Studies: Lessons from a Study of Rampage School Shootings. *Sociological Methods & Research* 31(2), 174–217.

Harter, S., Low, S. M. and Whitesell, N. R. (2003). What Have We Learned from Columbine: The Impact of the Self-System on Suicidal and Violent Ideation Among Adolescents. *Journal of School Violence* 2(3), 3–26.

Hawdon, J., Oksanen, A. and Räsänen, P. (2012). Media Coverage and Solidarity after Tragedies: The Reporting of School Shootings in Two Nations. *Comparative Sociology* 11(6), 845–874.

38 Focusing events and public policy

Hepburn, L. M. and Hemenway, D. (2004). Firearm Availability and Homicide: A Review of the Literature. *Aggression and Violent Behavior* 9(4), 417–440.

Hurka, S. and Nebel, K. (2013). Framing and Policy Change after Shooting Rampages: A Comparative Analysis of Discourse Networks. *Journal of European Public Policy* 20(3), 390–406.

Jensen, C. (2011). Focusing Events, Policy Dictators and the Dynamics of Reform. *Policy Studies* 32(2), 143–158.

John, P. (2003). Is there Life after Policy Streams, Advocacy Coalitions, and Punctuations: Using Evolutionary Theory to Explain Policy Change? *Policy Studies Journal* 31(4), 481–498.

Kiilakoski, T. and Oksanen, A. (2011). Soundtrack of the School Shootings: Cultural Script, Music and Male Rage. *Young* 19(3), 247–269.

Kingdon, J. W. (1984). *Agendas, Alternatives, and Public Policies*. Boston: Little, Brown.

Kingdon, J. W. (2003). *Agendas, Alternatives, and Public Policies* (2nd edn). New York: Longman.

Knill, C. (2013). The Study of Morality Policy: Analytical Implications from a Public Policy Perspective. *Journal of European Public Policy* 20(3), 309–317.

Knill, C., Adam, C. and Hurka, S. (eds). (2015). *On the Road to Permissiveness? Change and Convergence of Moral Regulation in Europe*. Oxford: Oxford University Press.

Krug, E., Powell, K. and Dahlberg, L. (1998). Firearm-related Deaths in the United States and 35 Other High- and Upper-middle-income Countries. *International Journal of Epidemiology* 27(2), 214–221.

Lankford, A. (2016). Public Mass Shooters and Firearms: A Cross-National Study of 171 Countries. *Violence and Victims* 31(2), 187–199.

Lawrence, R. G. (2001). Defining Events: Problem Definition in the Media Arena. In R. P. Hart and B. Sparrow (eds), *Politics, Discourse, and American Society: New Agendas* (pp. 91–110). New York: Rowman & Littlefield.

Lawrence, R. G. and Birkland, T. A. (2004). Guns, Hollywood, and School Safety: Defining the School-Shooting Problem across Public Arenas. *Social Science Quarterly* 85(5), 1193–1207.

Leary, M. R., Kowalski, R. M., Smith, L. and Phillips, S. (2003). Teasing, Rejection, and Violence: Case Studies of the School Shootings. *Aggressive Behavior* 29(3), 202–214.

Levin, J. and Madfis, E. (2009). Mass Murder at School and Cumulative Strain: A Sequential Model. *American Behavioral Scientist* 52(9), 1227–1245.

Lindblom, C. E. (1959). The Science of 'Muddling Through'. *Public Administration Review* 19(2), 79–88.

Lindblom, C. E. (1979). Still Muddling, Not Yet Through. *Public Administration Review* 39(6), 517–526.

Lodge, M. (2011). Risk, Regulation and Crisis: Comparing National Responses in Food Safety Regulation. *Journal of Public Policy* 31(1), 25–50.

Lodge, M. and Hood, C. (2002). Pavlovian Policy Responses to Media Feeding Frenzies? Dangerous Dogs Regulation in Comparative Perspective. *Journal of Contingencies and Crisis Management* 10(1), 1–13.

Lowi, T. J. (1972). Four Systems of Policy, Politics, and Choice. *Public Administration Review* 32(4), 298–310.

Maesschalck, J. (2002). When Do Scandals Have an Impact on Policy Making? A Case Study of the Police Reform Following the Dutroux Scandal in Belgium. *International Public Management Journal* 5(2), 169–193.

Focusing events and public policy 39

May, P. J. (1992). Policy Learning and Failure. *Journal of Public Policy* 12(04), 331–354.

Mintrom, M. and Norman, P. (2009). Policy Entrepreneurship and Policy Change. *Policy Studies Journal* 37(4), 649–667.

Mooney, C. Z. and Schuldt, R. G. (2008). Does Morality Policy Exist? Testing a Basic Assumption. *Policy Studies Journal* 36(2), 199–218.

Mucciaroni, G. (1992). The Garbage Can Model & the Study of Policy Making: A Critique. *Polity* 24(3), 459–482.

Muschert, G. W. (2007). Research in School Shootings. *Sociology Compass* 1(1), 60–80.

Muschert, G. W. (2009). Frame-changing in the Media Coverage of a School Shooting: The Rise of Columbine as a National Concern. *The Social Science Journal* 46(1), 164–170.

Muschert, G. W. and Carr, D. (2006). Media Salience and Frame Changing across Events: Coverage of Nine School Shootings, 1997–2001. *Journalism & Mass Communication Quarterly* 83(4), 747–766.

Muschert, G. W. and Peguero, A. A. (2010). The 'Columbine Effect' and School Anti-violence Policy. *Research in Social Problems and Public Policy* 17, 117–148.

Muschert, G. W. and Ragnedda, M. (2011). Media and Control of Violence: Communication in School Shootings. In W. Heitmeyer, H.-G. Haupt, S. Malthaner and A. Kirschner (eds), *Control of Violence: Historical and International Perspectives on Violence in Modern Societies* (pp. 345–361): Springer New York.

Muschert, G. W. and Sumiala, J. (eds). (2012). *School Shootings: Mediatized Violence in a Global Age*. Bingley: Emerald Books.

Newman, K. and Fox, C. (2009). Repeat Tragedy: Rampage Shootings in American High School and College Settings, 2002–2008. *American Behavioral Scientist* 52(9), 1286–1308.

Newman, K., Fox, C., Harding, D. J., Mehta, J. D. and Roth, W. (2004). *Rampage: The Social Roots of School Shootings*. New York: Basic Books.

Nohrstedt, D. (2005). External Shocks and Policy Change: Three Mile Island and Swedish Nuclear Energy Policy. *Journal of European Public Policy* 12(6), 1041–1059.

Nohrstedt, D. (2008). The Politics of Crisis Policymaking: Chernobyl and Swedish Nuclear Energy Policy. *Policy Studies Journal* 36(2), 257–278.

Nohrstedt, D. (2010). Do Advocacy Coalitions Matter? Crisis and Change in Swedish Nuclear Energy Policy. *Journal of Public Administration Research and Theory* 20(2), 309–333.

Nohrstedt, D. and Weible, C. M. (2010). The Logic of Policy Change after Crisis: Proximity and Subsystem Interaction. *Risk, Hazards & Crisis in Public Policy* 1(2), 1–32.

Park, S.-Y., Holody, K. J. and Zhang, X. (2012). Race in Media Coverage of School Shootings: A Parallel Application of Framing Theory and Attribute Agenda Setting. *Journalism & Mass Communication Quarterly* 89(3), 475–494.

Prindle, D. F. (2012). Importing Concepts from Biology into Political Science: The Case of Punctuated Equilibrium. *Policy Studies Journal* 40(1), 21–44.

Savage, J. (2004). Does Viewing Violent Media Really Cause Criminal Violence? A Methodological Review. *Aggression and Violent Behavior* 10(1), 99–128.

Scharpf, F. W. (1997). *Games Real Actors Play*. Boulder, CO: Westview Press.

Schildkraut, J. and Cox Hernandez, T. (2014). Laws that Bit the Bullet: A Review of Legislative Responses to School Shootings. *American Journal of Criminal Justice* 39(2), 358–374.

40 *Focusing events and public policy*

Schildkraut, J. and Muschert, G. W. (2014). Media Salience and the Framing of Mass Murder in Schools: A Comparison of the Columbine and Sandy Hook Massacres. *Homicide Studies* 18(1), 23–43.

Simon, H. A. (1955). A Behavioral Model of Rational Choice. *The Quarterly Journal of Economics* 69(1), 99–118.

Spitzer, R. J. (2012). *The Politics of Gun Control* (5th edn). Boulder, CO: Paradigm.

Stone, D. A. (1989). Causal Stories and the Formation of Policy Agendas. *Political Science Quarterly* 104(2), 281–300.

Tatalovich, R. and Daynes, B. W. (eds). (2011). *Moral Controversies in American Politics* (4th edn). Armonk: M.E. Sharpe.

True, J. L. and Utter, G. H. (2002). Saying 'Yes', 'No', and 'Load Me Up' to Guns in America. *The American Review of Public Administration* 32(2), 216–241.

Verlinden, S., Hersen, M. and Thomas, J. (2000). Risk Factors in School Shootings. *Clinical Psychology Review* 20(1), 3–56.

Vizzard, W. J. (1995). The Impact of Agenda Conflict on Policy Formulation and Implementation: The Case of Gun Control. *Public Administration Review* 55(4), 341–347.

Walgrave, S. and Varone, F. (2008). Punctuated Equilibrium and Agenda-Setting: Bringing Parties Back in: Policy Change after the Dutroux Crisis in Belgium. *Governance* 21(3), 365–395.

Williams, R. A. (2009). Exogenous Shocks in Subsystem Adjustment and Policy Change: The Credit Crunch and Canadian Banking Regulation. *Journal of Public Policy* 29(1), 29–53.

Wilson, J. Q. (1973). *Political Organizations*. New York: Basic Books.

Wood, R. S. (2006). Tobacco's Tipping Point: The Master Settlement Agreement as a Focusing Event. *Policy Studies Journal* 34(3), 419–436.

Ybarra, M. L., Diener-West, M., Markow, D., Leaf, P. J., Hamburger, M. and Boxer, P. (2008). Linkages between Internet and Other Media Violence with Seriously Violent Behavior by Youth. *Pediatrics* 122(5), 929–937.

4 Theorizing conditions for politicization, policy change and stability

This chapter develops a set of theoretical expectations which guide the empirical analysis. It should be pointed out from the outset that the theoretical expectations developed in this chapter should not be read as full-blown, deductively derived research hypotheses, but as a theoretical grid structuring the remainder of the book. In this context, it is critically important to emphasize that this book makes the assumption that the processes generated by potential focusing events are highly context-specific and complex. This implies that we will hardly find a 'one-size-fits-all' explanation of politicization and policy change after rampage shootings. Instead, it is more reasonable to assume that both politicization and policy change can result from different causal configurations. In other words, we should not assume that any of the theoretical arguments presented below work in total isolation from one another. Instead, the configuration of different conditions may be critically important and as a logical corollary of this notion of causal complexity, both politicization and policy change can be the result of equifinal processes. Unlike in many other empirical studies in the social sciences, however, equifinality is not conceived of as a basic epistemological problem, but as a chance to make more precise statements about the different paths that can result in one and the same outcome. As the empirical section of the book will demonstrate, such a perspective provides us with insights that we might have missed otherwise. Thus, the theoretical expectations below should be read as 'baseline expectations', whose precise impact on politicization and policy change may be conditioned by the configuration of the other factors.

4.1 Theoretical expectations on the politicization of gun control

This first sub-section presents theoretical expectations on the factors driving the politicization of gun control after rampage shootings. The discussion starts with the implications of an event's 'objective' severity for the politicization process, then turns to the role of the mass media as drivers of moral panics and closes with a discussion of party politics and the timing of the event in the electoral cycle.

42 Theoretical framework

4.1.1 Pavlovian politics? The role of 'objective' event severity

Some scholars have emphasized that the political impact of potential focusing events critically depends on the magnitude of the implied shock (Birkland 2006; Cortell and Peterson 1999; Keeler 1993; Worrall 1999). When a stone is thrown into a pond, the size of the stone determines the size of the resulting waves. Analogically, the main event-related condition that should contribute to the politicization of gun control in the aftermath of a potential focusing event is the event's severity in objective terms. As far as rampage shootings are concerned, there is one indicator in particular which measures such objective event severity: the number of fatalities resulting from the rampage shooting. This argument not only makes intuitive sense, it is also bolstered by empirical findings from other policy areas prone to disaster. For example, the regulation of nuclear power plants has sparked considerable political debates in many countries after the disasters at Three Mile Island (Nohrstedt 2005, 2010), Chernobyl (Nohrstedt 2008, 2010) and Fukushima (Wittneben 2012), while the many other technical failures which occurred in other nuclear facilities hardly generated any sustained public interest. Also terrorist attacks are a case in point (compare, for example, the scope of the political debate in the wake of 9/11 and the Boston Bombings of 2013). Further examples include natural disasters like flash floods (e.g. Voss and Wagner 2010) or technical failures like plane crashes (Birkland 2006). All of these events have in common that they can vary significantly in scale, in particular in terms of how many people they affect and there is good reason to assume that this difference with regard to objective event severity is directly related to the scope of ensuing efforts of politicization.

The causal mechanism that drives this relationship is rooted in the notion of 'Pavlovian politics' (Lodge 2011; Lodge and Hood 2002). According to this logic, policymaking are conditioned to react to external stimuli. However, the simple fact that there is a plethora of simultaneous external stimuli requires policy makers to prioritize the incoming information. In this contest for attention, the stimuli which exert the most power have the best chance to evoke a reaction. Accordingly, the relative size of the damage resulting from a potential focusing event should bear relevance for the extent to which policy makers are willing to invest in efforts of politicization as a reaction to the shock. While relatively small stimuli always imply the potential to be ignored, larger stimuli can hardly be absorbed due to their mere scope. Unlike the argument on the meaning making of the mass media presented in the following sub-section, the argument on the impact of objective event severity is not based on any social constructivist claims, but builds on the assumption that actors are boundedly rational. As such, they filter incoming information for relevance and act according to the strongest stimulus. Accordingly, the first theoretical baseline expectation on politicization after potential focusing events reads as follows.

Theoretical expectation 1: Events of high objective severity lead to politicization in the affected policy area, whereas events of relatively low objective severity do not.

4.1.2 The mass media as drivers of moral panics

On a societal level, varying increases in media attention in the wake of a potential focusing event should be understood as one particularly important societal condition which can potentially promote the politicization of policy failures. After a potential focusing event, the mass media often occupy a central role in the political process by expressing and transmitting the public opinion about the shock's implications to the political actors (Birkland 1998; Birkland and Lawrence 2009). In addition to their role as conveyors of the public mood, the mass media are also independent societal actors which can decide on whether an event is relevant politically or not. By deciding over the newsworthiness of an event, they directly challenge political actors to position themselves on the event's potential political implications. One might be tempted to think that media attention is a direct corollary of objective event severity, but this assumption is not only questionable theoretically, but also not tenable in empirical terms. As social constructivism suggests, what really matters for the setting of the political agenda is not the objective size of a problem but the way the severity of a problem is perceived by societal actors. Following this logic, media attention does not measure objective, but perceived event severity. For instance, school shootings are generally perceived as particularly gruesome sub-types of rampage shootings, because they affect an especially vulnerable target population, namely children (Hawdon *et al.* 2012). As a corollary, those events should lead to a much greater increase in media attention than events outside of educational institutions, regardless of their objective severity.

Thus, by their ability to devote disproportionate attention to an isolated incident, the media have the power to contribute to the development of a moral panic, during which a small part of the population is targeted as the 'folk devils' (Cohen 1972). During a moral panic, a formerly largely ignored type of deviant behaviour can become the subject of intense political debate that is often based upon a conflict of 'us versus them'. In the seminal contribution by Cohen (1972), drug users were the empirical example for the illustration of the argumentation, but others have argued that also gun owners have become the subject of moral panics in the wake of school shootings (Burns and Crawford 1999). Accordingly, unlike the argument on the direct effect of objective indicators of problem pressure on the politicization of corresponding policy failures presented in the previous section, the notion of moral panics is firmly rooted in social constructivism. The central factor that drives the development of moral panics is the extreme reaction of the media to isolated events, whose probability of swift re-occurrence is negligible. Thus, the media do not merely react automatically to objective indicators of newsworthiness, but can either decide to ignore objectively severe events or blow events of smaller objective severity out of proportion. As we will discover later, Western European media outlets have done both over the course of the past 20 years, implying that media attention should not be equated with objective event severity.

44 *Theoretical framework*

According to those considerations, we can summarize the second theoretical expectation on the politicization of policy failures after potential focusing events as follows.

Theoretical expectation 2: Events that lead to extreme increases in media attention lead to politicization in the affected policy area, whereas events that are not covered extensively by the media do not.

4.1.3 Partisan cleavages, issue ownership and the electoral cycle

Finally, two political conditions and their interplay should be expected to play a prominent role for politicization efforts in the area of gun control after rampage shootings: party politics and the timing of the event in the electoral cycle.

First, whether or not a particular issue becomes subject to political controversy should not the least depend on the extent to which it touches upon an existing cleavage in the party system. If no party has an incentive to politicize a given issue, it will most likely be dealt with in expert circles and not be subject to intense public debates. If, however, a party has something to gain from highlighting a certain problem, it will do so. It may either do so because it wants to signal to its constituents that it cares about the same issues, or it may do so in order to expose the ignorance of the other parties. In addition to these political goals, parties may of course also want to politicize a given issue because they really want to change the state of affairs, i.e. act as policy seekers. Empirically, the relevance of those claims has recently been underscored by research in the area of morality policy making. While issues like abortion or euthanasia hardly ever become politicized in secular party systems, they often become subject to political debates in religious party systems, where some parties base their ideology on religious values while others do not (Engeli 2012). As a corollary of those different levels of politicization, morality policies tend to be more stable in the secular world than in the religious world.

Thus, the presence of a partisan cleavage on a given policy issue should facilitate politicization and it is reasonable to expect that the process should even be accelerated by the occurrence of a potential focusing event that signifies a policy failure in the respective issue area. When it comes to the identification of public problems, political parties assume a central role, especially in parliamentary democracies. Based on their ideological orientation, they filter and interpret incoming information and derive desirable courses of action for public policies. In the US context, it has been demonstrated by research on the micro-level that the attribution of causes for rampage shootings depends heavily on party affiliations. While supporters of the Republican Party tend to blame the individual perpetrator, Democrats tend to blame the social and political environment (Joslyn and Haider-Markel 2013). As a result of these different perceptions, the supporters of the two parties often draw fundamentally different lessons from one and the same event. When transferred to the meso-level of political parties, those findings relate to existing arguments on 'issue ownership' (Petrocik 1996) and 'selective issue emphasis'. According to this logic, parties (and in the US

Theoretical framework 45

context individual politicians) attempt to emphasize policy issues they are generally positively associated with by the population and downplay the importance of issues owned by other parties. However, as recent research has demonstrated, issue ownership only works to the benefit of the owner if the respective issue enjoys a certain amount of public salience (Bélanger and Meguid 2008). While gun control is typically not the most salient issue to voters in Europe most of the time, the issue's salience can increase rapidly if a potential focusing event challenges the legitimacy of the regulatory status quo. Therefore, if a party owns the issue of gun control and the status quo is challenged by a potential focusing event, we should expect the party that owns the issue to try to exploit the developing crisis politically. Yet, which parties generally own the issue of gun control in the European context?

Unlike in the areas of morality policy cited previously, the main cleavage between political parties in the area of firearm regulation probably does not run along religious lines. Instead, we should expect different incentives for politicizing gun control in conservative, liberal and rural parties on the one hand, and 'progressive' parties on the other hand. Let us first consider the former three types of parties. Conservative parties are by definition interested in defending the status quo (after all that is why they are called conservative). Accordingly, we should not expect conservative parties to be particularly proactive in pushing for stricter rules for gun ownership after a rampage shooting. The same goes with liberal parties, but for a different reason.[1] Liberal parties are based on the conviction that individual freedom and the right for self-determination should be maximized and that governmental infringements on personal liberties should be as minimal as possible. For this reason, we should expect liberal parties to side with conservative parties in the aftermath of rampage shootings on the matter of gun control. Finally, rurally based parties usually draw their support from farmers or hunters, who often possess firearms. In order to avoid an alienation of their support base, we should also expect rural parties to remain silent on the gun issue after rampage shootings or deflect public attention to other plausible causal stories.

The incentive structure looks different for parties that are strongly attached to pacifism and therefore condemn violence in general. Such parties arguably primarily conceive of firearms as instruments of conducting violence, not as tools for sports or hunting. Accordingly, we should expect such parties to exploit windows of opportunity opened by rampage shootings and push the regulatory status quo towards their own preferences. Some progressive parties may even question the very need for civilian gun possession and demand the prohibition of private firearms.

In Europe, especially green parties have earned a reputation of believing in pacifism and condemning the possession and use of weapons. Evidence from an original online expert survey carried out in 2013 support this argument (see Figure 4.1). While green parties tend to be consistently in opposition to civilian gun ownership, other parties scatter much more strongly across the preference range. Socialist and Social Democratic parties tend to be rather critical of private

46 *Theoretical framework*

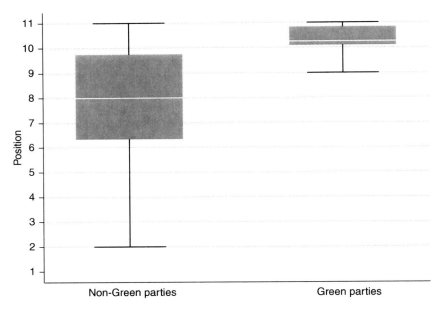

Figure 4.1 Party positions on gun control.

Note
The measured dimension runs from permissive (1) to restrictive (11). Experts were asked the question 'Where would you locate the following parties on a dimension that ranges from permissive (no constraints on private firearm ownership) to restrictive (total prohibition of private firearm ownership)?' N: 56 non-green parties and 8 green parties in 10 European countries (Austria, Belgium, Denmark, Finland, Germany, Great Britain, Greece, Ireland, Norway and Switzerland).

gun possession, but are usually much more divided on the issue. With regard to green parties, however, there is hardly any ideological variance across countries as far as gun control is concerned. There is variance, however, in the extent to which green parties existed at all during the time period under investigation and in particular, the extent to which they were represented in parliament.

Thus, we should expect that the existence and parliamentary representation of a green party contributes to the politicization of gun control in the aftermath of rampage shootings. In fact, it is possible that the presence of a green party is sufficient for the politicization of gun control. While this is a theoretically interesting proposition, it is already clear from the outset that the presence of a conservative party cannot be sufficient for the *absence* of politicization. This is true almost by default because there are hardly any national parliaments in democratic systems which lack a conservative party. Moreover, it is hardly possible for any individual party to prevent other parties from politicizing an issue. While the extent to which change-averse governments are cohesive in their opposition to policy change may have important repercussions when it comes to decision-making (see section 4.2.3 below), governments are not the only actors

Theoretical framework 47

who can set the political agenda in democratic systems (see section 2.2). Also the opposition can choose to politicize a given issue if it considers the associated benefits higher than the costs.

Theoretical expectation 3: An event will lead to politicization if it affects a political issue for which a partisan cleavage already exists. If a clear-cut partisan cleavage is absent, the policy failure implied by the event will not be politicized.

The second political condition which is deemed important for the politicization of the policy failure implied by a potential focusing event is the event's timing in the electoral cycle. Some previous research suggests that external shocks have a particularly strong impact on politicization if elections are looming on the horizon (Boin *et al.* 2009: 99). Building on a comparative analysis of 15 crisis episodes, the authors conclude that

> on balance, the cases studied suggest that the closer a crisis hits to the (anticipated) time of a forthcoming election, the more likely that crisis exploitation attempts to change advocates will be successful, and thus the higher the likelihood of elite damage, policy reform and institutional change.
>
> (Boin *et al.* 2009: 99)

Thus, if elections are close, political parties will have an incentive to exploit the crisis as an opportunity to present themselves as the ones who care for the population and save them from harm. As Boin *et al.*'s study suggests, this should be particularly true for minority coalitions that have a track record of criticizing the status quo in the affected policy area. Thus, national elections do not only function as events altering the power constellation in the political arena (i.e. as parts of Kingdon's political stream), but can influence the strategic considerations of political elites through anticipation.

This argument is further supported by another empirical study on the treatment of the Dutroux scandal in Belgium (Walgrave and Varone 2008). During the first period of the scandal, the involved political actors 'could afford to let the storm blow over and await better times' (Walgrave and Varone 2008: 388). This situation changed two years later when the scandal again became a public issue due to the escape of the perpetrator from prison. This time, however, elections were approaching which, according to the authors, contributed to the more pronounced political reaction. Additional evidence for the positive effect of proximate elections on the politicization of policy failures has been provided by Brändström and Kuipers (2003: 289) in their analysis of the impact of the Srebrenica massacre on Dutch politics.

Thus, the existing literature suggests that political actors will be more inclined to highlight the deficiencies of a given policy arrangement if the event that puts the spotlight on the policy issue occurs in the context of an election campaign. The causal mechanism for this argument is related to the anticipation of electoral gains by the involved political stakeholders. If an external shock can be framed as an indicator of a policy failure (as it is the case for all rampage shootings

48 Theoretical framework

committed with legal firearms), such attempts will rather be made if electoral rewards can be anticipated in the near future. Given these considerations, we can formulate the final theoretical expectation on politicization as follows.

Theoretical expectation 4: An event will lead to politicization if it occurs in close temporal proximity to a national election. If elections are temporally distant, the event will not lead to politicization.

To sum up, this section developed four theoretical expectations on the drivers of the politicization of policy failures in the aftermath of potential focusing events. First, the shock's severity in objective terms should be important. In the present empirical context, objective event severity can be approximated by the total number of people harmed by the respective event. Second, the mass media were argued to be driving forces of politicization as they have the power to create a moral panic which in turn creates the urge to act politically on behalf of the responsible political actors. Finally, the extent to which a potential focusing event becomes politicized should be related to the existence of a partisan cleavage in the affected policy area and the proximity of national elections. In the following sub-section, the theoretical expectations on the drivers of policy change and stability are developed.

4.2 Theoretical expectations on policy change and stability

As outlined previously, not all potential focusing events that get politicized ultimately result in regulatory changes of the status quo. Therefore, this section develops theoretical expectations on the factors which facilitate and impede policy change, given a policy failure has been identified and politicized. First, varying degrees of an event's causal complexity and resulting varying opportunities for framing are presented as factors that have the potential to either facilitate the political process or bring it to a deadlock. Second, the emergence and commitment of social movements is argued to play a decisive role for keeping the issue on the political agenda, when the issue attention cycle is about to kick in. Finally, the cohesiveness of the status quo advocates and decision hurdles set by the affected country's political and socio-cultural institutions are discussed as political factors that can impede and accelerate the reform process.

4.2.1 Perceived event complexity as a driver of policy change and stability

As mentioned in the previous chapter, existing research on the policy impacts of external shocks places a strong emphasis on the relevance of framing.[2] For the most part, however, the focus of these studies is centred on the distinct ways the media make sense of an event (e.g. Birkland and Lawrence 2009; Chyi and McCombs 2004; Muschert 2009). In contrast, deliberate framing efforts by the involved political actors have only received scant attention and have predominantly been associated with agenda-setting dynamics (Rochefort and Cobb 1993; Stone 1989). In this context, the elevation of social conditions to social problems

Theoretical framework 49

was argued to be the product of 'problem definition', which is composed of arguments on a certain problem causation, the portrayal of the nature of the problem along the dimensions of severity, incidence, novelty, proximity and crisis, arguments on the characteristics of the problem population, ends-means orientations of the problem definer, and the nature of the solution, which can vary in terms of availability, acceptability and affordability (Rochefort and Cobb 1993: 62). Despite the great influence of this problem definition perspective on agenda-setting studies, it involves a certain inconsistency with regard to the aspects of 'problem causation' and the 'nature of the solution'. In fact, if we acknowledge that multiple causes can be brought to bear, this directly implies that multiple potential solutions can co-exist. Accordingly, the critical question for policy change is not only whether or not a solution is available, as Rochefort and Cobb (1993: 69) suggest, but how many solutions are available at the same time and compete for political acceptance. As a result, the public and political discourse on a certain problem can vary in complexity depending on the number and quality of the problem's available solutions. The more potential solutions compete for support among decision-makers and the public, the stronger the political attention is dispersed among different policy areas. If we assume that the amount of attention devoted to a certain policy area is related to the scope of political action in that area, then there is good reason to believe that the dynamics of problem definition extend beyond the agenda-setting stage and can impact upon the decision-making process. However, research that connects the intensity of framing contests after external shocks to patterns of policy change has only developed more recently (Boin *et al.* 2009; Hurka and Nebel 2013).

This research suggests that the variety of interpretive frames that can be brought to bear in order to make sense of an event has implications for the scope of ensuing reform efforts. In other words, whether or not a focusing event eventually leads to policy change in a given policy area should to a certain extent be a function of the event's perceived causal complexity. The more policy areas a focusing event affects simultaneously, the smaller the political focus on any single one of those policy areas will eventually become and the smaller the eventual degree of policy change will be. As outlined above, however, the number of policy areas a focusing event affects is not necessarily an objectively determinable entity, but depends upon the framing skills of the involved political actors. This becomes particularly evident when we look at framing contests after rampage shootings. While legal access to guns is one of the causes which can invariably be brought to bear, policy makers often become quite creative with regard to the alternative causal attributions they attach to an event (Hurka and Nebel 2013; Stone 1989). As far as the empirical context of this inquiry is concerned, examples of such competing frames include the consumption of violent media content and ensuing calls for censoring or prohibition. Other frames include a lack of security measures in public spaces or buildings and the ensuing calls of their installation (e.g. video surveillance or metal detectors). Still other frames include the lack of medical treatment for mentally ill people or the lack of social cohesion and decay in moral values which all arguably contribute to the

50 *Theoretical framework*

occurrence of rampage shootings. If an event, by its simple idiosyncratic characteristics, invites the application of multiple causal stories which all share some face validity, it will become extremely difficult for change advocates in the area of gun control to focus the national debate on their issue. This is because opponents of the 'gun story' will find it easy to deflect the public debate to other causal frames. In such situations, policy stability should be the more likely result in the area of gun control. If, however, status quo advocates in the area of gun control cannot provide a convincing alternative causal story, firearm-related policy change becomes attainable.

Given those considerations, the corresponding theoretical expectation can be summarized as follows.

Theoretical expectation 5: If a focusing event is of high causal complexity and allows for multiple competing frames, policy stability will result. If an event is of low causal complexity and the debate focuses on one isolated policy issue, policy change will occur.

4.2.2 The role of societal mobilization – fighting the issue attention cycle

A second important factor that should have an impact on the degree of policy change after a focusing event is the extent to which societal actors commit themselves to the reform process. After large-scale events, the public sometimes becomes intricately involved in the political process by organizing into social movements and pressure groups (Birkland 1998; Gamson 1990; Giugni and Yamasaki 2009; Nathanson 1999). Collective anger, fear, or disappointment can result in concerted attempts of a few directly affected people to convince the broader public of the need for reform. Often led by charismatic 'policy entrepreneurs' (Kingdon 1984), they try to exploit the crisis and the resulting window of opportunity by advancing their cause and offering their solutions publicly. One of the most well-known historical examples of such movements is the antinuclear movement (Kitschelt 1986), a more recent one is the movement against allegedly neo-liberal financial institutions, popularly known as the Occupy movement. In the research program on social movements, Walgrave and Verhulst (2006) have additionally introduced the category of 'new emotional movements', which represents a very specific type of social movement that makes extensive use of emotions in their advocacy work. The authors explicitly discuss movements which originated out of rampage shootings (the Snowdrop Campaign in Great Britain and the Million Mom March in the United States) as instances of such new emotional movements.

Yet, how exactly do social movements exert their influence in the political processing of external shocks? In order to answer this question, it is useful to first recall Anthony Downs' arguments on the 'issue attention cycle' (1972). As Downs suggests, most public problems are usually dealt with by small circles of experts, but every now and then, problem pressure rises sharply and leads to 'alarmed discovery and euphoric enthusiasm' among the population that the

Theoretical framework 51

problem can and should be solved. However, it usually does not take a very long time until public interest in the problem wanes due to the recognition of the costs associated with the solution and other downsides. As a result 'an issue that has been replaced at the centre of public concern moves into a prolonged limbo – a twilight realm of lesser attention or spasmodic recurrences of interest' (Downs 1972: 40).

In the aftermath of focusing events in general and rampage shootings in particular, Downs' notion of 'alarmed discovery' characterizes the typical public reaction very well.[3] However, the short attention span of the general public is often blamed for the petering out of reform efforts. In other words, if the public loses interest in a reform of the gun laws, the window of opportunity closes and policy makers will turn their attention away to other issues, as predicted by the Downsian issue attention cycle. Therefore, the commitment of political actors to pursue political reforms should depend to a great extent on the commitment of societal actors to demand those reforms in a sustained manner. In such a situation, it may be the case that even unwilling governments will feel the urge to act. Unlike rapid increases in media attention, societal mobilization does not necessarily help to raise awareness over an issue in the short run. This is because social movements that emerge in response to potential focusing events usually take some time to develop and find ways to coordinate and organize. The critical question in terms of policy change becomes whether the initial commitment within the social movement can actually be sustained over a longer period of time. If it cannot, public attention to the issue will eventually fade as predicted by the 'issue attention cycle' (Downs 1972). Accordingly, sustained societal demand is argued to be critically important in order to keep an issue on the political agenda when the media have turned their attention to new stories and thereby increase the probability of policy change. The corresponding theoretical expectation following from these considerations can be formulated as follows.

Theoretical expectation 6: A focusing event will lead to policy change if societal actors demand such change in a sustained manner. An event will lead to policy stability if such societal mobilization is lacking.

4.2.3 The cohesion of reform opponents and institutional arrangements

As far as political conditions are concerned, two factors appear particularly relevant for the explanation of policy change and stability: the cohesion of the status quo coalition and the decision hurdles set by the affected country's political and socio-cultural institutions.

Since the occurrence of a rampage shooting invariably challenges the legitimacy of the status quo in the area of gun control, it is safe to assume that the actor coalition which had favoured stricter regulations in the first place will not suffer from major defections in its ranks. In other words, the policy failure indicated by the rampage shooting should rather reinforce the existing policy preferences of the change coalition, instead of destabilizing them. Given this

52 Theoretical framework

assumption, we should observe relatively high cohesion among change advocates after rampage shootings. After all, the rampage shooting underscores the legitimacy of their policy goal and opens a window of opportunity for the pursuit of their objective. Accordingly, we can assume that high cohesion among change advocates is rather a constant than a variable in the wake of rampage shootings. This theoretical assumption has recently also been buttressed empirically (Hurka and Nebel 2013).

Therefore, whether or not an initiated reform effort is successful should rather depend on the cohesion of the reform opponents in the area of gun control. If status quo advocates manage to keep their ranks closed and oppose the reform effort cohesively, chances are that the commitment of the change advocates ultimately wanes and policy stability will be the result. In other words, attempts to introduce tighter gun control measures will be unsuccessful if the reform opponents speak with one voice and central actors do not defect. If, however, important actors from the status quo coalition side with the change advocates early on during the political debate, the remaining status quo advocates will find it exceedingly difficult to contain the reform process. Actors of the status quo coalition may want to defect for various reasons. For instance, they may want to try to take advantage of public opinion and expect electoral benefits of their defecting behaviour. Alternatively, they may simply be change advocates 'in disguise', i.e. actors who are generally conservative on many other issues but hold strong preferences on the particular matter of gun control. Based on these considerations, we arrive at theoretical expectation 7.

Theoretical expectation 7: A potential focusing event will lead to policy change if the coalition of reform opponents is incohesive. An event will lead to policy stability if the coalition of reform opponents is cohesive.

Regardless of the precise composition of the change and status quo coalitions, however, the extent to which actors are able to translate their preferences into public policies is critically constrained by the way national political institutions are designed (Immergut 1990; Lijphart 1999, 2012; Siaroff 2003; Tsebelis 2002). By providing a legal framework for decision-making procedures, political institutions set the rules of the game which political actors must take into account when they engage in policy making (Scharpf 1997, 2000). This classical perspective on the role of institutional configurations has found many followers in political science and hardly any explanation of political processes ignores the central role of formal rules set by political institutions. One major characteristic of political institutions is their relatively high stability over time. Once a state has adopted certain institutional configurations, it is very unlikely that those configurations will be altered meaningfully, at least in the short run. Thus, institutional configurations are typically highly persistent and can be described as structural factors, which determine the range of opportunities actors face when they engage in political negotiations. This interpretation of political institutions as 'rules of the game' has been defended most prominently by Fritz W. Scharpf, who distinguished between actors as proximate and institutions as remote causes of policy change (Scharpf 2000: 764).

Theoretical framework 53

However, the design of political institutions varies across countries. While some countries impose very high institutional hurdles which need to be overcome in order to change the course of a public policy, other countries provide more room to manoeuvre for political actors, in particular governments. The most prominent attempt to measure patterns of political institutions cross-nationally has been carried out by Lijphart (1999, 2012), who has introduced the distinction between majoritarian and consensual democracies in order to make sense of those different approaches and facilitate theory building on their effects on public policies. While majoritarian democracies are characterized by a concentration of political power in the hands of the elected government, consensual democracies disperse power both horizontally and vertically in order to avoid too rapid and extreme policy shifts. As a result of these different approaches, changes in the composition of a national government should lead to faster and more profound alterations of public policies in majoritarian systems than in consensual systems (Lijphart 2012: 255f.).

Politico-institutional hurdles come in different forms, such as constitutional constraints, federalism, decentralization, bicameralism, and different types of electoral or party systems. Taken together, such institutional arrangements strongly influence the extent to which a government can react quickly and decisively to newly arising challenges. Fleming (2012) identified the presidential system of the United States and the parliamentary system of Canada as key drivers of policy stability and change in the aftermath of rampage shootings in the two countries. According to the author, the Canadian parliamentary system has helped to bring about gun-related policy changes while the presidential US system has obstructed similar efforts. However, there are 'varieties of parliamentarism' (Siaroff 2003) and different parliamentary systems can be made up of highly diverse political institutions. Therefore, parliamentary democracies should not be regarded as a uniform class of political systems, but should be distinguished according to the extent their political institutions facilitate or obstruct efforts of policy change. Most importantly, parliamentary democracies vary with regard to the relationship between the executive and legislative branches of government. In some countries, the executive is relatively weak and greatly depends on the support of the legislative branch; in other states the government dominates the legislature. For the present research purpose, it is reasonable to expect that the extent to which an executive is institutionally constrained should bear much relevance for the speed and scope of policy change dynamics in general and after focusing events in particular. As Immergut (1990: 397) has put it: 'The key variable is the independence of the political executive from vetoes at subsequent points in the chain of decision.' Based on these considerations, we arrive at the following theoretical expectation.

Theoretical expectation 8a: A focusing event will lead to policy change if the decision hurdles set by the affected country's political institutions are low. If these decision hurdles are high, policy stability will result.

Yet, this narrow view on institutions as political constraints for governments does not take into account other types of institutional hurdles which may be

54 Theoretical framework

equally important with regard to their capacity to facilitate or obstruct policy reforms after focusing events. Specifically, institutional hurdles are not necessarily only of a political nature; they can as well be based on socio-cultural norms concerning the affected area of regulation. In general, every modern nation-state is the product of a distinct cultural heritage, which often manifests itself in varying designs of public policies. Traditions and conventions exert their impact over centuries, establishing culturally distinct perceptions of the world. In some countries, certain practices become culturally entrenched and thereby universally accepted, while the same practices are continuously challenged elsewhere. Historical institutionalists have put a strong emphasis on the important role of past political decisions for subsequent policy developments (Mahoney 2000; Pierson 2000; Thelen 1999). In this logic, self-reinforcing dynamics lead to stability of the status quo, whereas 'critical junctures' can challenge existing arrangements and lead to a break with the past (Pierson 2000). Thus, political actors will often find it extremely diffcult to change a long established policy program fundamentally within the regular policy process and in the absence of some external shock. Yet, even if such a shock occurs, cultural factors will mediate its policy impact by affecting the way it is perceived by various actors, including societal actors, the media, and politicians. Thus, the implications of very similar events can be interpreted in dramatically different ways, depending on the cultural and historical background against which they occur.

Within the realm of political science, this notion of culture as an influential factor for policy designs is closely connected to sociological institutionalism (Hall and Taylor 1996: 946–950; March and Olsen 1996). According to this line of thought, societies set up their institutional arrangements not solely due to functional considerations, but also according to a 'logic of appropriateness' (March and Olsen 1996: 252). If a given policy approach is incompatible with a nation's cultural heritage, it will not be adopted regardless of its potential efficiency in solving a social problem. Also gun policies are heavily influenced by cultural factors. About 40 years ago, Richard Hofstadter (1970) coined the term 'gun culture' in order to describe the deep affection towards firearms in the United States, which can only be understood against the background of the country's fight for independence and the resulting mistrust against government in general. Also a pronounced hunting tradition and the frontier spirit of the early settlers have contributed to this unparalleled US gun culture (Spitzer 2012: 9f.). Eventually, the cultural affection towards guns was enshrined into the second amendment of the US constitution. Even though the relationship between easy availability of firearms and high crime rates is well established (Hepburn and Hemenway 2004), attempts to introduce stricter gun control have repeatedly failed, even after devastating school shootings (Schildkraut and Cox Hernandez 2014). A country which is often cited as a counter-example to the United States is Great Britain (Squires 2000), where firearm ownership used to be regarded as a privilege of the 'upper echelons and the landed gentry' (Lilly 2001: 69). In Great Britain, the mere possibility of an emergence of an US-style gun culture evoked strong public sentiment in the wake of the shootings at Hungerford and

Dunblane and eventually contributed to the comparably strong political reactions to those events (see the respective case study on Dunblane in section 7.1.1).

The most straightforward indicator that captures the extent to which firearms permeate a society is the availability of firearms in a given country. The higher the number of firearms in circulation, the higher is the number of people potentially affected by new firearm regulations. As a result, the cultural phenomenon of high firearm ownership can affect the tangible electoral considerations of responsible politicians. Thus, it should be expected that attempts to tighten gun laws in the wake of rampage shootings should be more successful the less the population is culturally attached to guns. If socio-cultural ties to firearms are strong, however, such attempts should be less successful. Thus, given the considerations in this section, the theoretical arguments on the effects of institutional arrangements can be formulated as follows.

Theoretical expectation 8b: A focusing event will lead to policy change if the decision hurdles set by the affected country's socio-cultural institutions are low. If these decision hurdles are high, policy stability will result.

4.3 Summary of the theoretical expectations

Figure 4.2 summarizes the theoretical expectations outlined above graphically. It is important to note that the line of argumentation followed throughout this book implies that the political process following a potential focusing event should be thought of as a selection process. In other words, political and societal actors first single out events they deem worthy of a political discussion and then engage in a quest to find an appropriate political response. As a logical implication,

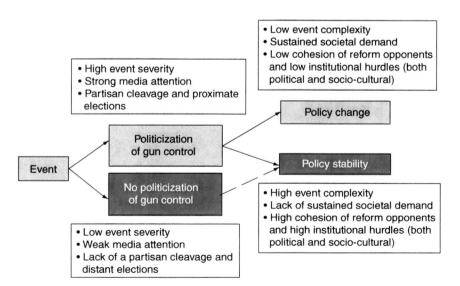

Figure 4.2 Summary of theoretical expectations.

56 *Theoretical framework*

politicization is considered necessary for policy change, but it is not sufficient. Accordingly, the question of policy change is downstream to the question of politicization and it is therefore critically important to evaluate both separately. This is because the outcome policy stability can be the result of two (equifinal) paths: either the event leads to a political discussion but does not result in any political reaction, or the event is being ignored by political actors in the first place.

After these theoretical considerations, the next chapter explains the case selection, provides some information on the data sources, and discusses the methodological approach of the analytical part of the book.

Notes

1 It should be pointed out here that the term 'liberal' is used in its European connotation, not in the US connotation.
2 No universal and uncontested definition of the term 'framing' has emerged, yet. However, a very useful definition has been provided by Entman (1993: 52) who argues that framing 'is to select some aspects of a perceived reality and make them more salient in a communicating text, in such a way as to promote a particular problem definition, causal interpretation, moral evaluation, and/or treatment recommendation.' While this definition is generally used by communication scholars, is equally applicable to applications of political science if we drop the requirement of a 'communicating text'.
3 Needless to say, the notion of 'euphoric enthusiasm' is rather inappropriate in the context of rampage shootings.

References

Bélanger, É. and Meguid, B. M. (2008). Issue Salience, Issue Qwnership, and Issue-based Vote Choice. *Electoral Studies* 27(3), 477–491.

Birkland, T. A. (1998). Focusing Events, Mobilization, and Agenda Setting. *Journal of Public Policy* 18(1), 53–74.

Birkland, T. A. (2006). *Lessons of Disaster: Policy Change after Catastrophic Events.* Washington, D.C.: Georgetown University Press.

Birkland, T. A. and Lawrence, R. G. (2009). Media Framing and Policy Change after Columbine. *American Behavioral Scientist* 52(10), 1405–1425.

Boin, A., t'Hart, P. and McConnell, A. (2009). Crisis Exploitation: Political and Policy Impacts of Framing Contests. *Journal of European Public Policy* 16(1), 81–106.

Brändström, A. and Kuipers, S. (2003). From 'Normal Incidents' to Political Crises: Understanding the Selective Politicization of Policy Failures. *Government and Opposition* 38(3), 279–305.

Burns, R. and Crawford, C. (1999). School Shootings, the Media, and Public Fear: Ingredients for a Moral Panic. *Crime, Law and Social Change* 32(2), 147–168.

Chyi, H. I. and McCombs, M. (2004). Media Salience and the Process of Framing: Coverage of the Columbine School Shootings. *Journalism & Mass Communication Quarterly* 81(1), 22–35.

Cohen, S. (1972). *Folk Devils and Moral Panics: The Creation of the Mods and Rockers.* London: MacGibbon and Kee.

Cortell, A. P. and Peterson, S. (1999). Altered States: Explaining Domestic Institutional Change. *British Journal of Political Science* 29(1), 177–203.

Theoretical framework 57

Downs, A. (1972). Up and Down with Ecology: The Issue Attention Cycle. *Public Interest* 28(1), 38–50.

Engeli, I. (2012). Policy Struggle on Reproduction: Doctors, Women, and Christians. *Political Research Quarterly* 65(2), 330–345.

Entman, R. M. (1993). Framing: Toward Clarification of a Fractured Paradigm. *Journal of Communication* 43(4), 51–58.

Fleming, A. K. (2012). *Gun Policy in the United States and Canada: The Impact of Mass Murders and Assassinations on Gun Policy*. New York: Continuum International Publishing Group.

Gamson, W. A. (1990). *The Strategy of Social Protest* (2nd edn). Belmont: Wadsworth.

Giugni, M. and Yamasaki, S. (2009). The Policy Impact of Social Movements: A Replication through Qualitative Comparative Analysis. *Mobilization: An International Journal* 14(4), 467–484.

Hall, P. A. and Taylor, R. C. R. (1996). Political Science and the Three New Institutionalisms. *Political Studies* 44(5), 936–957.

Hawdon, J., Oksanen, A. and Räsänen, P. (2012). Media Coverage and Solidarity after Tragedies: The Reporting of School Shootings in Two Nations. *Comparative Sociology* 11(6), 845–874.

Hepburn, L. M. and Hemenway, D. (2004). Firearm Availability and Homicide: A Review of the Literature. *Aggression and Violent Behavior* 9(4), 417–440.

Hofstadter, R. (1970). America as a Gun Culture. *American Heritage* 21(6), 4–10.

Hurka, S. and Nebel, K. (2013). Framing and Policy Change after Shooting Rampages: A Comparative Analysis of Discourse Networks. *Journal of European Public Policy* 20(3), 390–406.

Immergut, E. M. (1990). Institutions, Veto Points, and Policy Results: A Comparative Analysis of Health Care. *Journal of Public Policy* 10(4), 391–416.

Joslyn, M. R. and Haider-Markel, D. P. (2013). The Politics of Causes: Mass Shootings and the Cases of the Virginia Tech and Tucson Tragedies. *Social Science Quarterly* 94(2), 410–423.

Keeler, J. T. S. (1993). Opening the Window for Reform: Mandates, Crises, and Extraordinary Policy-Making. *Comparative Political Studies* 25(4), 433–486.

Kingdon, J. W. (1984). *Agendas, Alternatives, and Public Policies*. Boston: Little, Brown.

Kitschelt, H. P. (1986). Political Opportunity Structures and Political Protest: Anti-Nuclear Movements in Four Democracies. *British Journal of Political Science* 16(1), 57–85.

Lijphart, A. (1999). *Patterns of Democracy: Government Forms and Performance in Thirty-Six Countries*. New Haven and London: Yale University Press.

Lijphart, A. (2012). *Patterns of Democracy: Government Forms and Performance in Thirty-Six Countries* (2nd edn). New Haven and London: Yale University Press.

Lilly, J. R. (2001). Constructing a 'Dangerous Gun Culture' in Britain – New Gun Control Laws, 1997. In J. Best (ed.), *How Claims Spread: Cross-National Diffusion of Social Problems*. New York: De Gruyter.

Lodge, M. (2011). Risk, Regulation and Crisis: Comparing National Responses in Food Safety Regulation. *Journal of Public Policy* 31(1), 25–50.

Lodge, M. and Hood, C. (2002). Pavlovian Policy Responses to Media Feeding Frenzies? Dangerous Dogs Regulation in Comparative Perspective. *Journal of Contingencies and Crisis Management* 10(1), 1–13.

Mahoney, J. (2000). Path Dependence in Historical Sociology. *Theory and Society* 29(4), 507–548.

58 Theoretical framework

March, J. G. and Olsen, J. P. (1996). Institutional Perspectives on Political Institutions. *Governance* 9(3), 247–264.

Muschert, G. W. (2009). Frame-changing in the Media Coverage of a School Shooting: The Rise of Columbine as a National Concern. *The Social Science Journal* 46(1), 164–170.

Nathanson, C. A. (1999). Social Movements as Catalysts for Policy Change: The Case of Smoking and Guns. *Journal of Health Politics, Policy and Law* 24(3), 421–488.

Nohrstedt, D. (2005). External Shocks and Policy Change: Three Mile Island and Swedish Nuclear Energy Policy. *Journal of European Public Policy* 12(6), 1041–1059.

Nohrstedt, D. (2008). The Politics of Crisis Policymaking: Chernobyl and Swedish Nuclear Energy Policy. *Policy Studies Journal* 36(2), 257–278.

Nohrstedt, D. (2010). Do Advocacy Coalitions Matter? Crisis and Change in Swedish Nuclear Energy Policy. *Journal of Public Administration Research and Theory* 20(2), 309–333.

Petrocik, J. R. (1996). Issue Ownership in Presidential Elections, with a 1980 Case Study. *American Journal of Political Science* 40(3), 825–850.

Pierson, P. (2000). Increasing Returns, Path Dependence, and the Study of Politics. *The American Political Science Review* 94(2), 251–267.

Rochefort, D. A. and Cobb, R. W. (1993). Problem Definition, Agenda Access, and Policy Choice. *Policy Studies Journal* 21(1), 56–71.

Scharpf, F. W. (1997). *Games Real Actors Play*. Boulder, CO: Westview Press.

Scharpf, F. W. (2000). Institutions in Comparative Policy Research. *Comparative Political Studies* 33(6–7), 762–790.

Schildkraut, J. and Cox Hernandez, T. (2014). Laws that Bit the Bullet: A Review of Legislative Responses to School Shootings. *American Journal of Criminal Justice* 39(2), 358–374.

Siaroff, A. (2003). Varieties of Parliamentarianism in the Advanced Industrial Democracies. *International Political Science Review* 24(4), 445–464.

Spitzer, R. J. (2012). *The Politics of Gun Control* (5th edn). Boulder, CO: Paradigm.

Squires, P. (2000). *Gun Culture or Gun Control? Firearms, Violence and Society*. London: Routledge.

Stone, D. A. (1989). Causal Stories and the Formation of Policy Agendas. *Political Science Quarterly* 104(2), 281–300.

Thelen, K. (1999). Historical Institutionalism in Comparative Politics. *Annual Review of Political Science* 2(1), 369–404.

Tsebelis, G. (2002). *Veto Players: How Political Institutions Work*. Princeton: Princeton University Press.

Voss, M. and Wagner, K. (2010). Learning from (Small) Disasters. *Natural Hazards* 55(3), 657–669.

Walgrave, S. and Varone, F. (2008). Punctuated Equilibrium and Agenda-Setting: Bringing Parties Back in: Policy Change after the Dutroux Crisis in Belgium. *Governance* 21(3), 365–395.

Walgrave, S. and Verhulst, J. (2006). Towards 'New Emotional Movements'? A Comparative Exploration into a Specific Movement Type. *Social Movement Studies* 5(3), 275–304.

Wittneben, B. B. F. (2012). The Impact of the Fukushima Nuclear Accident on European Energy Policy. *Environmental Science & Policy* 15(1), 1–3.

Worrall, J. L. (1999). Focusing Event Characteristics and Issue Accompaniment: The Case of Domestic Terrorism. *Criminal Justice Policy Review* 10(3), 319–341.

5 How to study the political impact of rampage shootings

This chapter has three central objectives. First, it introduces a range of important scope conditions that delineate the scope of the empirical analysis. Second, the resulting pool of 17 rampage shootings will be presented briefly and some descriptive information will be provided. This step is important as it further helps to familiarize the reader with the empirical evidence that forms the basis of the empirical section of the book. Finally, the methodological approach of the book will be outlined in the last part of the chapter. Most importantly, this last section includes a short introduction to the terminology, epistemology and technique of (fuzzy set) Qualitative Comparative Analysis (fsQCA). It also contains arguments on why the method is considered useful for the analysis of politicization, but not equally helpful for the evaluation of the theoretical expectations on policy change.

5.1 Scope conditions

In order to be able to identify necessary and sufficient conditions in a comparative research design, it is of critical importance that both the conditions and the outcome vary across cases. There are two straightforward reasons for this: first, a problem occurs if only cases are selected which display the outcome of interest, a strategy which has been described as sampling on the dependent variable (Geddes 1990). Translated into the present research context, this would mean than only rampage shootings that led to politicization and policy change are selected and all other rampage shootings are ignored. In such a situation, all present conditions would automatically be sufficient for the outcome and accordingly, statements of sufficiency could no longer be falsified. A few years ago, Emmenegger (2010) has taken up this discussion and pointed to the need to take non-events seriously. He defines non-events as 'critical junctures during which the policy path is not changed although the counterfactual case of policy change was a likely possibility' (Emmenegger 2010: 3). Such cases must be taken into account in order to arrive at sustainable causal claims. The second reason for the need of a diverse pool of cases is related to the first one, but is more closely related to the notion of necessity. If a certain condition does not vary across cases, the condition is trivial and by definition necessary (see also Schneider and

60 *Research design*

Wagemann (2012: 232f.)). Of course, such trivial statements of necessity should be avoided at any cost. One viable way to reduce the risk of making trivial statements of necessity is to properly define the universal set by setting scope conditions, which are deliberately held constant across all cases and are not further considered interesting from a theoretical point of view (Walker and Cohen 1985).

These scope conditions pertain to the characteristics of the unit of analysis as well as the geographical and temporal focus of the study. It is important for the reader to understand that only rampage shootings which fulfil all of the scope conditions defined below will be considered in the empirical analysis. All other rampage shootings are not of interest for the purpose of this study.

5.1.1 Delineating the unit of analysis

While the central defining characteristics of rampage shootings have already been spelt out in section 2.1, they shall be repeated briefly once again, because they are crucially important. An event must be characterized by four features in order to be included into the comparison: first, as implied by the term rampage shooting, the weapon used for the massacre must have been a firearm, i.e. 'a weapon from which a shot is discharged by gunpowder' (Merriam Webster Dictionary 2014). While rampages with knives, explosives or even motor vehicles do occur on a regular basis (in particular in Asia, where firearms are banned in many countries), they are not of further concern here. Second, the firearm must have been acquired legally either by the perpetrator himself or made easily accessible by people in the perpetrator's immediate environment. Third, the shooting must have been carried out either in an open public space or in a public building, such as a school or a courthouse. Finally, the shooting must have resulted in at least two fatalities excluding the perpetrator. The final three criteria primarily serve as a means to make sure that an event can actually be detected by systematic research. Shootings carried out with illegal weapons are arguably often the by-product of some other criminal activities. Shootings in private homes are often simple murders and do not necessarily arouse political attention. In addition to the criteria which delineate the unit of analysis, I also impose a geographical and a temporal criterion in order to clarify the limits of the book. I explain and justify both in the following.

5.1.2 Geographical criterion: Western Europe

One central scope condition for the statements made in the empirical part of the book is a geographical one: only rampage shootings which occurred in Western Europe are considered. This decision is based on two reasons: First, as outlined in Chapter 3, the existing literature already has a strong bias towards the United States and the geographical focus should be broadened. However, what is even more important in this regard is the fact that Western European countries share the characteristic that they all regulate firearm ownership exclusively on the

Research design 61

national level, which allows us to hold one very important factor constant.[1] The advantage of this case selection becomes particularly evident if we briefly take a look at two countries which regulate guns at least partially on a sub-national level: the United States and Australia.

Even though the general legislative framework on firearm ownership is determined by a range of national gun laws in the United States, most importantly the right to bear arms which is enshrined in the second amendment of the country's constitution (Spitzer 2012: 19ff.), all 50 states have separate gun laws and those laws exhibit strong variance (Bruce and Wilcox 1998; Open Society Institute 2000). These mixed legislative competences make it difficult to establish a common ground for comparing the United States to other countries. Most problematically, it is not possible to establish a-priori, which level of government should be examined in the United States if we are interested in firearm-related policy change. As Wilson (2007: 213) notes:

> In the case of gun control, it is a situation of pure federalism, in that states often wish to follow their own path with regard to guns and gun control legislation. [...] It recognizes that circumstances regarding firearms are very different in California than they are in North Dakota.

Accordingly, it would be a big mistake to treat the national political institutions in the US as the key players in policymaking as far as the regulation of firearms is concerned. More importantly, however, in order to arrive at a good understanding of the political reactions following rampage shootings in the US, it would be necessary to investigate cross-level interactions within the same country. Therefore, instead of comparing US shootings with shootings in other countries solely focusing on the national level, it would be much more adequate to compare their respective state-level consequences holding the national legal framework constant.

Another example that demonstrates the complexity generated by mixed legislative competences is Australia. The regulation of the possession, use and sale of firearms is the sole responsibility of the Australian territories (Bricknell 2012: 6). Despite this fact, it is often claimed that Australia as a nation tightened its gun laws as a response to the shooting at Port Arthur in 1996. In reality, however, some laggard states (among them Tasmania) were more or less forced by the national government to tighten their rules for firearms by means of a 'National Firearms Agreement' (Howard 2013). Thus, the Australian legal framework is very special as far as guns are concerned. The Port Arthur massacre prompted a legislative reaction on the state level, which was clearly made under pressure from the national level. Yet, this should not tempt us to conclude that the national government changed the Australian gun laws in the wake of the Port Arthur massacre.

This brief discussion illustrates the problems federal countries like the United States and Australia generate for the comparative research design as it is employed in this book. In some countries, the national level is responsible for

62 *Research design*

the regulation of firearms, but the countries are excluded from the case selection for the reason that they either are or were not democratic throughout the time period under observation. Since the theoretical expectations developed in the previous chapter require a certain amount of freedom of speech and the press in order to work, only states that were democratic throughout the entire time period under observation are considered. Also states in which the democratic transition was still underway during the 1990s are excluded in order to obtain a homogeneous country sample. In combination, these selection rules disqualify all Eastern European states, most African states and many Asian states. Accordingly, Western Europe is chosen as the geographical area of interest in order to establish a common ground for comparison.

5.1.3 Temporal criterion: 1990–2010

In the empirical part of the book, only events which occurred between 1990 and 2010 will be considered. The choice for the starting point has an empirical, a pragmatic and a theoretical reason. The empirical reason relates to the fact that before 1990, rampage shootings were an almost completely unknown phenomenon in Western Europe. For the most part, gun violence carried out in Europe before 1990 was either state sponsored (in particular during the two world wars) or originated from terrorist activities (for example the Red Brigades in Italy or the Red Army Faction in Germany). Rampage shootings as they are under scrutiny in this book were considered a distinctly American phenomenon before the first major shooting occurred in Hungerford (Great Britain) in 1987. Given this fact, the reader may wonder why 1987 was not chosen as a starting point. This is where the practical reason comes in: good data are very hard to come by for events that occurred prior to 1990. In particular, several media sources are not available electronically. While the significant Hungerford event is a formidable exception to this general rule, the lack of data particularly applies to events of smaller magnitude, such as the shootings in Rauma (Finland, 1989) or Bogaarden (Belgium, 1987). Since it is necessary to apply a common period of observation for all countries in Western Europe, the cut is made in 1990. This has the unfortunate implication that the Hungerford case is not part of the comparative analysis, but the positive implication that we can rely on a reasonably comparable data foundation. Finally, from a theoretical standpoint, 1990 is a good starting point because it allows us to hold the general status quo constant, at least for the EU countries. In 1991, the European Union introduced a firearms directive which bound all EU member states to obey to some minimum standards with regard to their firearm regulations.[2] In particular, this concerns the 'genuine reason requirement' and the minimum age threshold of 18 years for gun ownership.[3]

The reason why the observation period ends on 31 December 2010 mainly relates to the fact that this book project was started in May 2011. While some events occurred in 2011 and would have fulfilled the other scope conditions, they could not be integrated into the empirical analysis. These events might, however, be included in an updated version of this book at some later point in time.[4]

5.2 Case identification procedure

One theoretically plausible way of identifying focusing events would be a search for spikes in the amount of media attention to a given policy area. However, apart from the fact that this proceeding would imply that potential focusing events (Birkland 1997) would be less likely to be found, there are two more practical problems associated with the proceeding: first, not all national newspapers uphold digital archives dating back to the year 1990. Second, and more fundamentally, language barriers make a good and systematic search hardly feasible. Moreover, the following example illustrates the downsides from inferring relevant cases solely from spikes in media attention.

Figure 5.1 illustrates the German case, more specifically the number of articles devoted to the regulation of firearms in the *Frankfurter Allgemeine Zeitung* between 1990 and 2010 on a monthly basis. Like many other national newspapers in Europe, the newspaper is not available electronically for free before 1990. The figure clearly demonstrates that the attention devoted to the firearms issue has not been distributed normally across time in Germany. Instead,

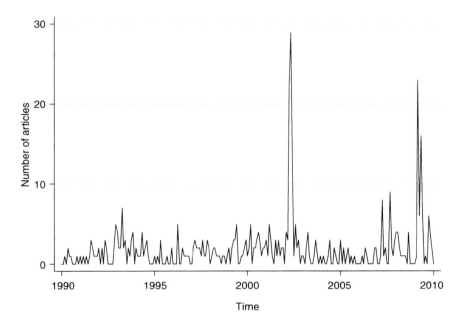

Figure 5.1 Media attention towards gun laws in Germany.

Note
Data retrieved from the online archives of the *Frankfurter Allgemeine Zeitung* (FAZ): http://faz-archiv-approved.faz.net/intranet/biblionet/. Used search term: Waffengesetz* or Waffenrecht*.

64 *Research design*

the pattern of media attention towards the issue has been rather low for most of the time, but punctuated by two extreme increases. The two spikes not only provide clear visual evidence that the assumptions of the punctuated equilibrium framework seem to be very relevant in the context of gun policy, the spikes' origins are also fairly easy to identify. The first spike resulted from the massacre in the *Gutenberg Gymnasium* of Erfurt in April of 2002 and the second spike is a consequence of the school shooting in Winnenden in March of 2009.

However, it is even more interesting what the graph does not show: first, it does not show a significant increase of attention in the wake of the Columbine shooting in Littleton (Colorado) in 1999, which provides clear evidence that rampage shootings are typically dealt with as national tragedies, and accordingly, national policy failures. In addition, it does not show a spike in attention towards gun control after other potential focusing events, which occurred in a courtroom in the city of Euskirchen in 1994, in Bad Reichenhall in 1999 and in Lörrach in 2010. As we shall see in the empirical section of the book, these events fulfilled all conditions of a potential focusing event, but only partially led to politicization and none led to policy change in the area of gun control in Germany. Thus, searching for relevant cases via media outlets is not only hardly feasible for pragmatic reasons, it is also misleading because it implies the danger of selection bias by missing out on cases which do not display the outcomes of interest.

Thus, finding all relevant cases for the empirical validation of the theoretical expectations is a veritable challenge. As of today, there is only one database which comprises those cases in a fairly comprehensive manner and this database is upheld by the online platform Wikipedia (Wikipedia 2014a, 2014b). While Wikipedia is often criticized by academics with regard to its alleged lack of reliability, it is generally considered legitimate to use the information provided on the platform as a starting point as long as it is possible to cross-validate the information with other sources like news reports or academic research. Ultimately, there simply is no guarantee that every single case that fulfils the scope conditions outlined above is listed on the online platform. This is especially true for cases with comparably low numbers of casualties. However, even during the more intense work on the individual case studies presented in Chapter 7, no additional cases were detected, which can be interpreted as an encouraging sign that the analysed pool of cases is complete. Moreover, since it is very certain that all politicized rampage shootings have been detected, the potentially lacking cases can at best question the results on the statements of sufficiency derived in the first empirical analysis. However, rampage shootings with fewer than two fatalities hardly ever become subject to political scrutiny. Thus, while the solution adopted for the identification of relevant cases is certainly less than ideal, it was the most pragmatic and probably also the only one given the circumstance that no prior academic work has been done on the subject. Since this study is the first systematic attempt to compare the political consequences of rampage shootings on an international basis, it must start with the scarce and patchy information that already exists and proceed from there.

Research design 65

5.3 Pool of cases and some background information

When the scope conditions introduced above are systematically applied, the result is a pool of 17 relevant cases (see Table 5.1). Those are the cases that form the basis for the empirical section of the book.

How do the identified rampage shootings vary in terms of their main characteristics? First of all, there is clear evidence that rampage shootings, as they have been defined for the purpose of this inquiry, have occurred in several, but not all countries of Western Europe. In fact, some countries have experienced more than one rampage shooting over the course of the past 20 years, while others have not been hit by a single one. Germany, as the most populous country in Western Europe, has been hit by five rampage shootings between 1990 and 2010, France has experienced three, while Great Britain and Finland suffered from two rampage shootings each. One rampage shooting occurred in Austria, Belgium, Denmark, Italy and Switzerland respectively. Other countries have been spared the occurrence of rampage shootings that fulfil the criteria set out above. This pattern suggests that the occurrence of rampage shootings does not vary randomly across countries and this observation alone represents a veritable research puzzle that should be addressed by future studies. This inquiry, however, is solely concerned with the political processes that follow rampage shootings, not with the ones that potentially contribute to their occurrence.

In addition, Table 5.1 shows that with the exception of the shooting in Lörrach, all of the identified shootings were perpetrated by men. In contrast to this strong gender bias, the shootings varied more strongly in terms of their locational venue. Six shootings took place in educational institutions, ranging from primary schools (Dunblane) over secondary schools (Jokela, Kauhajoki, Erfurt and Winnenden) to universities (Aarhus). One shooting occurred in a courthouse (Euskirchen) and two occurred in local parliaments (Zug and Nanterre). All other eight shootings took place in public areas. The perpetrators varied strongly with regard to their age. The youngest perpetrators were Éric Borel and Martin Peyerl (aged 16), whereas Friedrich Leibacher was the oldest perpetrator (aged 57). The median age of the perpetrators was 35. Very often, rampage shooters commit their crimes accepting or even desiring their own death. Out of the 17 perpetrators, only four could be arrested by the police and only three could actually be convicted to a prison sentence, because Richard Durn (Nanterre) managed to commit suicide after his arrest by jumping out of a window. One perpetrator was shot to death by the police (Sabine Radmacher, Lörrach). The remaining 12 perpetrators committed suicide right after their rampage.

After having identified the empirical cases, the question arises which methodological approach is the most appropriate for the comparative assessment of the theoretical expectations. I argue below that fuzzy set Qualitative Comparative Analysis (fsQCA) (Ragin 1987, 2000, 2008) can be considered the most promising way to go for the analysis of politicization dynamics, while the format of comparative case studies appears more suitable for the analysis of policy

Table 5.1 Overview of cases

	Event	Date	Location	Perpetrator		
				Name	*Age*	*Aftermath*
Austria	Mauterndorf	21 November 1997	Public area	Johann Gautsch	36	Suicide
Belgium	Antwerp	9 May 2006	Public area	Hans van Themsche	18	Arrest
Denmark	Aarhus	5 April 1994	School	Flemming Nielsen	35	Suicide
Finland	Jokela	7 November 2007	School	Pekka-Eric Auvinen	18	Suicide
	Kauhajoki	23 September 2008	School	Matti Juhani Saari	22	Suicide
France	Solliès-Pont/Cuers	24 September 1995	Public area	Éric Borel	16	Suicide
	Tours	29 October 2001	Public area	Jean-Pierre Roux-Durrafourt	44	Arrest
	Nanterre	27 March 2002	Parliament	Richard Durn	33	Arrest+suicide
Germany	Euskirchen	9 March 1994	Courthouse	Erwin Mikolajczyk	39	Suicide
	Bad Reichenhall	1 November 1999	Public area	Martin Peyerl	16	Suicide
	Erfurt	26 April 2002	School	Robert Steinhäuser	19	Suicide
	Winnenden	11 March 2009	School	Tim Kretschmer	17	Suicide
	Lörrach	19 September 2010	Public area	Sabine Radmacher	41	Shot by police
Italy	Bogogno	28 June 2005	Public area	Angelo Sacco	54	Arrest
Switzerland	Zug	27 September 2001	Parliament	Friedrich Leibacher	57	Suicide
Great Britain	Dunblane	13 March 1996	School	Thomas Hamilton	43	Suicide
	Cumbria	2 June 2010	Public area	Derrick Bird	52	Suicide

Research design 67

change. Before developing on this argument, however, the remainder of the chapter first provides a brief introduction to fsQCA in order to familiarize the reader with the method's terminology and functioning.

5.4 The methodology of (fs)QCA

Many statistical models applied in political science rest on the assumption that individual explanatory variables have an additive and often linear net effect on a dependent variable. This expectation finds its numerical expression in corresponding measures of association (regression coefficients) and measures of significance (p-values). The quantitative, variable-oriented approach which underpins those models has produced a wealth of highly interesting insights into a broad range of social phenomena. Yet, it is not equally practicable and helpful for every kind of theoretical setup and type of empirical evidence. As soon as our theory leaves room for combinations of causal conditions to be relevant for the occurrence of an outcome, statistical models become very hard to interpret and as soon as a comparatively low number of cases are being analysed, our trust in regression coefficients and significance levels diminishes.

In-depth case studies have always been presented as the main alternative to this quantitative research program. In contrast to the quantitative approach, this method puts a strong emphasis on the identification of causal mechanisms in order to acquire a precise understanding of how specific outcomes are produced. Those intensive and deep examinations of cases can reveal substantial insights about complex social processes. But despite the indisputable fact that this logic of scientific inquiry has its virtues, its findings also often suffer from a lack of generalizability and sometimes selection bias.

Inspired by the inadequacies of both research traditions and building on set theory, Ragin (1987, 2000, 2008) developed crisp set Qualitative Comparative Analysis (csQCA) and its refinement fuzzy set Qualitative Comparative Analysis (fsQCA) as a middle path between quantitative and qualitative strategies. Applications of both methods have been burgeoning over the past years and decades and have slowly but steadily gained increasing recognition among political scientists as a viable alternative to established strategies of scientific inquiry (Marx *et al.* 2014; Rihoux *et al.* 2011). Moreover, the method has been under constant development since its inception and has since experienced a wide range of improvements (Rihoux and Ragin 2009; Schneider and Wagemann 2006, 2012). Thus, despite its long history, QCA has only recently gained traction as a methodological approach in the social sciences and it still seems like the use of QCA requires more justification than the use of statistical methods. This is unfortunate, because statistical methods are not preferable by default in all research scenarios. In a situation with a small or medium amount of cases, a configurational approach can reveal deep insights into complex causal processes. However, while this argument rests on an important pragmatic consideration, it is not the most persuasive one in order to justify the use of QCA. In the present research context, the most important reason why QCA is used relates to the

68 *Research design*

method's ability to cope with equifinality and asymmetric causal relationships. Before we turn to the core concepts of QCA and a brief introduction to the method's operation, those important arguments should be laid out in some more detail.

This book is interested in the identification of causal paths that link the occurrence of a potential focusing event to the politicization of a policy failure in the affected policy area and to subsequent policy change. In order to tackle this analytical challenge, the comparison of similar potential focusing events does not aim to arrive at one single model that best describes the empirical evidence, but takes the possibility of equifinality into account. In other words, the politicization of gun control after a rampage shooting and ensuing policy change and stability can result from different individual causes and their interplay. Accordingly, there can be multiple paths leading to the same outcome. By drawing on the tools of formal logic, set theory and Boolean algebra, QCA provides the most intuitive theoretical concepts and vocabulary in order to identify and analyse such equifinal processes. However, in addition to QCA's built-in ability to conceive of and deal with equifinality as an asset instead of an analytical problem, there is a second important feature that makes QCA a useful method. This feature is the way the method copes with asymmetric causality.

The notion of asymmetric causal relationships is key in order to fully understand the central difference between set-theoretic methods such as QCA and most approaches of statistical inference. Briefly summarized, asymmetry should be understood as follows: if we know that a condition is causally related to the presence of a certain outcome if the condition is present, we do not know anything about the causal relationship if the condition is not present. The main implication of the notion of asymmetry is that set-theoretic methods require the separate analysis of the outcome and the non-occurrence of the outcome. In this study, this means that the explanation of politicization is not simply the inverse of the explanation of non-politicization (and vice versa). If, for example, we found out that high event severity facilitates politicization, we cannot validly conclude that low event severity impedes it. Therefore, we must identify the necessary and sufficient conditions for the outcome and its absence in separate analyses. The important aspect of asymmetric causal relationships often gets lost in statistical approaches, such as logistic regressions (Grofman and Schneider 2009: 669), in which an inversion of the dependent variable typically simply changes the sign of the estimated coefficient, thereby suggesting a symmetric relationship between the independent and dependent variable.

To sum up, QCA is chosen as the method for the analysis of politicization for three reasons: first, the method is best able to deal with an intermediate amount of cases. Second, it allows for the identification of equifinal processes and builds on the notion of causal complexity, which is arguably more in line with the political processes triggered by potential focusing events than the notions of linearity and additivity. Finally, QCA facilitates the evaluation of asymmetric causal relationships through its firm set-theoretic foundation and through a consistent terminology working with concepts like sufficiency and necessity.

5.5 QCA: a primer on terminology and technique

Since QCA is (still) not the most conventional data analysis technique in social science research, I consider it important to spend a few pages explaining how QCA works. In particular, I discuss the difference between sets and variables, the key concepts of necessity and sufficiency, INUS and SUIN conditions, the truth table algorithm and point to the two main challenges associated with QCA: limited empirical diversity and contradictory truth table rows. The parameters of consistency and coverage are briefly introduced in order to make the reader familiar with the most prominent technical approaches of tackling the aforementioned problems. Of course, this section is not meant to provide an exhaustive discussion of all the aspects associated with a proper QCA analysis. It does, however, provide a sufficient account in order to enable the reader to comprehend the empirical analysis on politicization.

5.5.1 Sets and variables

One of the most often disregarded features of QCA is the fact that it does not operate with variables, but with sets. Unlike a variable, which often describes a simple, objectively measureable entity like 'weight' or 'height', a set is composed of an adjective and a noun, like 'heavy person' or 'tall person'. Obviously, in order to transform a variable into a set, qualitative anchors must be imposed. At what threshold value does a person move from being 'not heavy' to being 'heavy'? At what height does a person count as tall? Those questions cannot be answered without a clear understanding of the universal set, that is, the universe of cases which fulfil the scope conditions defined by the researcher. For example, if the universal set consists of basketball players, the threshold for a tall person will be different from a universal set that consists of children. Eventually, the decision of where the threshold should be located must be based on prior theoretical knowledge and a sound understanding of the empirical phenomenon under study. In csQCA, only two options for set membership exist: either a case is fully in the set or fully out of the set. In fsQCA, different degrees of set membership are possible. Thus, a fuzzy set consists of multiple thresholds which differentiate between individual cases. For example, while a country with a membership score of 0.9 in the set of democratic countries is close to fulfilling all standards we commonly associate with democracies, it is not fully democratic. On the other hand, however, we would never call the country undemocratic, because its membership score is far above the decisive 0.5 threshold. The process by which such qualitative anchors are defined is known as set calibration and will be performed in section 6.2.

For the sake of completeness, it should be mentioned that csQCA and fsQCA are not the only QCA variants available. Methodological developments have resulted in some additional approaches including for example multi-value QCA (mvQCA), which deals with ordered categorical outcomes (Cronqvist and Berg-Schlosser 2009); temporal QCA, which allows for a sequential ordering of the analysed conditions (Caren and Panofsky 2005); and finally two-step QCA,

70 Research design

which sub-divides the analysed conditions according to their causal proximity and remoteness with regard to the outcome (Schneider and Wagemann 2006). In particular the first two variants are associated with several problems that make their empirical application problematic. For the most part, those problems are associated with questionable set-theoretic foundations with regard to mvQCA (Vink and Van Vliet 2009) and the challenge to keep the complexity of the empirical analysis at a manageable level in temporal QCA (Schneider and Wagemann 2012: 273). Also this book relies on the classical approach of fsQCA, mainly because of its ability to manage causal complexity in a way that makes the analysis and the results much more accessible to the reader.

5.5.2 Necessity and sufficiency

In order to understand the way QCA operates, it is important to recall that the method is firmly based on set theory and formal logic, and thereby rests on the notions of necessity and sufficiency and their interplay (Schneider and Wagemann 2012: 56ff.). Both types of conditions may not be confused. First, in order to identify a necessary condition, only cases which display the outcome are relevant. In contrast, all cases that do not display the outcome can be disregarded in an analysis of necessity. A necessary condition exists, if it is always present when the outcome is present. In other words, a condition is necessary for an outcome if no case displays the outcome without the condition. If X denotes a condition and Y denotes an outcome, the conventional expression for a statement of necessity in a QCA-setting is the following:

$$X \leftarrow Y$$

Compared to such a relationship of necessity, the logic of a sufficient condition is different. Here, only present conditions are relevant for the analysis, while absent conditions may be disregarded. A condition is sufficient if the outcome always occurs while the condition is present. In other words, a sufficient condition can produce an outcome by itself. In QCA studies, statements of sufficiency are usually denoted as follows:

$$X \rightarrow Y$$

Table 5.2 Logic of necessity

Y	Present	Violation	Confirmation
	Not present	Irrelevant	Irrelevant
		Not present	Present
			X

Note
Table adapted from Schneider and Wagemann (2012: 71).

Research design 71

Table 5.3 Logic of sufficiency

Y	*Present*	Irrelevant		Confirmation
	Not present	Irrelevant		Violation
		Not present		*Present*
			X	

Note
Table adapted from Schneider and Wagemann (2012: 59).

Thus, while necessary and sufficient conditions are by no means equivalent, they are two sides of the same coin. It should be pointed out clearly that while it is very well conceivable that a condition is either necessary or sufficient, it is hardly ever both at the same time. If a condition is both necessary and sufficient, the corresponding set relationship is almost certainly trivial and maybe even tautological.

5.5.3 INUS and SUIN conditions

In addition to the possibility of individual conditions being sufficient, it is also possible that a logical minimization reveals conjunctions of multiple conditions that jointly fulfil the requirements of sufficiency. In fact, applied QCA often identifies conditions that only exert their impact in combination with one or several other conditions. That is, the conjunction of conditions would not be sufficient, if any single one of its components were not present. Such conditions have been labelled '*insufficient* but *necessary* part of a condition which is itself *unnecessary* but *sufficient* for the result' and been assigned the acronym INUS condition (Mackie 1965: 245, italics in original).[5] Such INUS conditions are ubiquitous in applied QCA and it is therefore essential to understand what those conditions are. Going back to the notation used above, we could detect two INUS conditions in the following solution term:

$$X*Z + W \rightarrow Y$$

In this statement of sufficiency, both condition X and condition Z are INUS conditions.[6] While X cannot produce Y on its own and is therefore insufficient, it can produce Y in combination with Z. However, the conjunction $X*Z$ is unnecessary, because there is an alternative path to Y via condition W. This example illustrates that QCA is a method that does not treat causal complexity as a problem, but as an asset. It also shows that the method endorses the notion of equifinality, which implies that one and the same outcome can result from various causal conditions and their configurations. As a result, more than one causal path can lead to a given empirical phenomenon or its absence.

More recently, also the notion of SUIN conditions has found entry into QCA. Although such SUIN conditions are not as ubiquitous as INUS conditions, their

72 Research design

operation shall be briefly addressed for the sake of completeness. A SUIN condition has been defined as a '*sufficient*, but *unnecessary* part of a factor that is *insufficient*, but *necessary* for the result' (Mahoney *et al.* 2009: 126, italics in original).[7] The final part of the definition already suggests that SUIN conditions are relevant in analyses of necessity relationships. They occur if two or more individual conditions are mutually substitutable in constituting a complex necessary condition. The following generic solution formula contains SUIN conditions:

$$(X+Z)*(W+V) \leftarrow Y$$

In this scenario, various combinations of the individual conditions making up the two unions could be necessary, but at least one of the components in the respective parentheses must be present. If no condition is present in either of the parentheses, the entire expression is not necessary any longer. To sum up, an individual condition like X is sufficient in order to make the first parenthesis present, but X is not necessary for the presence of the parenthesis, because Z can take its place. Yet, even if either X or Z are present, we still need either W or V to be present in order to obtain a valid statement of necessity.

5.5.4 Consistency

Since the concepts of sufficiency and necessity are, in principle, deterministic concepts, we quickly encounter problems when the empirical evidence does not perfectly fit into our theoretical expectations. If several cases display the same configurations of causal conditions but vary in terms of their displayed outcome, the causal configuration is no longer sufficient. Likewise, if several cases display the outcome, but not all of those cases display a certain condition, then the condition is no longer necessary. In order to tackle this analytical problem, Ragin (2006) has developed a relatively simple indicator that expresses the extent to which statements of sufficiency and necessity are violated by the empirical evidence at hand: the consistency coefficient. To a certain extent, this coefficient relaxes the deterministic causal structure underlying the QCA approach and introduces a probabilistic element into the analysis. The coefficient shall be explained briefly.

The consistency coefficient has the major advantage that it is very straightforward and easy to calculate. For sufficiency statements, the coefficient simply expresses the relation between all cases that are in line with the postulated statement of sufficiency (i.e. all cases that display condition and outcome) and all cases which are relevant for the evaluation of the respective set theoretic claim (i.e. all cases that display the condition). If, in a crisp set scenario, 10 cases display a certain condition and only 9 of those cases display the outcome, then the consistency score for a sufficiency statement equals $9/10=0.9$. Note that cases that do not display the condition are entirely irrelevant for the calculation of this consistency score.

Research design 73

A consistency score for a necessity relationship, in turn, divides all cases that display both the outcome and the condition by all cases that display the outcome. If, for example, 10 cases display a certain outcome and only five of them also display the condition, the consistency value for the corresponding necessity relationship would equal $5/10 = 0.5$, which would signify that the condition is clearly not necessary for the outcome to occur. In this logic, cases that do not display the outcome are irrelevant and therefore cannot violate the statement of necessity.

Of course, the main task that must be solved by the researcher is the drawing of a consistency threshold that delineates causal conditions (or configurations) which are considered sufficient or necessary from those that are not. In contrast to the statistical method, where p-values are conventionally fixed at the levels of 0.01, 0.5 and 0.1 in order to indicate statistical significance, no universally applicable threshold exists in QCA research. While Schneider and Wagemann (2012: 129) recommend that the consistency threshold for sufficient conditions should at least be higher than 0.75, they also make the case that 'the exact location of the consistency threshold is heavily dependent on the specific research context' (Schneider and Wagemann 2012: 127). This is because in fsQCA, a consistency value of below 0.75 can still indicate a consistent statement of sufficiency if the value is not based on a 'true' logical contradiction, i.e. the presence of two or more cases that display the fuzzy set memberships in the conditions, but display different outcomes. Sometimes, a low consistency threshold can result if cases are only barely in or out of the analysed conditions. It would, however, be a big mistake to ignore those cases in the minimization of the truth table and therefore, it is essential to inspect the truth table closely by hand and resist the temptation to assign consistency thresholds in a mechanical manner.

Accordingly, it is up to the researcher to define a threshold and most importantly, to do so in a completely transparent way. Especially for the analysis of sufficiency statements (i.e. the logical reduction of the truth table), the decision of where to draw the threshold can have major implications for the resulting solution term, because it implies a decision about the truth table rows which are included into the minimization process. Therefore, robustness checks for QCA results can be based upon the deliberate changing of consistency thresholds within a reasonable range (Skaaning 2011).

5.5.5 Coverage

A second issue that affects the quality of the solutions obtained in a QCA is the share of cases covered by a certain statement of sufficiency or necessity. This share can be described with the help of the coverage coefficient (Ragin 2006). While the calculation is of similar simplicity like the calculation of the consistency value, its interpretation is different for relationships of sufficiency and necessity respectively. Before turning to the explanation of the coverage value, it should be pointed out that coverage is of downstream importance and is always considered after consistency. This is because even the highest coverage value is

74 *Research design*

of no use if the statement to which it applies is inconsistent with the empirical evidence at hand. In such a situation, we are able to explain a lot with a wrong explanation. Accordingly, if we cannot confirm consistency, coverage is of no further concern. If we can confirm consistency, however, the corresponding coverage value can teach us a lot about the empirical importance of the evaluated set-theoretic claim. Yet, how is the coverage value calculated?

For sufficiency statements, the coverage value of a certain condition is calculated by dividing the number of cases which display both outcome and condition by the number of all cases that display the outcome.[8] In so doing, we obtain the share of cases which are covered by a certain condition or a certain causal configuration. Essentially, there are three types of coverage values for sufficiency relationships: the unique coverage, the raw coverage and the solution coverage. The unique coverage displays the share of cases that are covered by one condition or causal configuration uniquely. For example, if a certain condition has a unique coverage value of 0.4, 40 per cent of the relevant cases are covered only by this particular condition. The raw coverage, in turn, also includes cases that are covered by other conditions simultaneously. As a logical corollary, a condition's raw coverage value can never be lower than its unique coverage value. Finally, the solution coverage expresses the share of cases which are covered by an entire solution term.

The coverage value of a necessary condition is calculated by dividing the number of cases that display both the condition and the outcome by all cases which display the condition. Coverage values for relationships of necessity require an interpretation that is different from the interpretations explained above. If a relationship of necessity is found to be consistent, the corresponding necessary condition always covers all cases that display the outcome. Therefore, what matters is no longer the question of whether condition and outcome are in a subset-relationship (in fact, the analysis of consistency has shown that they are), but the relative size of the two sets. If the condition set is disproportionately large in comparison to the outcome set, then chances are that the condition we have identified as necessary is trivial (Goertz 2006). In other words, if a condition is always present, it is by default necessary and therefore probably not particularly interesting from an analytical point of view. Thus, a low coverage value of a consistent necessary condition indicates that the condition is almost always present, regardless of whether the outcome is present or not.

5.6 The varying applicability of QCA in the present research context

While the discussion of the basic foundations of QCA suggests that the method should be highly compatible with the analytical interest of this book, this is only partially the case. In fact, it was found during the research process that the approach is very useful for the evaluation of the theoretical expectations on politicization, but much less applicable to the comparative analysis of policy change and stability. While the theoretical concepts relevant for the analysis of

Research design 75

politicization can all be operationalized with solid, quantifiable data, this is not fully the case for the concepts relevant for the analysis of policy change. As a result, the theoretical expectations that form the basis for the analysis of policy change dynamics are hard to translate into set-theoretic language. This applies both to the outcome of interest and the conditions that are included in the theoretical expectations. More precisely, the degree of subsequent policy change hinges to a considerable extent on the policy configuration present at the status quo. Therefore, translating legislative changes into a set like 'major policy change' is complicated by the fact that 'major' can mean very different things under different accompanying circumstances. This implies that the question of where incrementalism ends and where major policy change begins is extremely difficult to resolve in the present research context. As far as the conditions of interest are concerned, especially the measurement of a potential focusing event's perceived causal complexity and the cohesion of reform opponents would require enormously difficult set calibrations, which could not be based on a clear, quantifiable measure. Yet, this unavailability of a good basis for measurement is not related to any conceptual ambiguities. On the contrary, recent studies have shown that the complexity of a political discourse and the cohesion of the participating discourse coalitions can be measured very well employing discourse network analysis (Hurka and Nebel 2013). However, while such an approach is well applicable if the number of cases is low and the required data are equally accessible, it quickly becomes unmanageable if the number of cases increases and the data are not available for all cases to the same extent. Accordingly, the application of QCA is sometimes complicated by simple research pragmatic constraints. In the present research context, the calibration of satisfactory sets for some theoretical concepts would require the analysis of large amounts of qualitative data on 12 cases published in a multitude of different languages (among them rather particular ones like Finnish or Flemish). Thus, a quantification of the discourses following rampage shootings would require substantial financial and human resources and would arguably constitute another book project by itself. Instead of giving in to the temptation of applying purely arbitrary rules of thumb for the allocation of individual cases into hypothetical sets, it is therefore considered more appropriate to analyse policy change and stability by conducting comparative case studies on the politicized events. In so doing, the specific characteristics of the individual cases can be put into the structural context in which they occur and the complex interplay of different conditions can be analysed.

Accordingly, the choice to apply fsQCA in the first empirical section of the book but not in the second is based on theoretical and research pragmatic grounds. First, not all theoretical concepts can be translated into set-theoretic language in a satisfactory way, which implies that a thorough examination of the causal mechanisms in the form of comparative case studies might sometimes constitute the better method of analysis. Second, the acquisition of a comprehensive data foundation for the precise measurement of discourse complexity and the cohesion of discourse coalitions would require a data collection effort

76 Research design

which is beyond the scope of this book. Accordingly, the following chapters first identify the necessary and sufficient conditions for politicization of gun control in the wake of rampage shootings with the help of fsQCA, before the politicized cases are analysed in greater detail in 12 case studies.

Notes

1 In Germany, the central government assumed legislative authority on the matter before the beginning of the observation period (1972). The only Western European country, which shifted legislative authority from the sub-national to the national level between 1985 and 2010 was Switzerland in 1997 (Wüst 1999).
2 Council Directive 91/477/EEC of 18 June 1991 on control of the acquisition and possession of weapons.
3 Two important Western European countries are not part of the EU (Norway and Switzerland) and some only joined the EU during the time period under observation (e.g. Finland and Austria).
4 For example, the Utøya massacre and the shooting in a shopping mall in the Dutch town Aalphen an den Rijn fall into this category.
5 I consider the formulation 'necessary part' in the original definition misleading as a quick reading would suggest that an INUS condition is necessary for the outcome. However, this is not the case. The reader is advised to think of an INUS condition as an indispensable part of a sufficient conjunction of conditions. In other words, the conjunction would not be sufficient without the INUS condition.
6 Throughout this study, I use the symbol * in order to indicate a logical AND combination and the symbol + when referring to a logical OR combination. A present condition is indicated by uppercase letters, an absent condition is indicated by lowercase letters.
7 Again, the terminology here is not optimal, because the term 'factor' suggests that multiplication is involved. Of course, this is not the case. In this context, the reader should rather think of a higher-order concept, which consists of mutually substitutable components.
8 It should be pointed out here that the formulas for the calculation of consistency and coverage are mirror images when applied to sufficiency and necessity relationships.

References

Birkland, T. A. (1997). *After Disaster – Agenda Setting, Public Policy, and Focusing Events*. Washington, D.C.: Georgetown University Press.
Bricknell, S. (2012). *Firearm Trafficking and Serious and Organised Crime Gangs*. Canberra: Australian Institute of Criminology.
Bruce, J. M. and Wilcox, C. (1998). Gun Control Laws in the States: Political and Apolitical Influences. In J. M. Bruce and C. Wilcox (eds), *The Changing Politics of Gun Control* (pp. 139–154). Lanham: Rowman & Littlefield.
Caren, N. and Panofsky, A. (2005). TQCA: A Technique for Adding Temporality to Qualitative Comparative Analysis. *Sociological Methods & Research* 34(2), 147–172.
Cronqvist, L. and Berg-Schlosser, D. (2009). Multi-Value QCA (mvQCA). In B. Rihoux and C. C. Ragin (eds), *Configurational Comparative Methods: Qualitative Comparative Analysis (QCA) and Related Techniques* (pp. 69–86). London: Sage Publications.
Emmenegger, P. (2010). Non-Events in Macro-Comparative Social Research: Why We Should Care and How We Can Analyze Them. *COMPASSS Working Paper Series 2010-60*.

Research design 77

Geddes, B. (1990). How the Cases You Choose Affect the Answers You Get: Selection Bias in Comparative Politics. *Political Analysis* 2(1), 131–150.

Goertz, G. (2006). Assessing the Trivialness, Relevance, and Relative Importance of Necessary or Sufficient Conditions in Social Science. *Studies in Comparative International Development* 41(2), 88–109.

Grofman, B. and Schneider, C. Q. (2009). An Introduction to Crisp Set QCA, with a Comparison to Binary Logistic Regression. *Political Research Quarterly* 62(4), 662–672.

Howard, J. (2013). I Went After Guns. Obama Can, Too, *New York Times*, 17 January 2013.

Hurka, S. and Nebel, K. (2013). Framing and Policy Change after Shooting Rampages: A Comparative Analysis of Discourse Networks. *Journal of European Public Policy* 20(3), 390–406.

Mackie, J. L. (1965). Causes and Conditions. *American Philosophical Quarterly* 2(4), 245–264.

Mahoney, J., Kimball, E. and Koivu, K. L. (2009). The Logic of Historical Explanation in the Social Sciences. *Comparative Political Studies* 42(1), 114–146.

Marx, A., Rihoux, B. and Ragin, C. (2014). The Origins, Development, and Application of Qualitative Comparative Analysis: The First 25 Years. *European Political Science Review* 6(1), 115–142.

Merriam Webster Dictionary. (2014). Firearm. Retrieved 27 February 2014 from www.merriam-webster.com/dictionary/firearm.

Open Society Institute. (2000). Gun Control in the United States – A Comparative Survey of State Firearm Laws. Retrieved 21 March 2013 from www.opensocietyfoundations.org/sites/default/files/GunReport.pdf.

Ragin, C. C. (1987). *The Comparative Method: Moving Beyond Qualitative and Quantitative Strategies*. Berkeley: University of California Press.

Ragin, C. C. (2000). *Fuzzy-Set Social Science*. Chicago: University of Chicago Press.

Ragin, C. C. (2006). Set Relations in Social Research: Evaluating Their Consistency and Coverage. *Political Analysis* 14(3), 291–310.

Ragin, C. C. (2008). *Redesigning Social Inquiry: Fuzzy Sets and Beyond*. Chicago: University of Chicago Press.

Rihoux, B. and Ragin, C. C. (2009). *Configurational Comparative Methods: Qualitative Comparative Analysis (QCA) and Related Techniques*. Thousand Oaks: Sage.

Rihoux, B., Rezsohazy, I. and Bol, D. (2011). Qualitative Comparative Analysis (QCA) in Public Policy Analysis: An Extensive Review. *German Policy Studies* 7(3), 9–82.

Schneider, C. Q. and Wagemann, C. (2006). Reducing Complexity in Qualitative Comparative Analysis (QCA): Remote and Proximate Factors and the Consolidation of Democracy. *European Journal of Political Research* 45(5), 751–786.

Schneider, C. Q. and Wagemann, C. (2012). *Set-Theoretic Methods for the Social Sciences: A Guide to Qualitative Comparative Analysis*. Cambridge: Cambridge University Press.

Skaaning, S.-E. (2011). Assessing the Robustness of Crisp-set and Fuzzy-set QCA Results. *Sociological Methods & Research* 40(2), 391–408.

Spitzer, R. J. (2012). *The Politics of Gun Control* (5th edn). Boulder, CO: Paradigm.

Vink, M. P. and Van Vliet, O. (2009). Not Quite Crisp, Not Yet Fuzzy? Assessing the Potentials and Pitfalls of Multi-value QCA. *Field Methods* 21(3), 265–289.

Walker, H. A. and Cohen, B. P. (1985). Scope Statements: Imperatives for Evaluating Theory. *American Sociological Review* 50(3), 288–301.

Wikipedia. (2014a). List of rampage killers (Europe). Retrieved 10 October 2014 from http://en.wikipedia.org/wiki/List_of_rampage_killers_(Europe).

78 *Research design*

Wikipedia. (2014b). List of rampage killers (school massacres). Retrieved 10 October 2014 from http://en.wikipedia.org/wiki/List_of_rampage_killers_(school_massacres).

Wilson, H. L. (2007). *Guns, Gun Control, and Elections: The Politics and Policy of Firearms*. Lanham: Rowman & Littlefield.

Wüst, H. (1999). *Schweizer Waffenrecht*. Zurich: FO Publishing.

6 Paths to the (non-)politicization of gun control

Why do some rampage shootings directly lead to the politicization of gun control whereas other events with similar characteristics go by without a political debate on this issue? In this chapter, this first research question of the book is addressed by conducting an fsQCA on the 17 potential focusing events identified previously. Before we move to the empirical analysis, let us recall and summarize the theoretical arguments made in Chapter 4. First, I argued that whether or not we observe the politicization of gun control after a rampage shooting should be related to the event's magnitude in objective terms (theoretical expectation 1). The more people are directly harmed by the event, the stronger the stimulus for political actors to respond with suggestions over the event's policy implications. Second, I argued that the relative amount of media coverage an event receives can be understood as an indicator of the event's perceived severity which is not necessarily solely related to the number of victims (theoretical expectation 2). Instead, it was argued that the media can generate 'moral panics' through extensive event coverage and thereby increase the pressure on the responsible political actors to satisfy the public's call to action. Third, the existence of a partisan cleavage on gun control should facilitate the political treatment of the issue after a rampage shooting (theoretical expectation 3). More specifically, given their pacifist ideology and their generally cohesive opposition to civilian gun ownership, the presence of green parties was argued to be a potentially important contributing factor to the politicization of gun control in the aftermath of a rampage shooting. Finally, the event's timing in the electoral calendar was identified as another potentially relevant explanatory factor for politicization dynamics (theoretical expectation 4). Specifically, it was argued that proximate national elections can facilitate politicization, because they provide politicians with an incentive to present themselves as the ones who save the population from harm. This should be the case especially if the previous condition is met, i.e. a political party is present who owns the issue of gun control.

Before we turn to the actual fsQCA, it is important to make the used data sources and the process of the set calibration as transparent as possible in order to enable the reader to gauge the soundness of the empirical analysis. Therefore, the following sub-sections introduce the way the concepts of event severity,

80 *Paths to (non-)politicization*

media attention, partisan cleavage and electoral cycle have been operationalized and measured. Afterwards, those data will be transformed into sets which can then be analysed systematically with the help of fsQCA.

6.1 Operationalization, measurement and descriptive information

In order to enable the comparative analysis of the identified cases, it is necessary to translate the theoretical concepts first into variables and then into sets. Let us first consider the four conditions under scrutiny. It has been outlined in the theoretical part of this book that the death toll resulting from a rampage shooting can be reasonably interpreted as an indicator for the event's severity in objective terms. The more people are physically harmed as the result from an incident, the stronger the impetus for politicians to ponder the event's policy implications. Therefore, the death toll is used as a measure that operationalizes the concept of objective event severity. Second, an event's perceived severity can be approximated by the amount of media coverage it receives. For the lack of a better measure, I use the number of articles devoted to the event in a leading national newspaper of the affected country within the first week after the incident. Of course, this measure is explicitly based on the assumption that the number of articles published by these newspapers is at least roughly comparable across countries and over time. Since the extent to which this assumption is realistic cannot be established beyond doubt, the robustness checks of the fsQCA assume a particularly important role here (consult Appendix B for a presentation of these robustness checks). Third, I use the seat share of the affected nation's green party in the national parliament as a measure indicating the presence of a partisan cleavage on the gun issue. While political parties that are not represented in parliament have the ability to contribute to the public debate, their chance to get heard is significantly reduced. Accordingly, this measure only exceeds zero if a green party is actually represented in parliament. Green parties were identified with the help of data from the Comparative Manifesto Project (Budge *et al.* 2001; Klingemann *et al.* 2006) and the figures for the seat shares were taken from PARLGOV (Döring and Manow 2012). Finally, I use the number of days that lie between the date of the rampage shooting and the next scheduled national parliamentary election as a measure that indicates the event's timing in the electoral cycle. Like the seat shares of green parties, the election dates were taken from the PARLGOV database (Döring and Manow 2012).

As far as the outcome of interest is concerned, it was established whether or not the event became subject of a political debate. The way this book conceives of politicization leaves relatively little room for interpretation on behalf of the observer in this regard. Either gun control becomes a subject of political scrutiny in the aftermath of the respective event or not. Accordingly, the outcome set of this fsQCA is dichotomous, whereas all conditions provide for membership scores other than 0 and 1. The references which prove the efforts of

Paths to (non-)politicization 81

politicization are all part of the case studies on the politicized events and will therefore only be referred to briefly below. Table 6.1 gives an overview of the empirical distributions of the measures introduced above.

With regard to the death toll, we can see that the cases vary from two fatalities in Antwerp and Aarhus to 17 in Dunblane. A total of seven cases resulted in a double-digit number of fatalities. The number of articles published on the event within the first week after its occurrence varies from only one article on the Aarhus shooting to 174 articles on the Erfurt school shooting. This enormous variance indicates that a massive increase in media attention after rampage shootings is by no means pre-determined, as conventional wisdom suggests. In addition, the data suggest that objective and perceived event severity are often, but not always related. Cases like Solliès-Pont/Cuers show that the media sometimes pay only minor attention to events of comparably strong severity, and sometimes cover other events more extensively. Accordingly, while the objective and perceived severity of an event are related most of the time, there is quite some leverage on behalf of the media. As far as the parliamentary representation of green parties is concerned, the data show that during 12 out of 17 rampage shootings, green parties were represented in the affected country's national parliament and thereby enjoyed a privileged position in terms of setting in motion a political debate. In only two instances, a green party was additionally part of the national government (during the shootings in Bad Reichenhall and Erfurt in Germany). Finally, the temporal distance to the next parliamentary elections varied from only 74 days after the Nanterre shooting to 1800 days after the Cumbria massacre. The latter shooting occurred right after the institution of the coalition between Conservatives and Liberal Democrats under the leadership of David Cameron in May 2010.

Let us now turn to the varying extents to which the identified events led to the politicization of gun control in their aftermath. As Table 6.1 indicates, 12 out of the 17 identified potential focusing events led to a political debate over the appropriateness of the affected country's gun control arrangements. In the Mauterndorf case, gun control was politicized primarily by parliamentarians from the Green Party (Terezija Stoisits and Dr. Madeleine Petrovic) with a motion to set a deadline for the government to draw up a proposal for a new and tighter gun law (Stoisits *et al.* 1998). After the Antwerp incident, gun control quickly became the subject of political scrutiny and the corresponding laws were tightened without much time delay and virtually unanimously (Expatica News 2006). After both Finnish rampage shootings, gun control immediately became a major subject of political debate, but legislative changes were only implemented in the wake of the second shooting (Lindström *et al.* 2011). In Germany, four out of five rampage shootings triggered a political debate over the country's gun control arrangements: Bad Reichenhall, Erfurt, Winnenden and Lörrach (see section 7.2). Rapid policy change occurred after the two school shootings in Erfurt and Winnenden. The shooting in the Swiss town of Zug in 2001 triggered a public and political debate over the country's permissive gun laws, but the debate did not result in any legislative changes (Hurka and Nebel 2013). Finally,

82 Paths to (non-)politicization

Table 6.1 Raw data matrix for the comparison of politicization patterns

Case	Death toll	Media attention	Seat share of green parties	Days until next elections	Politicization of gun control
Mauterndorf	6	12	4.9	682	Yes
Antwerp	2	41	2.7	397	Yes
Aarhus	2	1	0.0	169	No
Jokela	8	56	7.5	1,257	Yes
Kauhajoki	10	57	7.5	936	Yes
Solliès-Pont/ Cuers	15	4	0.0	610	No
Tours	4	2	0.0	223	No
Nanterre	8	73	1.4	74	Yes
Euskirchen	6	11	1.2	221	No
Bad Reichenhall	4	27	7.0	1,056	Yes
Erfurt	16	174	7.0	149	Yes
Winnenden	15	86	8.3	200	Yes
Lörrach	3	32	10.9	1,099	Yes
Bogogno	3	10	0.0	82	No
Zug	14	52	4.0	752	Yes
Dunblane	17	107	0.0	414	Yes
Cumbria	12	63	0.0	1,800	Yes

Note
The column 'death toll' displays the total number of fatalities resulting from the shooting, excluding the perpetrator. The column 'media attention' displays the number of newspaper articles mentioning either the perpetrator's name or the shooting's locality, corrected for irrelevant hits. Specifically, the newspapers examined were the *Guardian* (Great Britain), *Frankfurter Allgemeine Zeitung* (Germany), *Oberösterreichische Nachrichten* (Austria), *De Standaard* (Belgium), *Jyllands Posten* (Denmark), *Helsingin Sanomat* (Finland), *Le Monde* (France), *La Repubblica* (Italy), *Neue Zürcher Zeitung* (Switzerland). The column 'seat share of green parties' displays the seat share of green parties (in per cent) in the respective national parliament at the time of the shooting. The column 'days until next elections' displays the number of days until the next major national election.

two rampage shootings in Great Britain caused the politicization of gun control in the time period between 1990 and 2010: Dunblane and Cumbria (Squires 2014). While the former debate resulted in a policy change of paradigmatic proportions, the latter did not have any legislative impact.

6.2 Set calibration

In order to perform an fsQCA, we must transform the existing empirical information from variables to sets. As one of the most central components of QCA in general, this task is known as set calibration and requires a maximum of transparency (Schneider and Wagemann 2010: 7). Before the set calibration is performed, however, it should be underscored once again that set calibrations are sometimes easy and unambiguous, but sometimes involve delicate decisions on the setting on the thresholds. However, just like the coefficients gained from statistical models, also QCA results can be subject to robustness checks, which involve, among other procedures, the setting of different (reasonable) thresholds

Paths to (non-)politicization 83

(Skaaning 2011). Such robustness checks have been carried out and their results are reported in Appendix B.

The rationale behind the set calibration that guides the empirical analysis below is fairly straightforward with regard to the outcome of interest. The politicization of gun control can be understood as an empirical phenomenon that is either present or absent in the aftermath of a rampage shooting. In fact, the cases identified above leave relatively little room for interpretation on this matter. An event counts as politicized if at least one major political actor calls for tighter gun control as a direct lesson that should be drawn from the event. It is important to point out here that 'major political actors' are conceptualized in a narrow sense, referring to nationally relevant politicians, i.e. national party leaders or members of government. Thus, calls to action which are exclusively voiced by the media or interest groups are not considered indicators of politicization, unless they are taken up by a political actor. In this sense, every event can unambiguously be allocated to the outcome set POLIT or its absence.

Unlike the clear binary conceptualization and calibration of the outcome, the conditions are calibrated as fuzzy sets, because they are clearly based on quantitative information that is measured on an interval scale: the number of dead people, the number of newspaper articles, the seat share of green parties, and the temporal distance to the next national elections. If we dichotomized these data, we would lose interesting information on the examined cases. But where can we draw reasonable thresholds? First of all, the sets are calibrated using the direct method of calibration (Schneider and Wagemann 2012: 35f.), fitting a logistic function of membership scores with the help of three qualitative anchors: the threshold for full membership (1), the threshold for full non-membership (0), and the point of maximal ambiguity (0.5).

As far as the death toll is concerned (DEATH), the analysis applies a 0.5-threshold of seven fatalities in order to separate events of high severity from events of lower severity. For the most part, this decision has practical reasons. In order to illustrate the reasons for the decision, let us take a quick look at the events in Jokela and Kauhajoki. Both rampage shootings were very similar in many respects, but one led to eight fatalities and the other led to 10. If we decide to draw a threshold at eight or nine fatalities, we would introduce the assumption that the two shootings were qualitatively different as far as their objective severity is concerned. Since both shootings occurred in schools and led to fatalities among minors, it is probably more intuitive to classify them as severe shootings, instead of less severe shootings. This is also supported by qualitative case studies on the two events (Lindström *et al.* 2011; Oksanen *et al.* 2010). In addition, it should be noted that the shooting at Nanterre (8 fatalities) resulted in the very high number of 19 non-fatal injuries. Accordingly, the best choice for the 0.5-threshold is seven fatalities. In the empirical context of this inquiry, this threshold implies the additional advantage that no case must be assigned the 0.5 value, because no case resulted in exactly 7 fatalities. In the appendix of this book, alternative results for 0.5-thresholds at 5, 9 and 11 fatalities are reported. The thresholds of full set membership and non-membership are set at 14 and 3

84 *Paths to (non-)politicization*

fatalities respectively. It should be pointed out that the precise setting of these latter thresholds does not imply a massive impact on the obtained solutions, because they only affect the cases' differences in degree, not their differences in kind.

Next, the calibration of the green party set (GREEN) is fairly straightforward. The threshold for non-membership is simply set at a threshold of 0 per cent – a decision that probably requires no further justification. The cross-over point is set at 1 per cent in order to make sure that every green party that is represented in parliament is more in than out of the set. It hardly makes any sense to set the threshold higher and thereby introduce the assumption that a parliamentary represented green party is more out of than in the set. However, it does make sense to distinguish between green parties that are only marginally represented and those that hold more seats, because their respective ability to get heard in the political process may to a certain extent depend on their relative strength vis-à-vis the other parties. The value that distinguishes parliamentary represented green parties best can be set at a seat share of 5 per cent. Again, the reader is referred to Appendix B for the solution terms for other thresholds.

The calibration of the MEDIA set represents a bigger challenge. There is no external and perfectly valid theoretical yardstick in order to distinguish high from low media attention, especially given the fact that the raw data come from different newspapers. Therefore, the initial decision of where to draw the line is a delicate one and must to a certain extent be made on the basis of the empirical data at hand. Accordingly, the reader is urged to consult the appendix for the robustness checks on this set calibration, which clearly show that the obtained solution terms remain stable when we change the 0.5-threshold within a reasonable range. In order to calibrate the MEDIA-set, I start with a threshold of 21 articles for the 0.5-threshold. This choice can be justified with the existence of a comparably large gap in the distribution of the raw data between 12 articles (Mauterndorf) and 27 articles (Bad Reichenhall). In addition, more than 21 published articles imply that the respective newspaper published more than 3 articles per day on average. The threshold for full non-membership is put at seven articles, since this number corresponds to an average number of articles of one per day. Finally, I put the threshold of full membership at 63 articles (an average of 6 articles per day).

Finally, the election set (ELECTIONS) is calibrated by setting the 0.5-threshold at a temporal distance of 365 days until the next general election. Thus, the set distinguishes events which occur in an election year from those that do not (according to the calendar year). An event is fully in the set if it occurs fewer than 100 days before the election and the event is fully out of the set if it occurs more than 2 years before the election (730 days). Table 6.2 summarizes the set calibrations used in the fsQCA on the politicization of gun control.

Based on these qualitative anchors, the sets can be calibrated directly by fitting a logistic function to the distribution of the raw data. This procedure yields the results of the set calibration, which are illustrated in Figure 6.1.

What empirical patterns emerge when we interpret the resulting set relationships in terms of necessity and sufficiency? The analysis below will address this

Paths to (non-)politicization 85

Table 6.2 Sets used in the fsQCA on politicization

Concept	Set label	Set type	Case is member of the set if ...
Politicization of gun control	POLIT	Crisp	... as a direct result of the event, at least one major political actor calls for the revision and/ or tightening of the affected country's legislative framework for private firearm ownership.
High event severity	DEATH	Fuzzy	... the event resulted in more than seven fatalities.
Green Party	GREEN	Fuzzy	... a green party is represented in the national parliament at the time of the rampage shooting.
Proximate elections	ELECTIONS	Fuzzy	... national parliamentary elections are scheduled within the next year.
Strong media attention	MEDIA	Fuzzy	... within the first week after the shooting, a national newspaper published at least 21 articles that either contained the name of the perpetrator or the locality of the shooting (corrected for irrelevant hits).

question and provide the solution terms along with an interpretation. In order to make the analysis as methodologically sound as possible, its setup follows the advice on the best practices in QCA given by Schneider and Wagemann (2010). Several components are of particular importance. For instance, since causal relationships are by definition asymmetric in a QCA setting, the presence and the absence of the outcome must be analysed in separate steps. Accordingly, both the analysis of necessity and sufficiency are performed for the presence and the absence of politicization. In addition, it is generally considered best practice to start with the analysis of necessary conditions and then proceed to the minimization of the truth table (Schneider and Wagemann 2010: 8). This best practice is not purely a convention. In fact, if we try to derive necessary conditions from an analysis of sufficiency, we run the danger of overlooking hidden necessary conditions or finding false necessary conditions (for more information on this matter, consult Schneider and Wagemann 2012). Finally, I provide arguments on the most proper treatment of contradictory truth table rows, clarify how thresholds of consistency are applied, make my simplifying assumptions explicit and present all possible solution terms (conservative, intermediate and parsimonious). The analysis is carried out with the software fsQCA 2.0 (Ragin *et al.* 2006).[1]

6.3 Analysis of necessity

As the set calibration has demonstrated, 12 rampage shootings directly sparked political debates over the appropriateness of the affected countries' gun policies, whereas 5 rampage shootings did not. Yet, which characteristics are

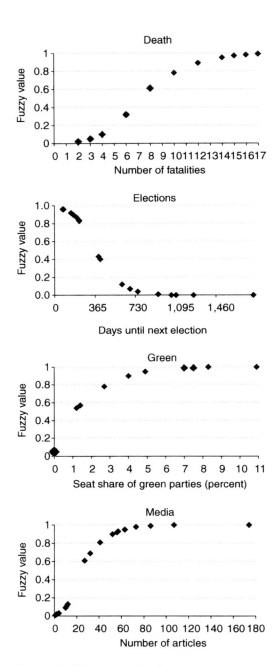

Figure 6.1 Direct set calibrations.

Paths to (non-)politicization 87

constituent elements of the two groups of cases? Which conditions are always present or absent within the sets of politicized and not politicized cases respectively? Can we identify functionally equivalent necessary conditions? These questions form the core challenge for the analysis of necessity relationships. In order to address the analytical challenge, we start with the analysis of the absence of the outcome.

6.3.1 Necessary conditions for the absence of politicization

In order to identify necessary conditions for the absence of politicization, we only need to take the five cases into account which are out of the set of politicized cases. All other cases are logically irrelevant for the analysis. Table 6.3 summarizes the results.

Are rampage shootings of rather low severity necessarily ignored by political actors? The answer to this question is clearly no, because the corresponding consistency value of this statement is only 0.71. If we tie the analysis back to the cases, we see that it is the rampage shooting at Solliès-Pont and Cuers (France) that violates this necessity relationship. In terms of casualties, the rampage shooting committed in the French villages Solliès-Pont and Cuers by 16-year-old Éric Borel on 23 September 1995 is the deadliest incidence in France up until today. First, the perpetrator killed his parents and his brother in his hometown Solliès-Pont, before carrying on with his rampage in the neighbouring village Cuers, where Borel killed another 12 people, including his best friend (Supp 1995). Borel used his father's hunting rifle for the carnage, which he had apparently taken from a wardrobe (Supp 1995). This proceeding resembles the way Tim Kretschmer, the Winnenden shooter (see section 7.2.3), acquired his weapons roughly 14 years later in Germany. Yet, despite the obvious simplicity with which Borel got hold of the weapon and the fact that the rampage was unprecedented in its scope on French soil, the event was completely ignored on a political level. In fact, the shooting in Solliès-Pont and Cuers did not evoke any legislative reactions and not a single demand for a change in French gun laws could be found. Instead, the media focused strongly on the reporting of

Table 6.3 Analysis of necessity: absence of politicization

Condition	Consistency	Coverage
DEATH	0.29	0.17
death	0.71	0.43
MEDIA	0.05	0.03
media	0.95	0.69
GREEN	0.15	0.07
green	0.85	0.61
ELECTIONS	0.73	0.50
elections	0.27	0.14

88   *Paths to (non-)politicization*

community grief and the perpetrator's alleged Nazi mind-set. French gun laws were entirely absent from the public discourse in the aftermath of the shooting. Accordingly, while most shootings that did not get politicized had resulted in a relatively low number of fatalities, the incident described above prevents us from concluding that low 'objective' event severity is a necessary condition for the absence of politicization.

However, the analysis of necessity clearly suggests that perceived event severity matters. As the figures on media attention show, events that did not get politicized were always accompanied by relatively low media attention. This is also true for the previously discussed shooting at Solliès-Pont and Cuers. As one of the leading French daily newspapers, *Le Monde* only published four articles on the shooting within the first week. If we compare this figure to the 73 articles published after the Nanterre shooting (see section 7.4.1), we can clearly identify a gap in perceived event severity. One possible reason for this comparably low attention might be related to the different types of firearms used in the respective shootings. While the Nanterre massacre was perpetrated with handguns, which are usually rather rare, the shooting at Solliès-Pont/Cuers was carried out with a hunting rifle, a weapon that is far more common, especially in rural areas. Thus, low media attention can reasonably be interpreted as a necessary condition for the absence of politicization. However, the condition is not by itself sufficient, as later sections will reveal.

As far as the political conditions are concerned, certain tendencies can be identified, but outright patterns of necessity are absent. While it seems that the absence of green parties indeed tends to coincide with the absence of politicization, the Euskirchen shooting violates the statement of necessity. Although the party *Bündnis 90/Die Grünen* maintained seats in the German *Bundestag*, the shooting did not lead to a national political debate on gun control.[2] In the nation's former capital Bonn, the *Bundestag* commemorated the victims of the rampage (Deutscher Bundestag 1994), but no party initiated political action in response to the event. Neither a representative of the Christian-Liberal government led by Helmut Kohl, nor any national politician of the opposition parties questioned the appropriateness of the German firearm law, although the event in Euskirchen could have been interpreted as a clear policy failure. A mentally unstable man had been in legal possession of a sizable arsenal of firearms and the police had not revoked his certificate despite the fact that even relatives had reported him to the authorities as being 'dangerous and abnormal' (Frankfurter Allgemeine Zeitung 1994). Gun control was only raised as a political issue on the local level, but also only to a limited extent. In North Rhine-Westphalia, the state in which Euskirchen is located, the Social Democrats and the Greens in the state's local parliament called for a stricter German gun law (Landtag intern 1994), but did not manage to elevate the political debate to the national level. This is probably due to the fact that as a sub-national entity, North Rhine-Westphalia would not have been allowed to take legislative action in the area of firearm regulation. In order to change the German weapons act, the state would have had to introduce a bill in the *Bundesrat*, where all 16 *Länder* governments are represented. Even though the North Rhine-Westphalian government was formed by Social Democrats at the time of the shooting, the left parties did not enjoy a majority in this chamber, which essentially rendered any effort of changing Germany's gun law doomed to fail. Instead, the state decided to focus only on security measures for public buildings and tightened those measures to a certain extent (Truscheit 2012).[3] No further political action was taken. This brief illustration demonstrates that rampage shootings can also have no impact on the politicization of gun control if green parties are represented in parliament. For the sake of completeness, it should nevertheless be underscored that the Euskirchen shooting represents an exception and not the rule. During the other four non-politicized shootings (Aarhus, Solliès-Pont/Cuers, Tours, Bogogno), green parties were not represented in parliament.

Finally, the analysis of necessity does not allow us to draw any clear lessons on the role of the electoral cycle. While four of the non-politicized shootings occurred in relatively close temporal proximity to national elections (Aarhus, Tours, Euskirchen, Bogogno), elections were not imminent after the remaining shooting (Solliès-Pont/Cuers). While this finding is inconclusive as far as necessity is concerned, it includes a certain tendency. More specifically, the observation suggests that political actors tend to hesitate in exploiting a crisis if elections are close. Accordingly, the figures tend to raise doubts over the validity of theoretical expectation 4 (see section 4.1.3) and suggest that the hypothesized relationship might be inverted. However, the shooting at Solliès-Pont again prevents us from deriving a clear-cut necessity relationship.

In set-theoretic terms, we can therefore conclude this first analysis of necessity with the claim that the set of non-politicized shootings is a subset of the shootings that received low media attention. In other words, low attention of the media can be considered a necessary, but not sufficient condition for the absence of politicization in the area of gun control after rampage shootings. This statement can be summarized as follows:

media ← politicization of gun control

(Consistency: 0.95; coverage: 0.69)

6.3.2 Necessary conditions for politicization

Let us now turn to the presence of the outcome and accordingly, to the remaining 12 rampage shootings. Table 6.4 lists the consistency and coverage values we obtain by analysing the necessity of the individual conditions for politicization. As a cursory glance over the consistency values indicates, none of the individual conditions surpasses a conventional threshold of consistency of 0.9. Accordingly, the analysis suggests that there are no necessary conditions for politicization, which implies that the politicization of gun control in the wake of rampage shootings cannot be attributed to one single causal mechanism alone. Instead, the absence of individually necessary conditions suggests that such

90 Paths to (non-)politicization

Table 6.4 Analysis of necessity: politicization

Condition	Consistency	Coverage
DEATH	0.61	0.83
death	0.39	0.57
MEDIA	0.83	0.97
media	0.17	0.31
GREEN	0.77	0.93
green	0.23	0.39
ELECTIONS	0.31	0.50
elections	0.69	0.86

politicization must probably be understood as the product of distinct causal combinations, which will be analysed in later steps of this fsQCA.

When we look at the individual conditions, the analysis of necessity therefore suggests that much conventional wisdom on the political effects of rampage shootings is demonstrably false. For example, the often-heard claim that politicians only react if the event's severity leaves them no other option is not supported by the empirical evidence. In fact, the issue of gun control has become subject to political controversy after events of both large and small magnitude. Specifically, a third of the politicized rampage shootings resulted in fewer than seven fatalities (Antwerp, Lörrach, Bad Reichenhall, Mauterndorf). The shootings in Antwerp even resulted in 'only' two fatalities, but nevertheless eventually led to the most fundamental policy shift in Belgium since 1933. Accordingly, the simple stimulus-response argument outlined in theoretical expectation 1 cannot account for patterns of politicization by itself. While many politicized rampage shootings had resulted in large numbers of fatalities, some were politicized despite their relatively low 'objective' severity. This implies that the politicization process is complex and requires us to take additional factors into account. In particular, the empirical evidence lends support to the social constructivist notion that the way a problem is perceived and portrayed often has more implications for the political process than objective measures of event severity.

As far as media attention is concerned, the analysis of necessity suggests that a strong interest of the media is a very common characteristic of politicized rampage shootings, but it is nevertheless not a necessary condition. In our empirical context, the Mauterndorf case challenges the necessity statement. When we compare the Mauterndorf shooting to many of the other shootings, the media's focus on the event was not particularly pronounced. Nevertheless, the event was taken as an opportunity by several change-friendly political actors to push the gun control issue. Thus, while the analysis suggests that the media are generally important actors when it comes to the formulation of policy implications of an event, their influence is not absolute. Despite this qualification that arises through the Mauterndorf case, the high coverage value of the MEDIA set indicates that the condition is far from trivial for the explanation of politicization patterns.

Paths to (non-)politicization 91

Next, the analysis of necessity demonstrates that there are many politicized events during whose occurrence green parties were in parliament. As we will discover in the case studies in Chapter 7, the previously mentioned Mauterndorf case is a prime example for an event whose policy implications were demanded primarily by the national green party (in coalition with the Social Democrats). Likewise, green parties played a major role for politicization in the Finnish and German cases as well as in the Swiss case. Despite those supportive cases, green parties are not necessary for politicization, because there are two prominent British events in the sample that violate the statement of necessity: Dunblane and Cumbria. Due to the two-party system of Great Britain, green parties have never managed to enter the national parliament. In terms of its opposition to private gun ownership, however, the British Labour Party has proven to be ideologically very close to the positions of many green parties in Europe. Accordingly, Labour has more or less taken over the role as the party demanding reforms in the area of gun control, a role that has been played by green parties in many other countries of Western Europe.

Do politicized rampage shootings typically occur in close temporal proximity to national elections or at a longer temporal distance? Since the analysis of necessity suggests that both scenarios have occurred, neither temporal proximity nor temporal distance can be interpreted as a necessary condition for politicization. Again, there is a certain tendency that suggests that politicization occurs more often if elections are not looming on the horizon (as is the case in 9 out of 12 events). However, three prominent events were politicized despite imminent national elections (Erfurt, Winnenden, and Nanterre). We will explore the cases in more detail in later sections of this book, but we should bear in mind for the moment that neither election proximity nor distance are by themselves necessary for politicization.

Before we turn to the truth tables and their logical minimization, let us have a quick look at plausible disjunctions (logical OR combinations) of the conditions analysed above. Table 6.5 lists some of those disjunctions. As a matter of fact, the chances for a case to become a member of a causal disjunction increase with every condition that is added. As a result, consistency usually increases (it cannot decrease by definition), but coverage often goes down, because the disjunction becomes trivially necessary. It is important to bear those important caveats in mind when interpreting the results.

Since the analysis above has shown that strong media attention is almost necessary for politicization (only Mauterndorf contradicted the necessity relationship), the addition of any other condition, except DEATH, leaves us with a

Table 6.5 Analysis of necessity: disjunctions of individual conditions

Disjunction	Consistency	Coverage
elections + MEDIA	0.97	0.89
MEDIA + GREEN	0.96	0.94

92 *Paths to (non-)politicization*

fully consistent statement of necessity. Spelt out, the first solution listed in Table 6.5 simply tells us that politicized events are either accompanied by extreme media attention or take place in temporal distance to national elections. In purely set-theoretic terms, the two conditions serve as functional equivalents. What is lacking for the solution's proper interpretation, however, is a common theoretical concept that captures both the absence of proximate elections and strong media attention. According to the second solution term, events that led to politicization were either accompanied by strong media attention or the presence of a green party. Given the particularities of the Mauterndorf case, which we will discover in more detail in section 7.5.1, it seems more appropriate to go with this second solution. This is also supported by the relatively high coverage value of the solution, which indicates that the causal disjunction is far from trivial. Thus, we can summarize the analysis of necessity with regard to politicization as follows:

MEDIA + GREEN ← POLITICIZATION OF GUN CONTROL

(Consistency: 0.96; coverage: 0.94)

6.4 Analysis of sufficiency

The analysis of necessity presented above has provided us with conditions that are necessary, but not sufficient for politicization and its absence. In order to arrive at these conditions, the analysis deliberately sampled on the dependent variable (or better, the outcome). Yet, while we now have a fairly clear understanding about the characteristics the groups of politicized and not politicized events share respectively, we have not yet acquired any knowledge about the causal interaction of individual conditions in producing the two outcomes. Therefore, the next analytical step consists of turning the analysis around and interpreting the empirical evidence in terms of sufficiency. Just like the analysis of necessity, this analysis starts with the absence of the outcome.

6.4.1 Sufficient conditions for the absence of politicization

In order to test for sufficiency relationships, we first need to construct the so-called truth table, which consists of all possible configurations of conditions. In a situation of four conditions, as it is encountered in our empirical context, a truth table thus consists of $2^4 = 16$ truth table rows (Table 6.6). Once the 16 causal configurations are listed, the next task consists of allocating the outcome (0 or 1) to every row that contains empirical evidence.[4] This decision is often based upon consistency values and the line is drawn where we can observe a major gap between two values. This procedure can be questioned if true logical contradictions are present in the truth table, i.e. if a single row includes both cases that do and do not display the outcome. This is, however, not the case in the present scenario. All five cases that lacked politicization can be allocated to

Table 6.6 Truth table: absence of politicization

Row	DEATH	MEDIA	GREEN	ELEC	Non-politicization	Consistency	Cases
1	0	0	0	1	1	0.91	3 (Aarhus, Tours, Bogogno)
2	1	0	0	0	1	0.82	1 (Solliès-Pont/Cuers)
3	0	0	1	1	1	0.68	1 (Euskirchen)
4	1	1	1	1	0	0.29	3 (Erfurt, Winnenden, Nanterre)
5	0	0	1	0	0	0.16	1 (Mauterndorf)
6	1	1	0	0	0	0.13	2 (Dunblane, Cumbria)
7	0	1	1	0	0	0.08	3 (Antwerp, Bad Reichenhall, Lörrach)
8	1	1	1	0	0	0.08	3 (Zug, Jokela, Kauhajoki)
9	0	1	1	1	?	–	–
10	0	1	0	0	?	–	–
11	1	0	1	0	?	–	–
12	1	1	0	1	?	–	–
13	0	0	0	0	?	–	–
14	0	1	0	1	?	–	–
15	1	0	1	1	?	–	–
16	1	0	0	1	?	–	–

94 *Paths to (non-)politicization*

the first three causal configurations, while all others fall into five other truth table rows. Accordingly, the first major challenge many existing QCA applications have to struggle with, inconsistent truth table rows, is not an issue in this particular analysis. This is also true for the third truth table row, although it displays a relatively low consistency score of 0.68. However, this value is a result of the fact that we are dealing with fuzzy sets and does not relate to any true inconsistencies. In fact, there is only one case in this particular truth table row and the low consistency value primarily stems from the fact that this case (Euskirchen) is only barely a member of the GREEN set and only barely a non-member of the DEATH set. However, there is no true logical contradiction involved, which implies that we can safely allocate the row to the presence of the outcome (non-politicization of gun control).

Thus, while inconsistent truth table rows do not cause problems in the analysis, we do encounter the problem that not all theoretically possible causal combinations are actually represented empirically. Exactly half of the 16 theoretically possible causal combinations are represented by at least one case, a situation of limited empirical diversity that is rather the rule than the exception in applied QCA (and implicitly in most studies of social science). Nevertheless, the existence of logical remainders requires us to work with assumptions, which, depending on their plausibility, lead us to different solution terms (conservative, intermediate and parsimonious). All of these solution terms will be presented and discussed, based on varying amounts of simplifying assumptions.

The goal of the minimization process is the identification of so-called prime implicants by means of Boolean algebra. Put simply, the primitive expressions presented in the previous sub-section (i.e. the individual truth table rows that imply the outcome) are compared pairwise in order to eliminate logically redundant conditions. The end of this minimization process yields three different solution formulas, which vary according to the number of simplifying assumptions we impose on the logical remainders. The conservative solution does not involve any simplifying assumptions on the logical remainders in the minimization process. In other words, only empirically represented rows are included in the minimization process and the outcome value is set to 0 for the logical remainders, which are thereby not considered for minimization. This has the advantage that the solution only includes the actual empirical evidence, but typically implies the downside that the resulting solution is extremely complex and hard to interpret substantively. At the other end of the extreme, we can derive a parsimonious solution term, which includes all logical remainders that contribute to parsimony. This has the advantage that the resulting solution formula becomes much easier to interpret, but the downside that it may rest upon assumptions that run counter to existing knowledge or even common sense (so-called difficult counterfactuals). In order to reach the goal of making relatively straightforward statements of sufficiency, which do not rest upon unrealistic assumptions, we can derive the intermediate solution term. This solution term only includes logical remainders for which we can safely make 'easy' counterfactuals. Such easy counterfactuals are both in line with directional expectations and contribute

Paths to (non-)politicization 95

to parsimony (whereas the 'difficult' counterfactuals used for the parsimonious solution only contribute to parsimony). While all three solutions will be presented in the remainder of this chapter, it may be considered most appropriate and useful to focus on the intermediate solution term which is based on the theoretical expectations outlined in Chapter 4.

Table 6.7 presents the results of the analysis of sufficiency. As the intermediate solution term demonstrates, there are two paths to non-politicization, whereby not both paths are equally important empirically as their respective coverage values indicate. While the first path exclusively covers four out of five cases (Bogogno, Aarhus, Tours, and Euskirchen), the second path only covers the remaining case (Solliès-Pont/Cuers). The first path consists of a conjunction of low event severity (both objective and perceived) with proximate elections. If all three of those conditions are jointly present in the context of a rampage shooting, the empirical evidence clearly suggests that political actors refrain from politicizing gun control. Not a single case contradicts this statement of sufficiency and accordingly, the consistency value of 0.91 is very high. Thus, if the shock waves generated by the rampage shooting are not large in objective terms and are accordingly not covered extensively by the news media, political actors will choose to ignore the event in the context of imminent elections regardless of their political ideology. The reasons for this non-politicization are arguably different for conservative and progressive forces of the political system.

If political actors have a conservative position on gun control, they have no incentive to politicize an event of comparably small magnitude anyway. In particular, they have even less of an incentive to do so in the context of a proximate election, because they are running the danger of alienating parts of their core constituents (e.g. hunters or sports shooters). Thus, the electoral costs associated with a politicization of gun control arguably always outweigh the potential benefits for conservative parties. Therefore, we should expect efforts of politicization to originate in other areas of the party spectrum. As the solution term suggests, however, also progressive forces are generally very careful with the politicization of gun control when elections are looming on the horizon. How can this counterintuitive result be explained?

On the one hand, it may be the case that events of low magnitude are simply absorbed, because the transaction costs for building a political campaign around the gun control issue are prohibitively high. After all, it probably takes an enormous effort to build a sustainable change coalition on the basis on an event of comparably small magnitude and in the simultaneous absence of media attention. However, next to high transaction costs associated with the politicization of relatively small-scale events, it may also be the case that the electoral benefits of such politicization are unclear, even for progressive parties. Contrary to theoretical expectation 4, if political actors have a progressive position on gun control, they may choose to abstain from politicizing the event before an election, because they want to avoid being blamed as crisis exploiters. Such a reaction is arguably particularly likely if the potential focusing event is a human tragedy. In such a tragic context, when national grief dominates the public discourse, attempts to

Table 6.7 Analysis of sufficiency: absence of politicization

Type of solution	Causal paths	Raw coverage	Unique coverage	Consistency	Solution consistency	Solution coverage
Conservative	ELECTIONS * death * media	0.67	0.60	0.91	0.90	0.84
	+					
	elections * green * media * DEATH	0.24	0.17	0.82		
Intermediate	ELECTIONS * death * media	0.67	0.57	0.91	0.90	0.84
	+					
	elections * green * media	0.27	0.17	0.75		
Parsimonious	media * green	0.84	0.03	0.91		
	+					
	media * DEATH	0.29	0.00	0.64	0.74	0.93
	+					
	media ELECTIONS	0.72	0.03	0.91		
	+					
	death * ELECTIONS	0.68	0.01	0.77		

Paths to (non-)politicization 97

exploit the event politically can easily backfire on the change advocates. Therefore, in anticipation of reproaches of pursuing their interest 'on the backs of dead people', change advocates may choose not to politicize a rampage shooting if the proximity of national elections suggests that they only do so for their own political benefit. Instead, they may fear that their potential electoral losses from politicizing the event may exceed their potential electoral gains. In this logic, attempts of crisis exploitation should rather occur if elections are not imminent and the change advocates' motivation of policy seeking is not in direct confrontation with their office-seeking motivation. We will have a closer look at this argument when we evaluate the sufficiency relationships for politicization in the next sub-section.

The second path of the intermediate solution term covers only the case of Solliès-Pont, where no politicization occurred despite relatively high objective event severity. The Solliès-Pont case suggests that the lack of a green party, a lack of media attention and the absence of proximate elections contribute to a non-politicization of gun control, even if the objective event severity is high. All three conditions are in line with the initial theoretical expectations, although the previously discussed path has shown that the argument on the electoral cycle often runs into the opposite direction. However, the Solliès-Pont case shows that objective event severity does not always lead to politicization efforts in gun control if no partisan actor 'owns' the issue and if, in addition, the media by and large ignore the event. In sum, the analysis of sufficiency shows that one and the same outcome (non-politicization of gun control) can be the outcome of different causal combinations of conditions, although the empirical evidence clearly suggests that one path covers more cases than the other.

In both paths, the absence of strong media attention serves as an INUS condition for non-politicization. This important role of the media corresponds to the findings in the section on necessity, where we have identified the absence of strong media attention as a necessary condition for the absence of politicization. However, those results had not allowed us to make any further conclusions about the condition's sufficiency for non-politicization. What we have learned from the minimization of the truth table is that there are two scenarios under which the absence of media attention becomes sufficient for non-politicization. In the first scenario, the event itself is comparably low objective severity and elections are proximate. In the second scenario, elections are proximate, but no political party has a clear-cut incentive for politicization.

Thus, we can summarize the empirical evidence on the sufficiency relationships for non-politicization as follows:

**(ELECTIONS * death * media) + (elections * green * media) →
politicization of gun control**

(Solution consistency: 0.90; solution coverage: 0.84)

On a final note, it should be underlined that the conservative solution is not dramatically different from the intermediate one. In fact, the first path of the

98 *Paths to (non-)politicization*

conservative solution is even exactly identical to the first path of the intermediate solution. Only the second path becomes slightly more complex if we refrain from imposing directional expectations. This suggests that the obtained intermediate solution term is relatively close to the conservative solution and that the directional expectations we imposed did not alter the substance of the solution term tremendously. The parsimonious solution term, in contrast, is hardly interpretable and should be read with great caution. Once again, the reader is reminded that this solution term rests on a broad range of assumptions that contribute to parsimony, but are not necessarily in line with the initial theoretical expectations or common sense. This leads to the situation that none of the identified paths has any unique coverage and the overall solution consistency is relatively low. Therefore, the parsimonious solution is only reported for the sake of completeness, but its actual interpretation should rather be avoided.

6.4.2 Sufficient conditions for politicization

Now that we have acquired a better understanding of the paths that link the occurrence of a rampage shooting to political ignorance, let us explore the paths that link it to political activism. First, it should be recalled that we have not identified a single individual condition as necessary for politicization (section 6.3.2). Instead, several different causal disjunctions could be identified (e.g. MEDIA + GREEN), whose explanatory power is limited due to the simple fact that the addition of OR-conditions automatically increases consistency, but often drives down coverage. As a result, the obtained relationships become ever more trivial with every OR-condition that is added. However, what picture emerges if we turn the analysis around and interpret the empirical evidence in light of sufficiency?

Again, we first construct the corresponding truth table (Table 6.8). Since the empirical evidence does not contain any logical contradictions, the truth table is the exact inverse of the truth table displayed in the previous sub-section on the absence of politicization. This time, however, the gap between consistent and inconsistent truth table rows becomes clearer from a simple look at the consistency values, which display a very large gap between rows 5 and 6.

The minimization of the truth table again yields three types of solutions and again, we primarily pay attention to the intermediate solution (Table 6.9). The corresponding analysis suggests that again, there are two paths which lead to the politicization of gun control in the wake of rampage shootings. Those paths can be interpreted as a 'top-down'-path and a 'bottom-up' path. Interestingly, both paths cover a similar amount of cases exclusively (as indicated by the unique coverage value) and both represent fully consistent statements of sufficiency. While the 'top-down' path implies the strategic decision-making of political actors in the aftermath of a rampage shooting, the 'bottom-up' path rests more on the pressure exerted by the pure magnitude of the event and its treatment by the media. Three cases are covered by both paths at the same time (Zug, Jokela, and Kauhajoki), four cases are exclusively covered by the top-down path

Table 6.8 Truth table: politicization

Row	DEATH	MEDIA	GREEN	ELEC	POLITICIZATION	Consistency	Cases
1	1	1	1	0	1	0.93	3 (Zug, Jokela, Kauhajoki)
2	0	1	1	0	1	0.93	3 (Antwerp, Bad Reichenhall, Lörrach)
3	1	1	1	1	1	0.92	3 (Erfurt, Winnenden, Nanterre)
4	1	1	0	0	1	0.89	2 (Dunblane, Cumbria)
5	0	0	1	0	1	0.85	1 (Mauterndorf)
6	0	0	1	1	0	0.32	1 (Euskirchen)
7	1	0	0	0	0	0.18	1 (Solliès-Pont/Cuers)
8	0	0	0	1	0	0.09	3 (Aarhus, Tours, Bogogno)
9	0	1	1	1	?	–	–
10	0	1	0	0	?	–	–
11	1	0	1	0	?	–	–
12	1	1	0	1	?	–	–
13	0	0	0	0	?	–	–
14	0	1	0	1	?	–	–
15	1	0	1	1	?	–	–
16	1	0	0	1	?	–	–

Table 6.9 Analysis of sufficiency: politicization

Type of solution	Causal paths	Raw coverage	Unique coverage	Consistency	Solution consistency	Solution coverage
Conservative	elections * GREEN * death	0.33	0.23	0.92		
	+					
	elections * MEDIA * DEATH	0.36	0.12	0.95	0.97	0.78
	+					
	GREEN * MEDIA * DEATH	0.43	0.19	0.96		
Intermediate	elections * GREEN	0.56	0.32	0.95		
					0.97	0.90
	MEDIA * DEATH	0.59	0.34	0.97		
Parsimonious	MEDIA	0.83	0.40	0.97		
	+					
	elections * GREEN	0.56	0.04	0.95	0.95	0.96
	+					
	elections * death	0.33	0.00	0.89		

Paths to (non-)politicization 101

(Mauterndorf, Antwerp, Bad Reichenhall, and Lörrach) and five cases are exclusively covered by the bottom-up path (Erfurt, Winnenden, Nanterre, Dunblane, Cumbria). Yet, how exactly do the two causal paths exert their influence?

First, the top-down path consists of distant elections and the presence of a green political party in the affected country's national parliament. The data suggests that if a rampage shooting occurs under such a constellation, it will trigger a political debate over gun control. This finding provides the missing puzzle piece on the role of the electoral calendar for patterns of politicization. While previous results have shown that proximate elections impede politicization efforts, the top-down path suggests that distant elections facilitate politicization if the party system features a cleavage on the gun control issue. Accordingly, it seems like progressive forces in the party system are less hesitant about the politicization of gun control if such politicization does not interfere directly with their electoral campaign. If elections are far away, progressive political forces do not run the danger of being blamed for crisis exploitation and as a result, find it easier to use the event as an opportunity to push their cause as policy-seekers. In this top-down logic, change advocates take matters into their own hands and do not rely on third actors, such as the media or societal actors, to demand change. Instead, they pursue their own political program. In some instances, such politicization attempts are mainly made out of the opposition primarily for the symbolic purpose of blaming the current government of its reluctance to change the laws (such as in Mauterndorf or in Lörrach). In those situations, green parties only had a small chance to succeed with their goals in the legislative process from the outset, but nonetheless managed to draw the political attention to an issue they 'own'. In another scenario, the politicization efforts served the sincere purpose of bringing about policy change and were either made by the government coalition (as in the Bad Reichenhall case) or were made in the context of great party unity on the need for more stringent gun control (as in the Antwerp case).[5]

Another observation underscores the importance of the top-down logic as a path to politicization that is relevant on its own. When we take a closer look at the four cases covered by the top-down path, it is interesting to note that all four events resulted in a comparably low number of fatalities, while all of the events covered by the bottom-up path resulted in a comparably high death toll. This suggests that while some particularly severe events do not need a special political environment in order to become subject to political controversy, events that are covered by the top-down path only get politicized if the political conditions are favourable, i.e. if elections are not imminent and a political party has a clear incentive for politicization. Accordingly, while we can clearly identify a top-down logic of politicization in some of the empirical cases, other events exert their impact in a 'bottom-up' manner via their sheer magnitude and accompanying strong media attention.

How exactly does the bottom-up path lead to politicization? First of all, the term 'bottom-up' primarily implies that while political elites are ultimately responsible for the actual act of politicization, the origins of those politicization

102 *Paths to (non-)politicization*

efforts relate primarily to characteristics of the event itself and its perceived meaning as portrayed by the media. In other words, the bottom-up path to politicization works as a conjunction of objective and perceived event severity. If an event is severe in objective terms (e.g. by its high death toll) and also portrayed as such by the media, political actors will find it difficult to avoid a political debate over the event's implications for public policy, regardless of their ideological orientation. In this logic, political actors do not choose to engage in a political debate over gun control, as in the top-down path, but are forced to do so due to the overwhelming severity of the event. Empirically, this bottom-up constellation covers five cases exclusively (Erfurt, Winnenden, Nanterre, Dunblane, Cumbria). In the first three cases, elections were relatively close, but the sheer magnitude of the respective events made it politically infeasible to ignore them. In the latter two events, green parties were not part of the political spectrum, but the pressure that was generated by the events' objective and perceived severity was channelled into the political process primarily by the British Labour party, which has been demonstrating relatively strong opposition to private gun ownership over the course of the past decades. This shows that while the presence of green parties is an INUS condition in conjunction with distant elections, the parties' mere presence is by no means necessary for the politicization of gun control after rampage shootings (recall the results of the analysis of necessity in section 6.3). Instead, their place can be taken by other types of parties if only the event is severe enough. Again, the case studies presented in Chapter 7 will shed some more light on the political processes unfolding in the wake of the events discussed above.

To sum up, the politicization of gun control after rampage shootings can be the result of two equifinal causal paths. First, even events of rather small magnitude can be politicized as indicators of a policy failure if the partisan landscape includes a party that has a clear incentive to push the issue and if distant elections suggest that politicization will not backfire as an attempt to exploit a human tragedy solely for electoral purposes. Second, if an event surpasses a certain threshold of objective severity and the amount of media attention it generates, political scope conditions become less important, because ignoring the event's policy implications is simply no longer a viable option for all political actors. Thus, while the first path implies a clear and conscious political strategy of 'crisis exploitation', the latter path assumes relevance through a combination of the event's characteristics and the way the event is covered by the news media. Given the fsQCA on sufficient conditions for politicization, we can thus summarize the solution as follows:

(elections * GREEN) + (MEDIA * DEATH) → POLITICIZATION OF GUN CONTROL

(Solution consistency: 0.97; solution coverage: 0.90)

6.5 Summary of the findings on politicization

What general conclusions can be drawn from this fsQCA on the selective politicization of gun control in the aftermath of rampage shootings? First of all, we can safely conclude that an event's impact on the political agenda is anything but pre-determined. Instead, apart from their varying severity, events like rampage shootings occur in variant political and societal contexts and the way those contextual conditions are configured is important for the events' political processing. Accordingly, the results presented in this chapter lend strong support to the notion of causal complexity and underline the need to consider the possibility of equifinal processes in studies of politicization in general and after external shocks in particular. As expected in Chapter 4, we cannot confirm or disconfirm the relevance of any single theorized condition without taking into account the configuration of the other conditions. Instead, what we found is a complex interplay of different causal configurations that all suggest substantive interpretations. This general finding alone implies that we may miss important and interesting causal mechanisms if we unhesitatingly trade accuracy for parsimony.

Beyond those general points, the empirical evidence analysed in this chapter has yielded several important lessons on the politicization of gun control in the aftermath of rampage shootings (see Figure 6.2 for a graphical summary). First, it is remarkable that the extent to which the media react to a rampage shooting is included in every single solution term in one way or the other. For instance, we

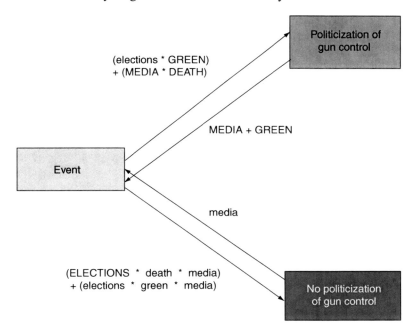

Figure 6.2 Summary of the findings on (non)-politicization.

104 *Paths to (non-)politicization*

have found that while strong media attention is almost necessary for politicization, it becomes sufficient if it is coupled with an overall high degree of objective event severity. Accordingly, we can safely expect a rampage shooting to get politicized if it is objectively severe and also perceived as such by the media as the most important societal actor delivering the first interpretation of the event's implications. In contrast, however, if the media decide to pay only marginal attention to an event, efforts of politicization must emerge on the political level.

The empirical evidence suggests that such efforts typically take place if a green party plays a prominent role in the affected country's party system and if elections are not temporally proximate. Green parties are particularly prone to attribute the occurrence of rampage shootings, as they are defined for the purposes of this book, to policy failures in the country's gun control system. As the expert survey presented in section 4.1.3 demonstrates, European green parties display exceptionally high cohesion in their rejection of private gun ownership. This strong scepticism primarily results from the general pacifist ideology prevalent in green parties. Accordingly, politicians from green parties should be the first political actors who call for stricter provisions in the area of gun control after rampage shootings, if such actors exist in the affected country's party system. The results of the QCA show that this pattern actually materializes empirically, but only under certain conditions. First, green parties politicize gun control if they can safely avoid the danger of being punished for crisis exploitation in proximate elections. According to this logic and contrary to the initially formulated theoretical expectation, temporally close national elections do not serve as catalysts for politicization, but as brakes. Even parties whose policy position is supported by the potential focusing event are thus hesitant to try and reap political benefit from a human tragedy if they must fear that such attempts could quickly backfire politically. In addition, the presence of green parties is irrelevant if the event's sheer magnitude and the media's strong coverage take the option to ignore the event's policy implications off the table for all political actors alike. In such a context of strong bottom-up pressure for politicization, the proximity of elections and the presence of green parties do not matter much. However, if the event is either not particularly severe in objective terms or largely ignored by the media, politicization takes a top-down path that works through green parties and distant elections.

When we look at the paths to non-politicization, it becomes evident that those paths are not simply the mirror image of the paths to politicization, although they partially come close to it. First of all, the media again play a prominent role. All non-politicized events analysed in this book were preceded by a lack of media attention and therefore, we can interpret ignorance of the media as a necessary condition for ignorance on behalf of the political actors. However, the condition is not by itself sufficient, since politicization also occurred in the context of low media attention (remember the Mauterndorf case). But, the condition does become sufficient if the death toll is simultaneously low and if elections are close. Thus, if the media ignore an event of already low objective severity and if the event interferes with proximate elections, the costs for seeking a political

Paths to (non-)politicization 105

confrontation outweigh the benefits for all political actors, regardless of their political colour. This logic has been found to be the most common path to non-politicization, covering a total of four out of five cases. While this number of cases may appear low on first sight, it should be kept in mind that the three conditions in this path (MEDIA, DEATH, ELECTIONS) could theoretically be configured in $2^3 = 8$ possible combinations. The fact that four out of five cases fall into the identical combination (media, death, ELECTIONS) is rather remarkable and suggests that this pattern seems to be a very relevant one for non-politicization. The remaining case, the shooting in Solliès-Pont/Cuers, is a puzzling outlier. Despite a high number of fatalities, it did not lead to politicization. The results suggest that this might primarily be due to the constellation that the French media hardly paid any attention to the event and that the French political system lacked a clear partisan cleavage on the issue of gun control at the time the shooting occurred. Thus, we can identify two paths to non-politicization, whereby the first path is clearly more relevant given the patterns found in the empirical evidence.

On a final methodological note, it may be concluded from this chapter that QCA provides a highly useful toolkit for the description and analysis of the processing of potential focusing events. If we conceptualize an event along some clearly specified definitional features instead of identifying it retrospectively through its political impact, we can open up interesting research avenues that avoid the confirmation bias inherent in many empirical studies on external shocks. Moreover, a systematic application of this approach enables the evaluation of complex theoretical relationships even in the context of a relatively low number of cases. As a methodological approach, fsQCA is well suited to deal with such theoretical and empirical situations and provides for the detection of complex empirical patterns that would otherwise easily evade scientific scrutiny. However, the method is especially useful if the theoretical concepts we are interested in can be translated meaningfully into set-theoretic language and the calibration of the sets rests on a solid data foundation. If this is not the case, the in-depth qualitative analysis of individual cases represents the better strategy to unravel the causal mechanisms at work. This methodological approach is chosen for the second empirical part of the book on policy change and stability.

Thus, we now have a certain understanding of the processes that lead to the politicization of gun control in the wake of rampage shootings, and the processes that lead to the absence of politicization. In those latter situations, any further political action is logically ruled out if we make the (realistic) assumption that politicization is a necessary pre-condition for policy change. Yet, the interesting variance that remains to be explained rests with the politicized cases. Although we now have a good picture of why those events lead to a political debate over the gun control issue, we still do not know why some of those debates eventually petered out without any legislative consequences and why others yielded policy change. This second research question will be dealt with in the following chapter by means of case studies on the 12 politicized events.

106 *Paths to (non-)politicization*

Notes

1 The software and the corresponding manual can be downloaded for free from Charles Ragin's website (www.u.arizona.edu/~cragin/fsQCA/software.shtml).
2 On 9 March 1994, Erwin Mikolajczyk shot six people to death and killed himself with a self-constructed bomb in the town's courthouse (Der Spiegel 1994). It was later established that Mikolajczyk, being a member of the local shooting club, had been in possession of a weapon possession card and therefore owned the murder weapon legally, along with a range of other firearms (Frankfurter Allgemeine Zeitung 1994).
3 This political reaction closely resembles Switzerland's handling of the Zug shooting (see section 7.6.1).
4 For the sake of completeness, it should be mentioned that the frequency threshold is one case. In other words, a row is empirically represented if at least one case can be allocated to this row.
5 The reader is referred to the case studies in Chapter 7 for more in-depth information about the political processes surrounding those cases.

References

Budge, I., Klingemann, H.-D., Volkens, A., Bara, J. and Tanenbaum, E. (2001). *Mapping Policy Preferences: Estimates for Parties, Electors, and Governments 1945–1998.* Oxford: Oxford University Press.

Der Spiegel. (1994). Schlimmes passiert. *DER SPIEGEL* 11/1994, 37.

Deutscher Bundestag. (1994). Plenarprotokoll 12/216: Deutscher Bundestag, Stenografischer Bericht 216. Sitzung. Retrieved 6 August 2014 from http://dipbt.bundestag.de/doc/btp/12/12216.pdf#P.18589.

Döring, H. and Manow, P. (2012). Parliament and Government Composition Database (ParlGov): An Infrastructure for Empirical Information on Parties, Elections and Governments in Modern Democracies. Version 12/10–15 October 2012. Retrieved 4 March 2014 from http://parlgov.org/.

Expatica News. (2006). MPs Give Green Light to New Gun Control Laws. Retrieved 10 July 2014 from www.expatica.com/be/news/local_news/mps-give-green-light-to-tighter-gun-control-laws-30144.html.

Frankfurter Allgemeine Zeitung. (1994). Schon 1991 vor Amokläufer gewarnt – Als Busfahrer entlassen, *Frankfurter Allgemeine Zeitung*, 12 March 1994.

Hurka, S. and Nebel, K. (2013). Framing and Policy Change after Shooting Rampages: A Comparative Analysis of Discourse Networks. *Journal of European Public Policy* 20(3), 390–406.

Klingemann, H.-D., Volkens, A., Bara, J., Budge, I. and McDonald, M. (2006). *Mapping Policy Preferences II: Estimates for Parties, Electors, and Governments in Eastern Europe, European Union, and OECD 1990–2003.* Oxford: Oxford University Press.

Landtag intern. (1994). Redner stellen Fragen nach einer Verschärfung des deutschen Waffenrechts. *Landtag intern* 25(6), 4.

Lindström, K., Räsänen, P., Oksanen, A. and Nurmi, J. (2011). Politiikkaprosessi ja aselainsäädännön uudistaminen Jokelan ja Kauhajoen koulusurmien jälkeen. In J. Saari and M. Niemelä (eds), *Politiikan polut ja hyvinvointiyhteiskunnan muutos* (pp. 254–271). Helsinki: Kela.

Oksanen, A., Räsänen, P., Nurmi, J. and Lindström, K. (2010). 'This Can't Happen Here!' Community Reactions to School Shootings in Finland. *Research on Finnish Society* 3(1), 19–27.

Ragin, C. C., Drass, K. A. and Davey, S. (2006). *Fuzzy Set/Qualitative Comparative Analysis 2.0*. Tucson, Arizona: Department of Sociology, University of Arizona.

Schneider, C. Q. and Wagemann, C. (2010). Standards of Good Practice in Qualitative Comparative Analysis (QCA) and Fuzzy-Sets. *Comparative Sociology* 9(3), 397–418.

Schneider, C. Q. and Wagemann, C. (2012). *Set-Theoretic Methods for the Social Sciences: A Guide to Qualitative Comparative Analysis*. Cambridge: Cambridge University Press.

Skaaning, S.-E. (2011). Assessing the Robustness of Crisp-set and Fuzzy-set QCA Results. *Sociological Methods & Research* 40(2), 391–408.

Squires, P. (2014). *Gun Crime in Global Contexts*. Abingdon, Oxon: Routledge.

Stoisits, T., Petrovic, M. and Colleagues. (1998). Entschließungsantrag betreffend Novelle zum Waffengesetz (656/AE XX.GP). Retrieved 11 April 2014 from www.parlament.gv.at/PAKT/VHG/XX/A/A_00656/fname_124994.pdf.

Supp, B. (1995). Eine Art von Rache. *DER SPIEGEL* 41/1995, 184–188.

Truscheit, K. (2012). Die Angst geht immer mit, *Frankfurter Allgemeine Sonntagszeitung*, 15 January 2012.

7 When laws bite the bullet (and when they do not)[*]

The previous chapter has demonstrated that equifinal paths to the politicization of gun control in the aftermath of rampage shootings exist. But which factors determine the extent to which those politicized events actually result in changes of the regulatory status quo? This question is the main focus of this second empirical chapter, which consists of a collection of case studies on the 12 politicized events discovered in the previous fsQCA. Applying the analytical framework presented in Chapter 4, these case studies take a closer look at the political processes that sometimes hit a dead end and sometimes resulted in more or less meaningful alterations of the existing policy arrangements.

In a comparative design based upon a medium sized amount of cases, certain trade-offs must be made with regard to the analytical depth of every individual case study. On the one hand, it is important to gain a sufficiently good overview of the empirical evidence at hand in order to evaluate the validity of the theoretical expectations. On the other hand, full-blown examinations of all 12 events would arguably overburden the reader and would hardly do justice to the analytical goal of this final empirical chapter of the book. Therefore, I opt for the middle way and present the cases in a 'mini' case study format. This primarily means that the case studies are strictly focused on the evaluation of the theoretical expectations developed in Chapter 4 and all of them are structured in the same concise manner. The case studies address the political processing of individual rampage shootings, but since multiple shootings sometimes occurred within the same country, the discussion of constant political and socio-cultural factors would create redundancies within some of the case studies. Therefore, the case studies are clustered by the countries in which they occurred. Each of the following seven sub-sections therefore starts with a general introduction on the affected country's socio-cultural and political institutions, in order to allow the reader to evaluate the extent to which the conditions outlined in theoretical expectations 8a and 8b are present. Building on the discussion of these structural factors, I first introduce the individual cases descriptively and analyse their political processing by focusing on the other, more case-specific conditions presented in theoretical expectations 5–7, i.e. the event's perceived causal complexity, the degree of social mobilization and the cohesion of the reform opponents. The chapter concludes with a comparative assessment and a

When laws bite the bullet 109

conclusion on the factors found to be important for policy change and stability after rampage shootings.

7.1 Great Britain

In 1689, the *Bill of Rights* explicitly stated a right for armed self-defence for every suitable protestant citizen of Great Britain. Despite this relatively permissive approach, firearms have traditionally been owned by the 'upper echelons and the landed gentry' (Lilly 2001: 70). Hence, although gun clubs have been spreading continuously over the country, their membership criteria were highly restrictive, which 'served to solidify gun ownership as a privilege for the relatively influential and wealthy' (Lilly 2001: 70). Evidence from the International Crime Victims Survey (ICVS) underscores the relatively low availability of firearms in general, and handguns in particular in Great Britain. Since 1989, ownership of firearms oscillated between 3 and 6 per cent, whereas handgun ownership was consistently well below 1 per cent (van Dijk *et al.* 2007: 279). These values are among the lowest in Europe. Of course, the low availability of firearms in Great Britain is also a corollary of the legislative development over the past centuries. Over time, the permissive approach originally outlined in the *Bill of Rights* was replaced by increasing restrictions on civilian firearms. In particular, licensing procedures were introduced in the nineteenth century and continuously tightened in the twentieth with the Firearm Acts of 1920 and 1968. Thus, when compared to other countries in Europe and around the world, the attachment of the majority of the British population to firearms has traditionally been rather low.

In terms of its political institutions, Great Britain is renowned for its Westminster Model, which is characterized by a dominance of the executive over the legislative process (Lijphart 1999: 10f.). Almost all governments in Great Britain have been run by a single party which can rely on an own legislative majority, reducing compromise pressures. Accordingly, the preferences of the government translate into policies more easily and quickly than in systems where the opposition enjoys more powers of veto and delay. Governments in Great Britain are neither constrained by any constitutional hurdles when it comes to gun policy, nor do their policies face systematic judicial review. As a result of these institutional configurations, cabinets in Great Britain are typically very stable (Lijphart 1999: 133). In the same vein, Siaroff (2003: 456f.) allocates Great Britain the highest possible score on the executive dominance dimension, which includes measures such as the government's control of the plenary agenda and the power of the Prime Minister vis-à-vis the legislative branch. All in all, therefore, the low politico-institutional obstacles in Great Britain should increase the speed and scope of policy change dynamics.

Thus, socio-cultural and political institutions are configured in a rather favourable manner for quick legislative responses to rampage shootings in Great Britain. Gun ownership is not prevalent across all social strata to the same extent and stricter regulations therefore only affect comparably small portions of the

110 *When laws bite the bullet*

population. In addition, the low consensus requirements implied by British political institutions should be expected to facilitate strong legislative reactions. And in fact, Great Britain had already shown such a relatively strong legislative reaction before the time period examined in this book. On 19 August 1987, Michael Ryan had shot at a random group of people from his hometown, resulting in 16 fatalities and 15 injured people (Williams 2012). After the rampage, the perpetrator committed suicide. Ryan had obtained all of the firearms he used for his rampage legally, including a semi-automatic rifle, a 9 mm Beretta and a carbine (Broome *et al.* 1988; Webster 1989: 183). The political debate following the incident eventually culminated in the Firearms (Amendment) Act of 1988, which changed the provisions of the Firearms Act of 1968 mainly by extending 'the class of prohibited weapons to include most semi-automatic rifles and smooth-bore shotguns, as well as self-loading or pump-action shotguns' (Parker 2011: 7). Thus, the British government showed a comparably strong legislative reaction to the Hungerford shooting.

Between 1990 and 2010, Great Britain experienced two other rampage shootings and as the previous chapter has demonstrated, both were politicized in a bottom-up manner. The shootings at Dunblane and Cumbria led to relatively high numbers of fatalities and the news media covered the events extensively. Yet, while the political process following the Dunblane shooting eventually culminated in a massive policy change, the shooting in Cumbria 17 years later did not have any legislative consequences, despite the fact that several suggestions for tighter gun control measures were initially put on the table. The following case studies assess the two events in more detail.

7.1.1 Dunblane: policy change under public pressure

The Dunblane shooting on 13 March 1996 has entered the collective memory of Great Britain as the most terrible rampage shooting which ever occurred on British soil (Karp 2003; Thomson *et al.* 1998). On the morning of that day, Thomas Hamilton, aged 43, entered the town's primary school and killed 16 children, one teacher, and himself. The crime was committed with four handguns, two 9 mm Browning pistols and two Smith & Wesson revolvers, Hamilton had acquired legally as a member of the local shooting club (Cullen 1996, Chapter 6). As Squires (2000: 137) notes, 'the event was discussed as a largely domestic, national tragedy'. As such, Dunblane spurred a controversial and intense political debate over the appropriateness of Great Britain's gun policy arrangements, which were 'hitherto regarded as beyond reproach, the toughest in the world' (Squires 2000: 137). After the shooting, all major newspapers of the country focused instantly on the event and covered the ensuing reactions extensively. For the most part, the newspapers were also quite clear about their recommendations for political action. The leading daily newspaper of Great Britain, *The Times*, endorsed demands for tighter firearm laws soon after the incident, which is rather surprising given the fact that the newspaper is typically known for its conservative positions. In an editorial on 15 March 1996, it was stated that

'The Times is instinctively wary of hasty legislation, never anxious to see liberties curtailed. Grief may lend urgency to the case, but, after calm reflection, the arguments for a ban on the private use of handguns now seem compelling' (*The Times* 1996). Similar calls for tighter controls on guns were voiced by the *Guardian*, while the *Independent* reported the political reactions to the shooting without taking a clear stance on the gun issue. Only the conservative *Daily Telegraph* clearly opposed any new legislation (Baber 1997: 27f.). Eventually, an inquiry commission was set up under the leadership of Lord Cullen. In its final report, the commission ultimately recommended changes to the British Firearms Act, but did not endorse a handgun ban (Cullen 1996). Nevertheless, the accompanying political debate on gun control eventually culminated in one of the most extreme policy responses rampage shootings have ever evoked – the prohibition of handguns for private ownership in Great Britain. This was achieved in two separate steps: first, the Conservative government 'banned 95 percent of handguns and required that the remainder (.22-caliber) be stored at gun clubs' (Cukier and Sidel 2006: 189). A few months later, the new Labour government extended this ban to small calibre handguns, making the handgun ban comprehensive, 'a measure unprecedented in a democratic country' (Malcolm 2002: 205). What factors contributed to this paradigm shift? The analytical lenses provided by the theoretical expectations developed in Chapter 4 can be used in order to answer this question.

Dunblane's perceived causal complexity

In the weeks following the Dunblane shooting, the gun issue clearly dominated the public discourse over the event's causes and other causal attributions did not arouse an even remotely comparable increase in public attention. As Hurka and Nebel (2013: 398) have demonstrated, more than half of the causal statements and calls for political action made by political stakeholders within the first month after the event referred to the need to revise the country's approach of regulating firearms. The remainder of the statements was scattered among a range of side aspects of the shooting, such as matters of criminal justice or the role of the media. However, none of those secondary aspects managed to attract any sustained attention and accordingly, none of those topics led to a broad national debate like the one over gun control. Only the issue of school security received some systematic attention in the public discourse and the debate ultimately led some schools to increase their expenditures on security measures (Champion 2006). It can therefore be safely concluded that Dunblane was a real focusing event in the original sense put forward by Kingdon (1984). The event instantly put the spotlight on a clearly defined policy failure in Great Britain's gun control system and despite some patchy attempts to allocate responsibility to other sources, the overwhelming focus of the discourse remained firmly centred on the gun issue. As a result of this strong focus of the public discourse, all political actors were forced to take a stand on the gun issue and they did so with varying cohesion.

112 *When laws bite the bullet*

The cohesion of reform opponents after Dunblane

At the time the shooting occurred, Great Britain was governed by the *Conservative Party* and its Prime Minister John Major. The parliamentary opposition was formed by the *Labour Party* and the *Liberal Democrats*. For two reasons, this actor constellation made sweeping policy change rather unlikely. First, the *Conservative Party* is based on 'classical liberal roots, a tradition greatly reinvigorated during the eleven-year rule of Margaret Thatcher' (Karp 2003: 196). Protecting the freedom from governmental intrusions into the private sphere was thus a constitutive element of the party's ideology. Second, John Major was not inclined to alienate rural voters, which formed a considerable part of the *Conservative Party*'s constituents (ibid.). Accordingly, a sweeping gun law reform was clearly not one of the government's priorities when the massacre at Dunblane happened and, as discussed above, the institutional environment would have given the government the power to fend off such reform initiatives. However, the *Conservative Party* was not united in its opposition to a handgun ban and several prominent Conservatives openly backed the proposed measures (Karp 2003: 198f.). Most prominently, David Mellor, a Conservative Member of Parliament, former cabinet minister and staunch supporter of tighter gun regulations warned the public that 'we must keep our anger burning bright. When the public has forgotten the horror of Dunblane, the gun lobbyists will be coming out with their garbage' (Pilger 1996). Such statements show that the *Conservative Party* faced significant internal dissent over the appropriate course of action and accordingly, could not sustain its opposition to policy change. Thus, a relatively low cohesion among those who should have been expected to act as veto players clearly contributed to the serious consideration of drastic policy measures in the wake of the Dunblane shooting. Unlike after the shootings in Mauterndorf and Zug, no cohesive conservative coalition formed and dedicated itself to a complete prevention of the handgun ban (Hurka and Nebel 2013). Yet, the explanation of the British government's reaction to the Dunblane shooting is not complete without taking into account the massive efforts of social mobilization that accompanied the political debate.

Societal demand for policy change after Dunblane

As outlined previously, the British news media generally voiced support for more stringent gun regulations. In so doing, they echoed an unprecedented effort of social mobilization carried out by the *Snowdrop Campaign*, which was formed in a direct response to the shooting (Karp 2003: 197f.). Inspired by the goal to ban all handguns in Great Britain, 'the Snowdrop campaign was run almost exclusively as a moral appeal and as one unwilling to compromise this moral stance' (Thomson *et al.* 1998: 333f.). In a short period of time, the movement managed to rally massive public support behind its goal to ban all handguns and collected a total of 750,000 signatures calling for a handgun ban in Great Britain (Campbell 1996). The constant lobbying efforts and the

When laws bite the bullet 113

campaign's public support kept the gun issue on the political agenda. Most importantly, however, the social movement quickly aligned itself with the *Labour Party*, especially after Ann Pearston, founder of the campaign, held an emotional speech at the party convention, forcefully demanding a complete handgun ban (Squires 2000: 149). Under such immense pressure, the government eventually proposed a partial handgun ban for calibres above .22, a measure that went beyond the recommendations put forward by the Cullen inquiry (Cullen 1996), but fell short of a total handgun ban. The measure was approved in the House of Commons with the help of the opposition parties and against the will of 63 Conservative Members of Parliament (Karp 2003: 200).

In sum, the Dunblane case illustrates that major policy change can result from a rampage shooting if several conditions are simultaneously present. Those conditions are change-friendly socio-cultural and political institutions, few possibilities for alternative causal attributions, an incohesive status quo coalition, and a massive effort of social mobilization. Taken together, those four factors led to a paradigm shift in the British approach of regulating handguns. Seventeen years later, Great Britain was again haunted by a severe rampage shooting. This time, however, the political reaction was different.

7.1.2 Cumbria: successful defence of the policy status quo

Even though Great Britain had repeatedly tightened its firearm regulations in the wake of the Hungerford and Dunblane shootings, another large-scale killing with a legal firearm could not be prevented. On 2 June 2010, taxi-driver Derrick Bird killed 12 people and injured 11 others with a shotgun and a small-calibre rifle (Carter 2011), both of which had been legally licensed despite the perpetrator's 'criminal record of theft, drink driving and allegations of threatening behaviour' (Wainwright 2010). The shooting was carried out over the course of a few hours in the north-western county of Cumbria in different places, which the perpetrator reached by car. Next to family members and colleagues, the victims also included 'random members of the public' (Carter 2011). Like many other rampage killers, Bird committed suicide after completing his rampage.

Unlike the event in Dunblane, the incident at Cumbria did not result in any changes to Great Britain's gun laws. On the one hand, observers noted that the existing regulatory framework already belonged to the strictest in the world and questioned whether it was even possible to tighten it further (Casciani 2010). On the other hand, while handguns and semi-automatic rifles had been prohibited in Great Britain, shotguns and hunting rifles were more easily available (Travis 2010). Accordingly, a debate over the need to introduce the mandatory provision of medical certificates by firearm applicants developed, but eventually did not result in any legislative action. Until today, licensing authorities only have the right to ask the applicant to produce such a certificate, but this authority is 'not routinely used' (Feikert-Ahalt 2013). Thus, unlike Germany and Austria, Great Britain did not introduce the mandatory requirement of a medical certificate for people interested in the possession of a firearm. Given the fact that the

114   *When laws bite the bullet*

institutional background remained stable between the shooting in Dunblane and the one in Cumbria, the question arises why the gun control arrangements were not changed this time, although the envisaged measures were by far not as fundamental as the ones debated after the Dunblane shooting.

Cumbria's perceived causal complexity

The causal complexity of the Cumbria incident cannot contribute to the solution of this puzzle, because the causal attributions brought forward were again closely centred on the legality of the used firearm. Just like in the context of the Dunblane shooting, the idiosyncratic features of the Cumbria massacre hardly allowed for any alternative framing of the event's causes. In fact, the entire discourse as it was portrayed in the leading British newspapers focused on the question of whether the mandatory provision of medical certificates can be considered a viable strategy for depriving mentally ill people of the ability to acquire firearms or whether the costs associated with such a measure would outweigh the potential benefits. Other policy implications were not pondered by the political actors and the remainder of the media coverage primarily focused on the criminal investigation of the shooting and the way the shooting impacted upon the local community. Accordingly, the political debate was focused on gun control to a similar extent like the debate following the Dunblane shooting, which should have increased the likelihood of policy change according to theoretical expectation 5. However, both the unequivocal opposition to 'knee-jerk legislation' on behalf of the *Conservative Party* (Morris 2010) and the lack of a sustained social movement pushing for policy change contributed to a deadlock of the political process.

The cohesion of reform opponents after Cumbria

Only a month prior to the Cumbria shooting, the general elections in Great Britain had resulted in the first coalition cabinet since the end of World War II. The coalition had been formed by the *Conservative Party* under the leadership of David Cameron and the *Liberal Democrats* led by Nick Clegg. On the day following the massacre, the newly elected Prime Minister David Cameron made his preferences regarding an overhaul of the British gun laws very clear: 'You can't legislate to stop a switch flicking in someone's head and for this dreadful sort of action to take place' (Davies *et al.* 2010). The Prime Minister only suggested that a review of the regulatory framework might take place once all circumstances of the shooting were known. In consequence, the government therefore demanded to put the focus on the investigation of the rampage, instead of drawing any pre-mature conclusions (Morris 2010). In contrast, the opposition was more vocal and demanded an immediate review of the licensing process in general and mental health checks in particular (Davies *et al.* 2010). Given this high cohesion on both sides of the political spectrum and the governmental advantage of the status quo advocates, real policy change was elusive in the

When laws bite the bullet 115

wake of the Cumbria shooting. In addition, the fact that the new government was still in its 'honeymoon' phase and accordingly well endowed with political capital also did not help the opposition to reach its policy goals.

Societal demand for policy change after Cumbria

Another factor that impeded a decisive response to the Cumbria shooting was the lack of a sustained effort of societal actors to keep the gun issue on the public and political agenda. Unlike after the Dunblane shooting discussed previously, no pressure groups formed and pushed for legislative change. The *Snowdrop Campaign*, which had successfully managed to put enormous pressure on the political actors in the aftermath of the Dunblane shooting, had dissolved after internal divisions over the campaign's long-term strategy had materialized (Rowe 1997). The campaign's successor organization, the *Gun Control Network* (GCN) could not influence the political debate after Cumbria in a decisive manner. No signatures were collected and in fact, the organization was not even mentioned once in the articles of two major British newspapers (the *Guardian* and the *Independent*) within the first year after the shooting, despite the otherwise high media coverage. This lack of societal pressure made it comparably easy for the change-averse government to delay the political process and even ignore investigation reports that suggested that an overhaul of British gun laws was in order (Morris 2011). With an increasingly uninvolved public, the matter faded from public conscience and could not be brought back despite some few attempts to do so (Morris 2012).

In sum, the political process following the Cumbria shooting demonstrates that without sustained pressure from the societal level, the issue attention cycle can hardly be overcome. Despite extensive media coverage on the event and a clear focus of the ensuing political debate on gun control, a cohesive status quo coalition could prevent policy change by simply waiting out. Thus, two commonalities and two differences stand out when we compare the events at Dunblane and at Cumbria. On the one hand, both events followed the bottom-up path of politicization and the political debate was clearly centred on gun control in both cases. On the other hand, the events differed in the extent to which the respective governments were able to keep their ranks closed and the extent to which societal actors got involved in the political process.

In the following sections, we move our empirical focus to continental Europe and start with the country that has experienced the most rampage shootings during the time period under investigation.

7.2 Germany

In general, and despite its traditionally stringent regulatory approach, Germany 'has a long history of civilian gun ownership, encouraged by militia-based armies in the 19th century, the side effects of two world wars, and interest in hunting and sport shooting' (Karp 2007: 51). As a corollary of those developments, the

116   *When laws bite the bullet*

number of firearms in the population rose sharply by the beginning of the 20th century and guns soon replaced knives as the most common weapons (Ellerbrock 2011: 192f.). After the disarmament of the German population by the allied forces after World War II, the ownership of guns for private use was re-authorized in 1956, but the right to make regulations on the acquisition and pos-session of firearms was first given to the German *Länder*. In 1972, however, the federal level took over legislative responsibility and crafted the first national German gun law since 1938.[1] This law practically remained unaltered until the events at Erfurt and Winnenden led to a tightening of several provisions after the turn of the century.

In terms of firearm availability, Germany occupies a middle position in the European context. On the one hand, gun ownership has never been as pervasive as in its neighbouring countries Austria and Switzerland (see sections 7.5 and 7.6 respectively). At the same time, however, gun ownership in Germany has also never been as rare as in Great Britain (see section 7.1). In the fifth sweep of the International Crime Victims Survey (ICVS), 12.5 per cent of all German citizens reported the possession of a firearm and 4.2 per cent reported the posses-sion of a handgun (van Dijk *et al.* 2007: 279). A recent survey found that the most common reason for gun ownership in Germany is target shooting (Flash Eurobarometer No. 383 2013: 11). Those target shooters enjoy the benefit of a highly professionalized interest representation. In particular, the Association of the German Sports Shooters (*Deutscher Schützenbund*), representing more than 1.4 million shooters in 2013, has regularly opposed attempts to tighten the German gun law. In addition to this long-standing multi-purpose lobby group, the founding of the specialized *Forum Waffenrecht* in 1997 has further con-tributed to a professionalization of the interest representation of legal German gun owners. Additional registered pro-gun interest groups are *prolegal e.V.* and the German hunting association (*Deutscher Jagdverband*) (Deutscher Bundestag 2013). Until the events at Erfurt, no meaningful anti-gun interest group had been formed, once again underlining the dominance of pro-gun interests in the German political system. Against this backdrop, the introduction of even stronger provisions into the already strict German gun laws should be expected to be a difficult challenge.

Also in terms of its political institutions, Germany is not the most likely place for profound policy change to occur. In fact, the politico-institutional hurdles embodied in the German political system are quite high and accordingly, Germany can be classified as a classical consensus democracy (Lijphart 2012). Its federal structure, its two-chambered national legislature, its strong judicial review, and its multi-party system which has almost always led to coalition gov-ernments are only a few examples for those hurdles. In the realm of gun policy, the consent of the *Bundesrat*, where the 16 *Länder* governments are represented, is required in order to change the regulatory approach. Those politico-institutional features imply that policy change processes typically take longer and require more compromise than in the majoritarian democracies like Great Britain.

When laws bite the bullet 117

Thus, both Germany's background in terms of gun culture and its political institutions make profound policy change difficult to achieve. Between 1990 and 2010, a total of four rampage shootings led to a political debate over the appropriateness of the German gun laws: Bad Reichenhall, Erfurt, Winnenden and Lörrach. While the two school shootings at Erfurt and Winnenden eventually resulted in several policy changes, the Lörrach shooting did not have any policy repercussions. The precise policy implications of the Bad Reichenhall shooting are more difficult to determine, as the following section will show.

7.2.1 Reichenhall: gun control's access to the political agenda

After the rampage shooting in Euskirchen in 1994, which had not led to a national political debate on gun control, Germany did not experience any comparable events until 1 November 1999. On that day, Martin Peyerl, a 16-year old student from Bad Reichenhall stole a rifle of large calibre from his father's gun cabinet and opened fire on randomly selected people out of his bedroom window (Finkenzeller 1999). Peyerl killed three people immediately, shot his sister when she came home from work and injured another eight people severely, among others the popular actor Günter Lamprecht, who had been in town for a play (ibid.). After completing his rampage, the perpetrator committed suicide with a shot in the head in the bathtub.

The events at Bad Reichenhall shocked the nation since a rampage shooting of such a young perpetrator had been unknown in Germany and had widely been perceived as an American problem. The fact that Peyerl simply stole the murder weapon from his father's gun cabinet resembles of the way the Winnenden shooter acquired his weapons 10 years later (see section 7.2.3). And in a similar way, stricter and more detailed safe storage requirements were quickly identified as possible policy solutions by some of the involved political actors, in particular from the *Social Democratic Party* (SPD) and the party *Bündnis 90/Die Grünen* (Frankfurter Allgemeine Zeitung 1999b). However, unlike after the Winnenden shooting, the events at Bad Reichenhall did not directly lead to changes in Germany's legislative framework for firearms. Even though Minister of the Interior Otto Schily announced his intention to present a suggestion for a revision of the German gun laws in the spring of 2000, no such suggestion was made at that time.

Bad Reichenhall's perceived causal complexity

The public debate following the Bad Reichenhall shooting featured several dimensions that competed for attention. As outlined above, the perpetrator's easy access to his father's guns was identified as a causal story and suggestions for stricter storage requirements were put on the table (Frankfurter Allgemeine Zeitung 1999b). However, the gun story only remained one among many causal stories. Another debate developed over the corrupting influence of excessive movie violence on young people when it transpired that the perpetrator had been

118 *When laws bite the bullet*

playing violent video games (Krach 1999). In later stages of the public debate, the focus centred on the release of a new Hollywood movie ('Killing Mrs. Tingle!'), that allegedly played down violence against teachers. The debate was further reinforced by the stabbing to death of a teacher in a school in the town of Meißen only eight days after the Bad Reichenhall shooting (Frankfurter Allgemeine Zeitung 1999a). As a result, the movie's title was changed to 'Saving Mrs. Tingle!' ('Rettet Mrs. Tingle!'), a reaction that followed the way the movie's title had been changed in the USA following the Columbine massacre ('Teaching Mrs. Tingle!'). Thus, media violence received relatively strong attention following the Bad Reichenhall massacre. However, the perpetrator's Nazi mind-set was also identified as a source that contributed to the rampage shooting, although experts refuted the thought that Peyerl's political views caused him to commit his crime (Deutsche Presse Agentur 1999). Finally, the perpetrator's social background, and in particular the alcoholism of his father, formed a causal story for the explanation of the rampage. In sum, the perceived causal complexity of the rampage shooting in Bad Reichenhall can be described as relatively high and accordingly, no single causal story emerged and gripped the unshared attention of the public and the involved political decision-makers.

The cohesion of reform opponents after Bad Reichenhall

Unlike after many other politicized rampage shootings, the political debate on gun control did not evolve in a particularly polarized way after the events at Bad Reichenhall. This absence of any stark polarization likely emerged as a result of the limited scope of the policy changes debated in the shooting's aftermath. However, a few rather progressive actors demanded that storing firearms at home should be prohibited, but conservative actors refuted this suggestion and demanded tighter sanctions for careless gun owners instead (Frankfurter Allgemeine Sonntagszeitung 1999). As far as the rules for private gun storage are concerned, conservatives were clearly opposed to prohibitive measures, but rather pushed for the clarification of existing rules. At the end of the political process, two and a half years after the shooting, storage requirements were somewhat tightened, but private storage was not prohibited. However, the measures were only a small part of a large-scale reform effort and can hardly be traced back in a monocausal way to the Bad Reichenhall shooting. Thus, policy change did eventually occur, but it was not the type of rapid policy change that could be detected in the context of other rampage shootings. Accordingly, while there was general agreement among all involved political actors that something should be done about the German regulatory framework for firearms, the scope and the degree of those changes was contested.

Societal demand for policy change after Bad Reichenhall

As a final important factor contributing to the rather quick disappearance of the Bad Reichenhall shooting from the political agenda, the public remained

When laws bite the bullet 119

comparably silent and no social movements formed and pushed for policy change. This absence of any broad public involvement allowed the political actors to go slowly on their stated commitment to reform Germany's gun laws. Just as predicted by the Downsian issue attention cycle, public attention quickly faded away and no sustained calls for action were voiced by the public. Unlike after similar rampage shootings both in Germany and the rest of Europe, no social policy entrepreneur emerged in the aftermath of Bad Reichenhall and mobilized the public either via the collection of signatures or by running a campaign in the media. This latter strategy was additionally hampered by the reluctance of the German news media to call for political action, despite the fact that the event was initially covered extensively.

Thus the rampage shooting in Bad Reichenhall raised the awareness among both the public and politicians that the German gun laws included certain loopholes and it became common sense that legislative action was necessary. However, unlike after other similar rampage shootings, the public pressure for policy change was insufficient and as a result, the momentum for change faded rather quickly. The public search for meaning centred on a multitude of causal stories and gun control was discussed as one aspect among many. Moreover, the debate quickly focused on limited measures on the safe storage of firearms, not on the legitimacy of gun ownership as such. Under those circumstances, the legislative process quickly faded from public conscience and was moved to expert circles. This process was ended on 26 April 2002, the day when the next, even more devastating rampage shooting hit Germany.

7.2.2 Erfurt: policy change after negotiation and compromise

On the morning of 26 April 2002, Robert Steinhäuser entered the *Gutenberg Gymnasium* in Erfurt, the school he had been expelled from a few months earlier, armed with a 9 mm Glock and a pump-gun. As a member of a shooting club, Steinhäuser had acquired the weapons legally (Kister 2002). The 19-year-old shot 16 people to death, before turning the gun on himself and committing suicide. The Bad Reichenhall shooting, along with a range of other events of lower magnitude (Scheithauer and Bondü 2011: 29ff.), had already put the gun issue 'in the back of people's minds' (Kingdon 2003: 98) and a certain amount of problem pressure had built up before the shooting in Erfurt. This is also documented by the fact that, as outlined previously, a review of the German firearm regulations had already been on the agenda before the Erfurt shooting and ironically, the German *Bundestag* passed a new firearms law on the very same morning the massacre occurred. Yet, the new law had been watered down in committee and many of the provisions originally foreseen by the government had been erased or weakened. In the parliamentary debate on the morning of 26 April 2002, the Christian Democrat Member of Parliament Hartmut Koschyk thanked the German shooters, hunters, gun collectors and producers, and the *Forum Waffenrecht* for helping in preventing the 'original, disgraceful' bill from becoming law (Deutscher Bundestag 2002: 23342). As a result of the Erfurt

120 *When laws bite the bullet*

shooting, the law was stopped in the *Bundesrat* and referred to conciliation, where several provisions were tightened. Among other changes, the age for acquiring a large calibre handgun was raised from 18 to 21, mandatory psychological tests were introduced for applicants below the age of 25, and pump-action shotguns with pistol-grips were prohibited. Original plans had foreseen a prohibition of pump-guns in general, but those plans were eventually defused in the political process. Thus, although parts of the governmental coalition, in particular the Green party, first aimed for prohibitive measures, the government finally adjusted the German gun law only in an incremental manner. How can this political reaction be explained?

Erfurt's perceived causal complexity

The shooting in Erfurt gave rise to a whole range of problem definitions. While the perpetrator's status as an authorized gun owner immediately led to calls for a review of the German gun laws, gun control was by far not the only issue in the ensuing public discourse. On the contrary, as Hurka and Nebel (2013) show, especially conservative stakeholders pointed to the perpetrator's consumption of violent video games and movies and thereby contributed an alternative causal story. In this context, calls for censorship and higher age thresholds for violent media content were brought forward as possible solutions to the problem of rampage violence. Another part of the discourse focused on deficiencies in the German education system and additional funds were demanded for school psychologists. As far as security measures for school buildings are concerned, decision makers generally agreed that 'schools should not become fortresses', a metaphor repeatedly used in the discourse (Hurka and Nebel 2013: 400). Thus, in comparison to other events studied in this chapter, the school shooting of Erfurt was relatively complex in terms of its causation and accordingly, the ensuing political debate was rather diffuse. Nevertheless, gun control was quickly identified as a possible area of political activity and it did not take more than a week until the major decision makers agreed that something should be done about the availability of firearms. Thus, despite the fact that the discourse surrounding the Erfurt shooting was extremely complex and multi-faceted, the gun issue did not fall prey to the issue attention cycle. For the most part, this can arguably be attributed to the fact that gun control had already been on the political agenda before the Erfurt shooting and the special circumstance that the German *Bundestag* had just passed a revision of the law on the morning the shooting took place. Yet, the window of opportunity for policy change also remained open because no cohesive coalition emerged to defend the status quo.

The cohesion of reform opponents after Erfurt

In April 2002, Germany was still governed by a left-wing coalition of Social Democrats and Greens, led by Chancellor Gerhard Schröder, the governmental coalition that had already been in place during the Bad Reichenhall shooting.

When laws bite the bullet 121

The conservative *Christian Democratic Union/Christian Social Union* (CDU/CSU), the liberal *Free Democratic Party* (FDP) and the *Party of Democratic Socialism* (PDS) formed the parliamentary opposition in the German Bundestag. The parties of the governmental coalition had already articulated their willingness to reform the German gun law in their coalition contract of 1998. After the Erfurt shooting, in particular the Green party displayed high internal cohesion in its demand for substantial revisions of the German gun laws (Hurka and Nebel 2013: 401). Within the ranks of its coalition partner SPD, only Minister of the Interior Otto Schily voiced some scepticism about the need for additional restrictions, but eventually cooperated as it became evident that a reaction to the Erfurt shooting was desired by the coalition partners. In addition, the coalition of reform opponents was not particularly cohesive:

> After initial efforts to frame the Erfurt shooting as a societal failure and the result of the corrupting influence of violent video games, the opposition moved towards accepting the need to change certain gun policies, including (among others) a lifting of age requirements and a prohibition of pump guns.
>
> (Hurka and Nebel 2013: 401)

In the second legislative chamber, the *Bundesrat*, the parties of the federal government had just lost their majority a few days before the Erfurt massacre and accordingly, substantial attempts to change the German gun law could have been vetoed there. As a result of this constellation, a wholesale handgun ban was not a viable option, as it was only supported by the Green party and unacceptable to the CDU and, in particular, the CSU. However, the conservative parties were not as cohesive in their rejection of less drastic measures and agreed to the forging of a compromise solution in the conciliation committee of the *Bundestag* and the *Bundesrat*.

Societal demand for policy change after Erfurt

In addition to the constraints described above, a more fundamental policy change after the Erfurt shooting was also prevented by the fact that other than in Great Britain, broad social mobilization did not occur. Only one notable attempt to influence the public debate from a societal actor could be established, the so-called Erfurt plea ('Erfurter Appell'), launched one week after the incident by the Catholic Church. This plea's intention, however, was multi-faceted and tighter gun control measures only played a sub-ordinated role. For the most part, the plea demanded stronger rules for the distribution of media content that glorified violence, stricter rules for the production of such material and stricter sanctions for non-compliance (Bistum Erfurt 2002). The build-up of a cohesive single-purpose social movement proved to be an elusive quest. After all, the government already supported policy change and could point to its previous efforts to reform the gun laws in order to underline its commitment. In addition, it

122 *When laws bite the bullet*

became evident quickly that the major parties would be able to strike a compromise based on the measures they had just agreed upon. Some additional measures were incorporated into the reform and voted on within a month after the shooting. This quick political process prevented the formation of a strong social movement as in Great Britain and satisfied the broad public sentiment that something should be done about the availability of guns in Germany.

In sum, the Erfurt case illustrates how difficult the achievement of fundamental policy change can be, even in the face of a major shock. If institutions make it difficult to form political majorities and gun owners are relatively numerous and well organized, even a change-friendly government can find it hard to achieve fundamental reforms, especially if the issue is not taken up on a societal level. Nevertheless, incremental changes were accomplished and this was clearly due to the fact that the coalition of reform opponents was porous. Especially when it was realized that a total deflection of the public debate to matters of school security, media violence and the education system would prove infeasible, compromises in the area of gun control became attainable. However, it should be mentioned that the issue attention cycle was not overcome completely, since the reform opponents were able to prevent the originally agreed upon total prohibition of pump-guns during the negotiations and water the prohibition down to only cover pump-guns with pistol grips.

7.2.3 *Winnenden: quick concessions and incremental change*

Roughly seven years after the Erfurt shooting, another large-scale school shooting incident grabbed the attention of the German public, media, and politicians.[2] On 11 March 2009, 17-year-old Tim Kretschmer, a former student of the *Albertville-Realschule* in Winnenden, shot 15 people in his former school and while fleeing from the police. Kretschmer committed suicide before the police could catch him (Frankfurter Allgemeine Zeitung 2009b). He had not owned the 9 mm Beretta he used for the massacre legally himself. Instead, he took the pistol from his father, a sports shooter who had failed to store the weapon correctly (Soldt and Eppelsheim 2009). This acquisition of the murder weapon is similar to the way the Bad Reichenhall shooter had acquired his gun (see section 7.2.1). However, in the latter case, the perpetrator used a hunting rifle, did not perpetrate his rampage in a school setting and only killed four people instead of 15.

Shortly after the rampage shooting, the Green party and the police asked for a total prohibition of the private storage of handguns (Frankfurter Allgemeine Zeitung 2009c), but the governing grand coalition of Christian Democrats and Social Democrats eventually only granted the police the right to search gun owners' homes and control whether all safe storage requirements are correctly applied, even without prior suspicions (Frankfurter Allgemeine Zeitung 2009a). Since the resources of the German police would hardly allow for a systematic enforcement of the newly introduced provision, the policy change was labelled 'cosmetic' by the union of German criminal officers (Frankfurter Allgemeine Zeitung 2009c). On the other hand, the fact that sports shooters later filed an

When laws bite the bullet 123

(unsuccessful) lawsuit against the measures in front of the German Constitutional Court (*Bundesverfassungsgericht*) indicates that the reform was not purely symbolic. Thus, unlike after the Bad Reichenhall shooting 10 years earlier, politicians reacted with rapid policy change to the event in Winnenden, although the measures were clearly not as far-reaching as the ones taken after the Erfurt shooting. Under which constellation of conditions did the political process after Winnenden unfold?

Winnenden's perceived causal complexity

Like all other previous rampage shootings on German soil, also the Winnenden massacre resulted in a rather complex and diffuse political debate. While the father's failure to store his weapons correctly was quickly identified as a central factor that contributed to the rampage shooting, the debate rapidly took a similar shape as the one that had developed in the wake of the Erfurt shooting seven years earlier. For example, the perpetrator's possession of horror videos and his consumption of the ego-shooter 'Counterstrike' was taken up especially by conservative observers in an attempt to construct an alternative causal story (FAZ.NET 2009a). Other conservatives expressed their diffuse concerns about the increasing societal glorification of violence and demanded a broad 'alliance against violence and brutalization' (FAZ.NET 2009a). Also the perpetrator's mental problems were identified as a cause of the rampage when the police announced that he had been under psychiatric treatment – a fact that was later denied by the perpetrator's parents (FAZ.NET 2009b). Finally, some observers pointed to the perpetrator's easy access to the school building and demanded increased security measures like entry controls or metal detectors (FAZ.NET 2009a). Those latter suggestions were, however, highly controversial and only supported by a minority of the discourse participants. Nevertheless, the multitude of framing opportunities outlined above clearly contributed to a dilution of the political debate after Winnenden, which made it difficult for change advocates in the area of gun control to focus the political debate on their causal story. The complexity of the debate also became strikingly evident in a parliamentary debate in the German *Bundestag* one week after the shooting, when parliamentarians from all across the political spectrum demanded consequences in a wide array of policy areas (Deutscher Bundestag 2009: 22686–22697). A few days after the massacre, Chancellor Angela Merkel announced her intention to strengthen police controls over the storage of private firearms – a measure that satisfied the general public mood that some sort of action should be taken, but fell short of being a decisive reform.

The cohesion of reform opponents after Winnenden

To a certain extent, this limited political reaction to the Winnenden shooting was due to the fact that within the two major conservative parties, the CDU and the CSU, the need for tighter gun control was contested. While Germany's Secretary

124 *When laws bite the bullet*

of the Interior, Wolfgang Schäuble, quickly refuted the rising demands for more gun control, other influential members of the CDU like the former Prime Minister of Thuringia Bernhard Vogel called for a debate over the appropriateness of the German gun laws (Frankfurter Allgemeine Zeitung 2009d). Within the CSU, new gun control measures were strongly rejected (Deutscher Bundestag 2009: 22686–22697). But the need for political action in the policy area of gun control was not only contested among conservatives, also members of the SPD underscored their scepticism with regard to 'knee-jerk reactions' (Deutscher Bundestag 2009: 22688). Only representatives of the parties *Bündnis 90/ Die Grünen* and *Die Linke* cohesively demanded stricter rules for gun owners, but were eventually unable to push through their positions due to their status as opposition groups. Accordingly, a decisive political reaction to the events in Winnenden was not only complicated by the enormous complexity of the political debate, but also by the fact that Germany was governed by a grand coalition with internally heterogeneous preferences. Nevertheless, the government did not leave the status quo untouched, but reacted with a modest, incremental policy measure, by increasing the enforcement rights of the police. This policy reaction quickly took the gun control issue off the political agenda and thereby prevented a further debate over more far-reaching measures, as they were later demanded by two social movements that developed in the wake of Winnenden.

Societal demand for policy change after Winnenden

On the evening of the rampage shooting in Winnenden, the initiative *Keine Sportwaffen als Mordwaffen!* was founded in Berlin under the leadership of the author and journalist Roman Grafe. Ever since its foundation, the group has been lobbying for a total prohibition of handguns in Germany, but unlike its counterpart the *Snowdrop Campaign* in Great Britain (section 7.1.1), the group has so far failed to accomplish its policy goals. After the grand coalition's announcement of the limited policy measures envisaged after the Winnenden shooting, the initiative attempted to put pressure on the responsible political actors to show a more far-reaching reaction. In order to rally public support, it attempted to mobilize students to stay home from school and thereby demonstrate their fear of another rampage shooting (Keine Mordwaffen als Sportwaffen! 2009a). However, the call did not evoke particularly strong societal reactions and it is safe to say that this mobilization attempt can be regarded as a clear failure. In the further process, the initiative launched a lawsuit against the German gun laws, but the German Constitutional Court did not even consider the lawsuit for a decision (Bundesverfassungsgericht 2013). Thus, the early incremental reaction of the German government to the event in Winnenden took the pressure out of the political debate and rendered further attempts to reignite public sentiment futile. This pattern also accounts for the other social movement that was founded in the wake of the massacre, the *Aktionsbündnis Winnenden*. Founded as a group of bereaved parents two weeks after the rampage shooting, the structure of this group is similar to the one of the *Snowdrop Campaign*, but its accomplishments

When laws bite the bullet 125

are not comparable. Both pressure groups eventually teamed up and managed to collect more than 100,000 signatures 'against deadly firearms', which were delivered to the German *Bundestag* 15 months after the Winnenden shooting in June 2010, at a time when the public salience of the gun issue was comparably low (Keine Mordwaffen als Sportwaffen! 2009b). Nevertheless, the Green party put forward a motion in the German *Bundestag*, demanding a fundamental revision of the German gun laws, which was referred to the committee level and later rejected (Deutscher Bundestag 2010). Only three months after the delivery of the signatures and the introduction of the motion, another rampage shooting brought the gun issue to the political agenda.

Before we turn to this final rampage shooting in Germany, the lessons of the Winnenden shooting can be summarized as follows. First, the extremely high perceived causal complexity of the rampage shooting did hardly facilitate a pronounced political debate over Germany's gun laws. A multitude of causal stories existed alongside each other, competing for attention. Second, the lines between the political camps were blurry and no cohesive reform opposition formed. Most importantly, however, the case demonstrates how pressure can be taken out of a political debate if a quick agreement on incremental measures can be forged among the political decision-makers. In such a scenario, the public demand for political action is at least ostensibly satisfied, the issue attention cycle works its way, and attempts to re-mobilize the public are doomed to fail.

7.2.4 Lörrach: cohesive status quo advocates and policy stability

On 19 September 2010, the rampage shooting in the German town Lörrach, close to the Swiss border, once again put the spotlight on Germany's gun laws. In the evening hours, Sabine Radmacher, aged 41, first strangled her son and shot her husband to death, before setting the flat on fire. Afterwards, she went to the nearby hospital, armed with a knife and her small-calibre Walther pistol. While on her way to the hospital, she opened fire on random passers-by, injuring two critically. In the hospital, the perpetrator killed a male nurse by shooting into his head multiple times and stabbing the man to death. After injuring a police officer who arrived on the crime scene, Radmacher was killed by the police in a shootout. As a registered sports shooter, Radmacher had owned the murder weapon legally (Soldt 2010).

The Green party immediately reacted to the rampage shooting in Lörrach by renewing its demands for a prohibition of private gun storage (Zeit Online 2010). Party leader Claudia Roth and the Green party's leading politician on internal security matters, Wolfgang Wieland, voiced their anger about the fact that 'one and a half years after Winnenden, we must again mourn the victims of a tragic rampage shooting' and concluded that sporting guns would have to be banned from private flats (Zeit Online 2010). The central policy solution put forward by the Green party was once again the decentralized storage of firearms in gun clubs. This suggestion, however, was met with fierce resistance from conservative decision-makers and the proposal's prospects for success were now

126 *When laws bite the bullet*

additionally hampered by a government coalition that now also comprised a sizeable amount of liberals who proved to be even more sceptical with regard to governmental intrusions into the private sphere than their conservative coalition partners. Yet, under what contextual conditions did the political process after the Lörrach shooting unfold?

Lörrach's perceived causal complexity

First, it is notable that attempts to formulate alternative causal stories were comparably rare after the rampage shooting. While the previous shootings in Bad Reichenhall, Erfurt, and Winnenden had invited the formulation of various interpretative frames, ranging from the consumption of violent media content, to failures in the education system and the security of public buildings, the shooting in Lörrach hardly allowed for many alternative causal interpretations. The precise motive for the rampage was quickly identified in private quarrels over child custody, but the ensuing political debate solely focused on gun control. Alternative causal frames, like violent video games or failures in the education system could simply not be activated in response to the event, which led to a much more focused debate on the event's implications for Germany's gun laws than the previous rampage shootings discussed above.

The cohesion of reform opponents after Lörrach

Yet, despite the fact that the debate's focus was firmly centred on the gun issue, no policy change occurred in response to the Lörrach shooting and this lack of a political response can clearly be attributed to the cohesion of reform opponents and their procedural advantages in the legislative process. After the national elections in September of 2009, the grand coalition had been replaced by a coalition of the CDU/CSU and the liberal FDP. Both coalition partners were quick to assure that the events in Lörrach would not result in any legislative changes. Several arguments were put forward in defence of the status quo. Most importantly, the reform opponents argued that the gun laws just had been reformed in response to the Winnenden massacre and that any further changes should not be considered before those changes are fully implemented (Die Welt 2010). In addition, the coalition partners jointly pointed to the potential dangers associated with a centralized storage of guns and ammunition in gun clubs. For instance, Wolfgang Bosbach, the CDU expert on internal security pointed out that such measures 'would create thousands of arms depots, which could serve to equip entire armies' (Zeit Online 2010). Thus, the opponents of another reform of Germany's gun laws were not only highly cohesive with regard to their framing of the Lörrach shooting, they also enjoyed the procedural advantage of forming the government. Yet, as the Dunblane case (section 7.1.1) demonstrates, even change-averse governments sometimes pursue large-scale reforms if they are put under significant pressure from societal actors. Such pressure, however, did not materialize after the shooting in Lörrach.

Societal demand for policy change after Lörrach

There is no evidence that would suggest that the pressure groups that had formed in the wake of the Winnenden massacre exerted any impact on the public debate after the Lörrach shooting. To a certain extent, this inability to influence the public debate was due to the timing of the Lörrach shooting. The signatures demanding a revision of the German gun laws been handed in at the *Bundestag* three months prior to the shooting and *Bündnis 90/Die Grünen* had already followed up on this call with a motion for stricter gun laws (Deutscher Bundestag 2010). While the Lörrach shooting could have served as an opportunity for the pressure groups to accelerate the political process in the *Bundestag* and put moral pressure on the reform opponents to act, they failed to have a decisive impact. However, this lack of a clear impact of societal actors was not only due to the inability of the existing pressure groups to keep the issue on the political agenda for more than a few days. It was also a result of the fact that even media outlets like the left-leaning *tageszeitung* (TAZ), that had a reputation of being in favour of stricter rules for gun owners, showed restraint in their interpretation of the Lörrach shooting (Arzt 2010). Also the *Frankfurter Allgemeine Zeitung* (FAZ) pointed out that 'experts' agreed that the new German gun laws would be sufficient, without clarifying the identity of those experts (Frankfurter Allgemeine Zeitung 2010). Only the *Süddeutsche Zeitung* (SZ) voiced concerns over sporting guns being 'ticking time bombs' in the hands of private citizens (Käppner 2010), but did not follow up on this initial interpretation with continued coverage once it became clear that no legislative reaction would occur.

Thus, the lack of a political reaction to the Lörrach shooting can be attributed to two central factors: On the one hand, unlike after the shootings in Erfurt and Winnenden, the German government now consisted of a cohesive coalition of reform opponents that was determined to defend the status quo. On the other hand, reform pressure from societal actors was lacking despite the fact that the shooting clearly highlighted deficiencies in the German gun control system. Accordingly, even under the condition of low perceived event complexity, policy change does not necessarily occur if willingness is lacking on behalf of the responsible decision-makers and if existing pressure groups fail to rally public support.

In general, the German cases discussed in this section illustrate that political responses to rampage shootings can vary dramatically within the same country, depending on the configuration of several conditions. The Bad Reichenhall case demonstrated that even reform-friendly governments can choose to delay the political process if the political discourse following a rampage shooting is diffuse and if pressure from the societal level is lacking. The Erfurt case showed how institutional consensus requirements can complicate decision-making if the event's causes are contested. Due to the fact that gun control had already been on the political agenda before the Erfurt massacre, this constellation yielded rapid, but incremental policy change. The second German school shooting in Winnenden demonstrated how change-averse decision-makers can absorb

128 *When laws bite the bullet*

increasing societal pressure by quickly agreeing to small and rather symbolic policy change. Finally, the Lörrach shooting illustrated how a change-averse government can defend the status quo if public pressure is entirely lacking. In the following sub-section, we turn to Finland, a country that experienced two high-profile school shootings in the past few years. In comparison to Germany, however, the country's gun political background could hardly be more different.

7.3 Finland

Like many other countries with abundant wildlife, Finland has always upheld a thriving hunting tradition. Over the centuries, hunting transformed from an economic activity to a recreational practice (Hallikainen 1995). Against this backdrop, it is not surprising that the prevalence of gun ownership in Finland is exceptionally high and the large majority of those firearms are hunting rifles (Liem *et al.* 2013: 79). In the most recent wave of the International Crime Victims Survey (ICVS), almost 38 per cent of all Finnish households reported the possession of at least one firearm, whereas 6.3 per cent reported the possession of at least one handgun (van Dijk *et al.* 2007: 279). In the European context, only Switzerland has a similarly high prevalence of firearm ownership (see section 7.6). The Finnish Ministry of Justice (2009: 135) summarizes the situation as follows: 'In Finland, the number of firearms relative to the population is large. It has been fairly easy to acquire a gun, and the atmosphere has traditionally been favourable for doing so.' This latter argument implies that the high availability of firearms in Finland is not the least a corollary of the country's relatively liberal regulatory framework. One of the most liberal elements of the Finnish gun laws used to be the possibility to grant the right to possess a handgun to minors above 15 years with parental consent. Finland had successfully withstood pressure from the EU to abolish this exception which was in violation with existing EU law (Reuters.com 2007). Accordingly, it was this measure in particular which came under attack after the school shootings discussed below.

In terms of its political institutions, empirical research clearly suggests that Finland can be considered a consensus democracy (Lijphart 2012). One important factor that supports this argument is Finland's highly fragmented party system and the resulting fact that governments in Finland typically consist of a broad coalition of several political parties. In the past, those coalitions have demonstrated their ability to forge compromises repeatedly (Ganghof and Bräuninger 2006: 530f.). In addition to the large amount of veto players typically present within Finnish governmental coalitions, however, the executive faces the obstacle of a relatively powerful legislature and therefore cannot translate its preferences into law easily. For example, unlike in several other European countries, the Finnish government cannot exert direct control over the parliament's agenda (Siaroff 2003: 456). Accordingly, executive dominance over the legislative branch can be regarded as low in Finland, which implies that rapid policy shifts should be expected to be the exception instead of the rule. In the following two case studies on the school shootings in Jokela and Kauhajoki, we will discover how those difficult structural conditions complicated the political reaction in the wake of the massacres.

7.3.1 Jokela: shock and delay

On 7 November 2007, Pekka-Eric Auvinen killed six students, the school nurse, a teacher and himself in his school at Jokela, using a semi-automatic handgun he had purchased legally (Raittila *et al.* 2010: 23). Inspired by similar shootings in the US, the perpetrator had gone to a shooting range, practicing the handling of handguns, before acquiring a handgun himself as a member of a shooting club only a few days before carrying out his rampage (Finland Ministry of Justice 2009: 17f.). The event immediately brought the hitherto dormant gun control issue to the public and political agenda. Yet, despite initial pledges by several involved actors, Finland did not amend its comparably lax firearm regulations in the wake of the Jokela shooting. Instead, the government set up a commission and instructed it to draw up a report on the shooting, including recommendations in order to prevent similar events in the future. The report was published in February 2009 and hence after the second Finnish school shooting at Kauhajoki on 23 September 2008 (see section 7.3.2).

The special circumstance that another high-profile school shooting occurred in Finland less than one year after the Jokela incident makes it practically impossible to establish whether or not the Jokela shooting would have eventually resulted in any meaningful policy change had the second school shooting not happened. It is important to note, however, that no direct legislative reaction was foreseeable in the 10 months between the two shootings. As a well-informed observer pointed out in a personal communication, 'between the Jokela and Kauhajoki shootings, no real efforts took place and the process was relatively slow.'[3] In fact, an initial plan by the government to raise the minimum age for gun ownership from 15 to 18 did not take effect and any momentum for policy change faded rather quickly (Tedmanson 2008).[4] How can this abandonment of the gun issue be explained?

Jokela's perceived causal complexity

As studies on community reactions to the Jokela shooting suggest, the event was broadly perceived as an 'isolated incident' that could not have been prevented by any means (Oksanen *et al.* 2010: 23). Nevertheless, the political search for meaning developed and it quickly turned out that a wide range of factors could be made responsible and addressed politically. As the investigation report on the Jokela shooting made clear, 'the reasons for the school shooting were multifarious and complex' (Finland Ministry of Justice 2009). Accordingly, the event was broadly conceived as the result of a complex combination of contributing factors. The accompanying public debate was extremely diffuse and thereby reminiscent of the debates that unfolded after similar school shootings in

130   *When laws bite the bullet*

Germany (see section 7.2). The best empirical evidence buttressing this argument on the perceived complexity of the Jokela shooting can be found in the 13 policy recommendations outlined by the investigation commission (Finland Ministry of Justice 2009: 133–139). Only recommendation no. 5 (ibid.: 135) included a range of policy measures whose implementation should reduce the availability of firearms, in particular handguns, in Finland. The other 12 recommendations covered a broad range of public policies and were predominantly designed to reduce the marginalization of individual students. The improvement of student welfare, better treatment options in the mental health sector, prevention measures against bullying, security measures in schools, more control over the internet,[5] encouragement of whistleblowing, changes in penal policies, better networking among involved authorities and the promotion of more self-regulation in the media formed the remainder of the recommendations put forward by the investigation commission. Thus, the Jokela shooting was first perceived as an unfortunate and isolated event that could have hardly been prevented. During the further debate, however, multiple policy solutions were discussed publicly, which implies that no single one of those policy solutions dominated the debate. Under those circumstances, a focused debate over Finland's liberal approach of regulation firearms could not develop and also pressure from the societal level remained marginal. Furthermore, in the political arena, the government's decision of installing an investigation commission further slowed down the political process.

The cohesion of reform opponents after Jokela

At the time the Jokela shooting occurred, Finland was governed by a four-party-coalition consisting of the *Centre Party* (KESK), the *National Coalition Party* (KOK), the *Green League* (VIHR) and the *Swedish People's Party* (SFP). The cabinet was headed by Prime Minister Matti Vanhanen (KESK) and the important ministry of the Interior was held by Anne Holmlund (KOK). As far as the regulation of firearms is concerned, the positions of the government parties were not in line. In particular the *Green League* has a reputation of favouring stricter gun laws, while the larger parties KESK and KOK tend to be sceptical on this matter (YLE.fi 2011). However, even though both the KESK and the KOK were not particularly renowned for a tough stance on private gun ownership, both the Prime Minister and the Minister of the Interior quickly voiced their readiness to address the Finnish gun control laws. More specifically, the government suggested that it would give up its opposition to the EU firearms directive, which would require Finland to prohibit the acquisition of guns for citizens below the age of 18, although the government tried to avoid giving the impression that this change in position was due to the Jokela shooting (YLE.fi 2007). The government's move to install an investigation commission, however, implied that those initial plans could easily be postponed. While the option to pursue policy change was still on the table, policy change became increasingly unlikely. Thus, quite similar to the Winnenden case (section 7.2.3), no coalition

When laws bite the bullet 131

of reform opponents emerged and tried to defend the pure status quo. However, the concessions made by the leading governmental actors were piecemeal in nature and more importantly, the work of the investigation commission was not accompanied with heightened attention and scrutiny by societal actors, as was the case after the Dunblane shooting (section 7.1.1).

Societal demand for policy change after Jokela

Even though the easy availability of firearms in Finland was quickly identified by some as a central policy problem that needs to be addressed, no united movement emerged and pushed for policy change. Also the country's leading newspaper, the *Helsingin Sanomat*, did not take clear sides on this matter and voiced contradictory views in the days following the Jokela murders (Tabermann 2011: 50f.). But also the Finnish public in general was divided on the question of whether tighter gun laws would be necessary as a result of the Jokela shooting. As noted above, most perceived the shooting as an isolated incident, lacking a broader narrative, while others interpreted it as an indicator of a policy failure. As media reports on the reactions of the Finnish populations suggest, however, the first view seemed to dominate the discourse in the wake of the Jokela shooting (Tanner 2007). However, no clear political demands were formulated by the news media. As Väliverronen *et al.* (2012: 170) observe, 'the license policy was considered problematic in the stories, but the politicians responsible for the matter were not really pushed into action'. As the authors further argue, this restraint of the news media resulted from the fact that journalists were themselves subject to massive criticisms for the way they covered the Jokela shooting (ibid.: 170). On the societal level, the pervasive presence of firearms in Finnish homes had prevented the development of a movement to tighten gun control even before the shooting. Even though some 'left-wing and pacifist groups' had started to lobby against the liberal Finnish gun laws prior to the shooting, the anti-gun lobby in Finland was judged to be 'weak' at the time the Jokela shooting occurred (Tanner 2007). In sum, the Jokela shooting dealt a blow to the Finnish gun culture, which, however, proved stable enough to weather the storm. It took another blow within a short time to further erode the opposition against more stringent gun laws.

7.3.2 Kauhajoki: tipping the balance

Only 10 months after the Jokela incident, another school shooting occurred in the Finnish town of Kauhajoki on 23 September 2008. The perpetrator, 22-year-old Matti Juhani Saari, entered the school in the morning, armed with his semi-automatic Walther P22 and shot to death 10 people before killing himself with a shot in the head. The similarities between the school shootings in Jokela and Kauhajoki and their respective perpetrators are numerous (Langman 2012). Both perpetrators had not only acquired their weapons legally, they even acquired them in the same gun store. In addition, both shooters had announced their

132 *When laws bite the bullet*

rampages online via YouTube and just like the Jokela shooting less than year before, the Kauhajoki rampage triggered the installation of an investigation commission by the Ministry of Justice (Oksanen *et al*. 2013). The revision of the Finnish gun laws had stalled between the two events and no further action was foreseeable at the time the Kauhajoki shooting occurred (Lindström *et al*. 2011). As described in the previous section, the Jokela inquiry commission published its recommendations in February 2009 and it took another year before the Kauhajoki commission came up with its report.[6]

Two firearm-related recommendations were issued: first, it was demanded that

> the Ministry of the Interior should take steps to ensure that all handguns allowing their user to fire a large number of shots within a short period of time are collected – against payment, for example – and that no new acquisition permits are granted for such firearms. Handing in illegally owned guns should be made more attractive for the owners.
>
> (Finland Ministry of Justice 2010: 162)

This recommendation implies a total ban on handguns and thereby goes much farther than the recommendations put forward in the wake of the Jokela shooting (and also farther than what the Cullen inquiry demanded after the Dunblane shooting in Great Britain). Second, for all other firearms, it was demanded that

> the Ministry of the Interior should take steps to raise the age limit for the possession of firearms to 20 years, to make all permits fixed-term, and to set two years of recreational shooting on a regular basis as a necessary condition for the granting of a permit.
>
> (Finland Ministry of Justice 2010: 163)

Those recommendations went quite far and only small parts of them were eventually realized. Most importantly, a handgun ban was declined by the government and in particular by Anne Holmlund, the country's Minister of the Interior, arguing that 'a complete ban was not the way to prevent mass murders' (YLE.fi 2010). Thus, the government proposed a range of incremental adjustments like higher age limits (from 18 to 20) and the mandatory provision of medical certificates. All in all, the quality of those measures was comparable to the measures taken by the German government in the wake of the Erfurt massacre (see section 7.2.2). Which accompanying circumstances made those policy changes possible, despite the relatively unfavourable socio-cultural and politico-institutional scope conditions in Finland described above?

Kauhajoki's perceived causal complexity

As the report of the Kauhajoki investigation commission clearly suggests, the shooting in Kauhajoki was of similar objective complexity as the Jokela shooting 10 months before: 'That the perpetrator ended up committing a school

When laws bite the bullet 133

shooting was the result of a long process involving many factors' (Finland Ministry of Justice 2010: 158). However, even though the Kauhajoki shooting was just as complex in terms of its causation as the Jokela shooting, 'much of the public attention was directed to the gun laws' (Oksanen *et al.* 2013: 209). This is also mirrored by the fact that reforming Finnish gun laws was now listed first among the nine recommendations put forward by the investigation commission (Finland Ministry of Justice 2010: 162). Thus, while several accompanying circumstances, such as the perpetrator's mental condition, his problematic relationship towards violent media content, his use of the internet as a platform for his rampage, and his social exclusion, were all identified as contributing factors, the gun control issue was clearly at the centre of public and political attention in the wake of the Kauhajoki shooting. Beyond any doubt, this increased focus on gun control can be attributed to the fact that while the Jokela shooting could be played down as a one-off incident that could have been prevented with more psychological counselling and more social awareness, the events at Kauhajoki made clear that access to high-powered firearms seems to be much more common than initially thought. The gun issue not only dominated the political discourse, but also became the main focus of the news media. Accordingly, even though the 'objective' complexity of the Kauhajoki shooting was comparable to the Jokela shooting, the two varied in terms of perceived complexity.

The cohesion of reform opponents after Kauhajoki

When we look at the way Kauhajoki was dealt with by the major political actors of Finland, we find that hopes for a major revision of the Finnish gun laws were first nourished shortly after the rampage shooting. Specifically, Finnish Prime Minister Matti Vanhanen suggested a far reaching reform and even called for a total handgun ban (Helsingin Sanomat International Edition 2008c). At the same time, however, Minister of the Interior Anne Holmlund was not as outspoken and merely demanded a thorough review of Finland's gun laws. In fact, she contradicted the Prime Minister by stating 'that she did not believe a ban on handguns as a first firearm would have prevented the Kauhajoki shootings from taking place' (Helsingin Sanomat International Edition 2008a). Accordingly, the government was composed of actors with different views on the event's implications for Finnish gun policy. When the investigation commission published its report in 2010, the recommendation to ban handguns (cited above) was not issued cohesively by all board members but came with a dissenting opinion. The Inspector General of the Police, Pekka Aho, opposed the ban and voiced his concerns 'that a ban would mean a violation of the Constitutional right of Finnish citizens to protection of property' (Finland Ministry of Justice 2010: 173). The government eventually adopted this latter position and rejected the commission's recommendations for a handgun ban. The suggestion for a handgun ban divided the Finnish party system (Helsingin Sanomat International Edition 2010), but a majority of the government parties opposed the ban. As the only outspoken party supporting a handgun ban, the *Green League* was marginalized in the coalition.

134 *When laws bite the bullet*

Thus, even though plans to ban handguns were advanced both by the Finnish head of state and an independent investigation commission, it did not materialize. Whether or not this rejection of the handgun ban was the result of intense lobbying efforts by shooting interests (a suspicion that was advanced by some observers but strongly denied by the Ministry of the Interior) cannot be established. For the most part, the opponents of a major reform were able to keep their ranks closed. However, the Prime Minister formed a significant exception to this general rule, by voicing his strong support for more stringent gun laws. Accordingly, one central political actor of the status quo coalition defected, which weakened the group's position significantly. As a result, a complete defence of the status quo quickly proved to be elusive. This was further aggravated by the fact that unlike after the Jokela shooting, societal actors were now much more vocal and organized in their demand for firearm-related policy change.

Societal demand for policy change after Kauhajoki

The dynamics unfolding on this societal level after the Kauhajoki shooting were markedly different from the ones following Jokela and therefore, it seems safe to argue that the varying policy consequences also have their roots at the societal level. Two observations buttress this argument. First, the news media took on a much more pro-active role after the Kauhajoki incident than they had after Jokela. As Väliverronen *et al.* (2012: 170) note, 'nearly every media outlet in Finland took up gun license issues in their stories on the day of the rampage' and 'the tone of the coverage was also far more critical than in Jokela' (ibid.: 171). The authors ascribe this to the fact that there was a sense of guilt among journalists for not having pushed the government harder on gun control after Jokela. Thus, the media pressure exerted after Kauhajoki was clearly higher than after Jokela, which is not the least due to the fact that the government had factually abandoned the gun control issue in the 10 months between the two shootings. Second, in addition to this comparably strong role of the media, the Kauhajoki shooting triggered much stronger social mobilization than the Jokela shooting had. This heightened public concern was powerfully demonstrated by the handing in of over 57,000 signatures calling for a handgun ban in Finland roughly one month after the Kauhajoki shooting (Helsingin Sanomat International Edition 2008b). The attention the petition received was amplified by the fact that it was signed by two prominent former Finnish politicians: Harri Holkeri, former Prime Minister of Finland and Elisabeth Rehn, former Minister of Defence. Despite this pressure from the societal level, the Finnish government was still able to wait out and refer to the pending investigation report. Nonetheless, the positions articulated by the news media and actors on the societal level made clear that the government would find it hard to get away without any legislative action, as it had after the Jokela shooting.

The Finnish cases illustrate that a comprehensive gun law reform can prove extremely difficult even after devastating shocks indicating clear policy failures. In Finland, the legislative reaction was first and foremost complicated by the fact

When laws bite the bullet 135

that guns are a crucial component of the Finnish national heritage. The wide availability of firearms implies that events that would quickly destabilize people's trust into the regulatory framework can more easily be absorbed if socio-cultural barriers to change are high. Similar patterns have been complicating policy change dynamics also in other countries with high firearm availability, such as the United States, Austria (see section 7.5) and Switzerland (see section 7.6). The varying political consequences of the two events can be explained by several contributing factors. First, the spotlight of the public debate was much more firmly centred on the gun issue after the Kauhajoki shooting than after the Jokela shooting. While the Jokela shooting was pre-dominantly perceived as an isolated and unfortunate incident, the occurrence of the second shooting within less than a year made it clear that there might be a structural problem related to the availability of firearms. Accordingly, the debate after Kauhajoki was much more focused and other side aspects received less attention than after Jokela. Second, the comparably pronounced mobilization efforts emerging after the Kauhajoki shooting contributed to a more prominent agenda status of the gun control issue. The news media had learned from their mistakes after Jokela and strengthened both their coverage and their anti-gun position. Moreover, the public became more mobilized and increasingly questioned the Finnish approach of regulating handguns. Finally, the role of the Finnish political actors is comparably ambiguous in the cases analysed above. In particular, the role of the Ministry of the Interior is difficult to evaluate, because it is hard to assess the extent to which concessions were made sincerely or strategically. More specifically, it is difficult to determine whether the installation of the investigation commissions were merely an attempt to win time or a sincere search for the best policy solution. The fact that the government rejected the investigation commission's suggestion to ban handguns after the Kauhajoki shooting tends to favour the first view. In general, however, the cases demonstrate that the Finnish multiparty system clearly works against major reforms, as at least one veto player will probably always be part of the governmental coalition.

On a final note, it must be pointed out that the impact of the two shootings is practically impossible to disentangle completely. While the independence assumption is generally hard to defend if more than one rampage shooting occurs within the same country, the two shootings in Finland occurred in a temporal proximity that is unparalleled on European soil. However, based on the empirical evidence, it is certainly not too far-fetched to argue that without the second rampage shooting, the gun-political status quo probably would have prevailed in Finland. In the following section, we explore another event in France that did not exert any legislative impact, albeit in an entirely different political environment.

136 *When laws bite the bullet*

7.4 France

In 1989, 25.3 per cent of the French population possessed a firearm and 7.2 per cent even possessed a handgun (van Dijk *et al.* 2007: 279). Compared to the rest of Europe at that time, those figures were extraordinarily high. The French firearm possession rate was similar to the availability of firearms in Finland and France was even the leading country in terms of handgun availability. In the following years, the firearm ownership rate in France declined, but the distribution of firearms is still rather high when compared with the rest of Europe. It is reasonable to suspect that the cultural roots of the comparably wide circulation of firearms essentially date back to the revolutionary France of the late eighteenth century and are thereby the result of a path-dependent development. During this time of turmoil, the citizens brought about the French Republic, not the least with the help of firearms. Up until today, the French citizens are called to arm themselves and resist tyranny in the country's national anthem ('aux armes, citoyens!'), an imagery that resembles closely the cultural roots of the United States. Despite this cultural background, however, France has been implementing a relatively strict gun policy since 1939,[7] when the French government feared internal rebellions due to the looming war against Germany. For the most part, the restrictive licensing procedures pertained to particularly dangerous weapons like handguns, while hunting rifles remained comparably easily accessible, as hunting has traditionally been an extremely popular pastime and profession in France (de La Chesnais and Hofstein 2013). Nevertheless, pistols and revolvers could still be obtained legally under certain conditions – a circumstance that eventually contributed to the worst rampage shooting France had to suffer.

In contrast to all other Western European countries, France has a semi-presidential political system, which implies that governmental tasks are divided between a President and a Prime Minister. The President is directly elected by the people and the Prime Minister relies on a majority in the National Assembly (*Assemblée Nationale*). Therefore, the extent to which the executive can exert its power depends considerably on the question of whether President and Prime Minister hail from the same political party. If this is the case, then the Prime Minister is basically at the service of the President in practically all areas of public policy. In a situation of cohabitation, however, the Prime Minister can put forward an own political agenda that may not always be in line with the President's preferences. Indeed, it has been shown empirically that governments under cohabitation tend to accept less far-reaching reforms than unified governments (Leuffen 2009). Such a situation of cohabitation was also present when France experienced its most devastating rampage shooting in 2002. The presidency was occupied by the conservative Jacques Chirac, while the socialist Lionel Jospin acted as Prime Minister. Given this complicated political environment, a profound policy change was thus unlikely. The following case study discusses why policy change materialized nevertheless.

When laws bite the bullet 137

7.4.1 Nanterre: policy change against all odds

Richard Durn's rampage shooting at the regional assembly of Nanterre, France, occurred on 27 March 2002 and accordingly only a few months after the similar Zug incident (section 7.6.1). Armed with two pistols and a revolver, the perpetrator shot and killed eight city council members and wounded 19 others. Despite a history of mental illness and signs of violent behaviour, the perpetrator had acquired a gun license and even managed to get it renewed. On the day following his arrest, Durn jumped out of the window of the police station, killing himself (Le Monde 2002b). Less than one year after the Nanterre incident, France passed a new law on internal security, which included, among many other (much more controversial) measures, several stricter rules for the acquisition and ownership of firearms.[8] How could this policy change be accomplished?

Nanterre's perceived causal complexity

First of all, the chances of a quick and decisive political reaction appeared rather slim when the Nanterre shooting occurred. This is not only due to the rather unfavourable political and cultural environment discussed above, but also a result of the event's high complexity and especially its dynamic aftermath. As far as the search for the event's causes was concerned, it quickly transpired that the French gun control system had failed. Despite the fact that the authorities had been aware of the problematic state of mind of Richard Durn, they failed to withdraw his weapons. Since the perpetrator managed to enter the regional parliament armed without any meaningful hurdles, however, the public discourse also focused on the safety of public buildings, but not to a similar degree as in the Zug case (section 7.6.1). Instead, what made the public discourse confusing and complex was not the search for the event's causes, but the dynamism of the events following the shooting. Unlike after most other rampage shootings, the Nanterre perpetrator did not commit suicide during his rampage, but was arrested by the police. When in custody, Durn managed to jump out the window of his interrogation room, killing himself. After the rampage shooting, this additional development quickly deflected the public interest from the actual shooting towards potential mistakes committed by the police (Ceaux 2002). Accordingly, the gun control story did not only have to compete for public attention with other causal frames, the search for the event's causes was also overshadowed by quickly unfolding events in the shooting's aftermath. Despite those developments, however, the gun control issue remained a central part of the public discourse and this was mainly due to the fact that several additional gun-related events of smaller magnitude occurred in the weeks following the Nanterre massacre. Most importantly, the attempted assassination of President Jacques Chirac by another legal gun owner reignited public concerns over the ineffectiveness of the French gun control system (Riding 2002). Thus, while the Nanterre massacre was of rather high complexity both in terms of its causation and its immediate aftermath, gun control did not quickly fade from the public discourse. Unlike in

138   *When laws bite the bullet*

the context of other cases discussed in this book, however, this persistence of the issue on the public and political agenda was not due to any sustained pressure emanating from the societal level, but resulted from several additional, highly mediatized acts of gun violence occurring in close temporal proximity to the Nanterre shooting.

The cohesion of reform opponents after Nanterre

However, the Nanterre shooting was not only highly complex in terms of its causation and as far as the ensuing public discourse is concerned. The event also took place in the context of a rather complicated political situation. Specifically, the shooting occurred in the middle of the French election campaigns for the presidency and the National Assembly. Since 1997, France had been governed in cohabitation by a conservative President (Jacques Chirac) and a socialist Prime Minister (Lionel Jospin). Both faced off as candidates for the presidency, while the battle for the National Assembly was led between the conservative Jean-Pierre Raffarin and the socialist François Hollande. Both campaigns took place under the impression of the terrorist attacks of 9/11 and Chirac managed to make law and order the top issue in his bid for the presidency (Bell and Criddle 2002: 650). Despite this complicated political situation, all political actors and competing candidates agreed that stricter gun laws would be necessary in response to the massacre. A few weeks after the massacre, the socialist Jospin government announced stricter rules for the acquisition of firearms in France, most importantly the introduction of a mandatory provision of medical certificates (Le Monde 2002a). Jospin was voted out of office before the new law could be adopted, but the incoming conservative Minister of the Interior Nicolas Sarkozy quickly took up the socialist government's proposal and included the provision into his controversial internal security law. The law was finalized and passed by the National Assembly on 18 March 2003, about one year after the Nanterre massacre. Thus, similar to several other rampage shootings discussed in this chapter, the cohesion of reform opponents was not a relevant variable in the political debate following the massacre, because such a coalition of reform opponents did not exist in the first place. Instead, stricter rules for gun ownership had been on the political agenda already before the Nanterre shooting and the event merely served as a catalyst for policy change. The specific political situation of the Nanterre case thus convincingly demonstrates that the precise composition and ideological orientation of the reigning government is of limited explanatory power when it comes to policy reactions to rampage violence. The original policy measures had been drafted by a socialist government and were finalized and implemented by its conservative successors. What matters much more is the extent to which an event's policy implications can be integrated by the political actors into an ongoing political discourse over internal security. In the context of the 2002 French election campaigns, which were dominated by security concerns, this could be easily accomplished.

Societal demand for policy change after Nanterre

As in many other rampage shootings discussed in this chapter, the public did not get deeply involved in the political process, because the responsible political actors reacted quickly. Only a few days after the massacre, it became clear that policy change would be desired by all relevant political actors. In addition, as noted above, further action on the societal level in order to break the issue attention cycle was not necessary, because the issue was kept on the agenda by repeated incidents of gun violence in the weeks following Nanterre.

In sum, the Nanterre incident provides evidence for a very special path towards firearm-related policy change after a rampage shooting. First, the shooting's implications for gun control were politicized despite an ongoing electoral campaign. Although several prominent governing politicians voiced pleas to refrain from abusing the event in an attempt to score electoral points (Albert 2002), also those actors later found themselves under pressure to ponder the event's consequences for public policy. Accordingly, politicization was primarily driven by an enormous increase in media attention and the sheer magnitude of the event. The fact that policy change ultimately materialized was primarily due to the fact that the issue had already been on the political agenda before the rampage shooting occurred and readymade policy solutions had been available. As in the context of other rampage shootings discussed in this chapter (e.g. Antwerp), the triggering event merely served as a catalyst for a political process that had already been going on. In such a scenario, policy change can occur despite an otherwise unfavourable political and cultural context.

7.5 Austria

In comparison to most other countries, Austrian citizens have traditionally been relatively well armed. In the mid-1990s, 15.3 per cent of all Austrian households possessed at least one firearm, 8.1 per cent even possessed at least one handgun, which roughly corresponds to the rate of handgun ownership in Finland (van Dijk *et al.* 2007: 279). According to the International Crime Victims Survey (ICVS), those figures have remained stable until 2005 (van Dijk *et al.* 2007: 279), but other surveys even find that roughly every third Austrian citizen is in possession of a firearm (Karp 2007). Regardless of the precise figures, it is safe to say that the Austrian population is comparably well endowed with firearms if we compare the possession rates to other European countries. To a certain extent, those high figures can certainly be attributed to the fact that Austria comprises large rural areas in which hunting continues to be a popular pastime and profession. In addition, Austria is home to some of the most successful producers of handguns in the world (e.g. Glock) and gun owners enjoy the benefit of a well-connected and influential lobbying organization, the *Interessengemeinschaft Liberales Waffenrecht in Österreich* (IWÖ). Not surprisingly, especially as far as handguns are concerned, Austria has been implementing one of the most lenient regulatory frameworks of all European countries. Every grown-up applicant,

140   *When laws bite the bullet*

who fulfilled the requirements set by the Austrian Firearms Law had to be granted a permit for the possession of a handgun and no genuine reason was explicitly required until 1997 except for applicants below the age of 21.[9] Although Austria's accession to the European Union led to the introduction of the requirement to prove a genuine reason, self-defence was explicitly acknowledged as a sufficient justification to acquire and own a handgun. Within the European Union, such a provision continues to be the exception. Taken together, this evidence clearly suggests that Austria maintains a relatively pronounced gun culture and that accordingly, the introduction of tighter gun regulations affect a larger share of the population than in most other European countries. Therefore, similar to the situation in Switzerland, substantial cultural barriers must be overcome by Austrian advocates of policy change in the wake of a rampage shooting.

In addition to the strong cultural attachment of the Austrian population to firearms, also the country's political institutions make radical policy changes difficult due to their relatively high consensus requirements. Those consensus requirements manifest themselves predominantly in Austria's multi-party system, which has often led to grand coalitions consisting of the two major political parties, the *Social Democratic Party of Austria* (SPÖ) and the *Austrian People's Party* (ÖVP). The two parties diverge rather strongly in their positions on gun control, which gives the ÖVP the power to veto any reform effort. In addition to those difficulties, the Austrian executive is not able to control the parliamentary proceedings to the same extent as in other countries. Accordingly, Siaroff (2003: 459) classifies Austria as a country in which the executive enjoys only low dominance over the legislative process. In a similar vein, the data provided by Lijphart (2012) clearly suggest that Austria should be regarded as a consensus democracy.

If we combine the evidence on the cultural and political hurdles present in Austria, we obtain a picture of a country in which policy change in general and firearm-related policy change in particular, are hard to achieve. Not only does relatively strong distribution of firearms among the Austrian population complicate the rallying of support for tighter regulations, also the design of the Austrian political institutions make the pursuit of policy change a difficult endeavour. In the context of the Mauterndorf shooting, we can observe how those difficult structural conditions translated into corresponding behaviour by the involved political actors.

7.5.1 Mauterndorf: veto players at work

The rampage shooting in the Austrian town Mauterndorf, near Salzburg, occurred on 20 November 1997 and resulted in six fatalities, excluding the perpetrator (Oberösterreichische Nachrichten 1997). The crime was committed by Johann Gautsch, a 36-year-old 'loner and gun fanatic' (Salzburg24.at 2007). The perpetrator used two legally registered handguns for his rampage – a Walther PPK 765 and a Smith & Wesson .357 Magnum (Oberösterreichische Nachrichten 1997;

When laws bite the bullet 141

Salzburg24.at 2007). In a letter later found by the police, Gautsch made demons in his head responsible for the shooting. On the morning after the rampage, the perpetrator committed suicide.

One week after the shooting, the interior committee of the Austrian National Council (*Nationalrat*) met and debated the possible causes and consequences of the shooting. During the debate, it became evident that both the SPÖ and the *Green Party* were strongly committed to pursuing a reform of the Austrian gun laws (Parlamentskorrespondenz 810 1997). Both parties had been critical of private gun ownership before the Mauterndorf incident and still uphold their scepticism about the need for private gun ownership today. As one contributor to the expert survey presented in section 4.1.3 remarked, 'in the four recent elections, only the SPÖ (in 1999, 2002, and 2006) and the Greens (2008) mentioned the private regulation of firearms in their manifestos, both parties advocating for a ban on firearms with exceptions for certain purposes'. Accordingly, a clear cleavage between the progressive and the conservative forces of the Austrian party system contributed to the top-down politicization described in the previous chapter. In addition, since the SPÖ enjoyed the advantage of leading the national government, actual policy change initially did not seem entirely elusive. In fact, Austria's Minister of the Interior Schlögl (SPÖ) even promised to put forward a suggestion on a reform of the gun laws before the end of the year 1997 (Parlamentskorrespondenz 810 1997), but failed to deliver such a proposal. When the *Green Party* realized that no further action would be taken, it tabled a parliamentary motion with the goal of setting a deadline for the government (Stoisits *et al.* 1998). However, the motion was rejected by the National Council and the momentum for reform faded. Which factors can account for the failure of the reform process?

Mauterndorf's perceived causal complexity

Already during the first meeting of the interior committee of the National Council, attempts to bring in alternative causal frames were made, although the gun issue still dominated the discourse (Parlamentskorrespondenz 810 1997). For example, a committee member from the liberal *Austrian Freedom Party* (FPÖ) blamed the media for contributing to excessive gun violence by broadcasting 'too many action- and psycho-thrillers' and consequently voiced the need to influence the media in that regard (Parlamentskorrespondenz 810 1997). Yet, even politicians from the SPÖ contributed to a deflection of the political focus by pointing to 'mounting aggression and increasing egoism' as societal causes of rampage violence and demanded parliamentary investigations into those matters. In general, however, the major focus of the political debate was still put on the gun issue and in particular the question of whether the recently introduced mental health checks for gun applicants should be expanded to all gun owners. After Minister of the Interior Schlögl had failed to come up with a proposal for reform, the National Council met and debated the Greens' suggestion for setting a deadline. During the corresponding parliamentary debate, the gun issue

142 *When laws bite the bullet*

remained at the centre of attention and the motion's initiator Mag. Terezija Stoisits challenged the government to keep its promise: 'What are you waiting for? Are you waiting for a new Mauterndorf?' (Nationalrat 1997: 114). Anton Leikam, the representative of the SPÖ, generally agreed with the Greens' political demands, but denied the urgency suggested by the motion (Nationalrat 1997: 116). However, both representatives from the ÖVP and the FPÖ increasingly rejected the progressive parties' causal reasoning and pointed to the broader social roots of violent behaviour and in particular, to the glorification of violence in the media (Nationalrat 1997: 116f.). Thus, despite the fact that gun control was at the centre of attention in the aftermath of the Mauterndorf shooting, attempts to deflect the political debate to other problems were numerous. Moreover, they were advanced in an exceptionally cohesive manner primarily by actors who were part of the national government.

The cohesion of reform opponents after Mauterndorf

As outlined in the introductory paragraph to this section, Austria has a long history of grand coalitions of the SPÖ and the ÖVP governing the country and such a coalition was also in place in 1997 when Johann Gautsch went on his murderous rampage. The coalition was led by the SPÖ under Chancellor Viktor Klima. While the SPÖ, as discussed above, was not opposed to changes in the Austrian legal framework, the ÖVP was. As a remark by one respondent in the expert survey (section 4.1.3) indicates, the ÖVP has always been strongly aligned with shooting interests: 'Traditionally, the ÖVP has very strong links to hunting associations ("Landesjagdverbände"), which are regularly headed by prominent ÖVP-politicians.' Thus, while the parliamentary opposition and in particular the Green Party politicized gun control in the wake of the Mauterndorf shooting, the ÖVP could block any envisioned policy changes being part of the Austrian government and its coalition partner SPÖ was not inclined to push the issue any further and risk the instability of the grand coalition. It is particularly striking that the ÖVP represented its interests in a highly cohesive manner. Unlike the Conservative Party in the wake of the Dunblane shooting, the ÖVP did not suffer from any defections within its ranks. All ÖVP politicians contributing to the political debate in the aftermath of the Mauterndorf shooting firmly rejected the need to revise the Austrian system for gun control. As its most vocal representative on the matter, the ÖVP parliamentarian Paul Kiss attacked the Green position for implying a total prohibition of firearm ownership. 'We are opposed to this. We will continue to oppose it within the coalition and there won't be any solution that includes the total prohibition of firearms in private hands' (Nationalrat 1997: 117). Accordingly, the cohesiveness of the ÖVP gave it the status of a veto player in the governmental coalition, which essentially made any substantive policy change elusive.

Societal demand for policy change after Mauterndorf

Outside of the political arena, the Mauterndorf massacre led to some lobbying activity on both sides of the debate. On the one hand, the shooting contributed to the creation of a movement demanding the curbing of private gun ownership in Austria called *Waffen weg!* (Guns away!). Politically, the new lobby group was strongly associated with the Greens and the SPÖ, as several of its supporters were at the same time leading members in those parties (Waffen weg! 1998). Also public opinion polls conducted in the wake of the Mauterndorf massacre supported the initiative's position (Oberösterreichische Nachrichten 1998) and the movement managed to collect 6,000 signatures in support of new restrictions in the Austrian legal framework for firearms. The list of signatures was submitted to the Austrian Minister of the Interior roughly two years after the Mauterndorf shooting (Waffen weg! 1999). However, despite its efforts to push for a reform of the Austrian gun regulations, the *Waffen weg!* initiative could hardly compete with the much better organized lobby of gun owners. In the wake of the Mauterndorf shooting, the IWÖ managed to collect 100,000 signatures against the tightening of Austria's gun laws (IWÖ 2002). Thus, while pro-change forces attempted to organize politically and mobilize the public, it became evident very quickly that the broadly institutionalized interests of gun owners would be impossible to overcome in terms of public support. As a result, while the *Waffen weg!* initiative still exists on paper, it has essentially given up its advocacy work.

To sum up, the Mauterndorf case suggests that policy change in the area of gun control can be complicated severely both by structural features of the affected country (both cultural and political) and by the resulting actor constellations. As after the shooting in Zug (section 7.6.1), the fact that the government in power was divided on the question of gun control made existing change efforts futile. In contrast to several other shootings which did not yield policy change, the Mauterndorf case resulted in some social mobilization. However, unlike after the shooting in Dunblane, the efforts were too small in scale in order to have an impact and were also not accompanied by supporting media coverage. Most importantly, however, the efforts were met by fierce resistance from gun owners and their organized interests – an obstacle that proved to be impossible to overcome.

7.6 Switzerland

In Europe, Switzerland has always been one of the most heavily armed societies. According to the International Crime Victims Survey (ICVS), 35.7 per cent of all Swiss households possessed firearms between 1999 and 2003 and 11.8 per cent even possessed handguns (van Dijk *et al.* 2007: 279). At this point in time, the availability of firearms in Switzerland was unmatched by any other European country.[10] Switzerland has a long history of shooting competitions (Halbrook 2003) and the Swiss militia system even requires able-bodied men to keep an assault rifle in their homes (Halbrook 2003: 146). This requirement led to an

144 *When laws bite the bullet*

enormous arsenal of private weapons in the Swiss population. As Kopel (1992: 284) puts it: 'Switzerland does not have an army; it is an army.' However, epidemiological studies show that this private arsenal is not only based on army firearms, but also on weapons which have been acquired via the regular process for civilians (Grabherr *et al.* 2010). Accordingly, Swiss citizens have a very strong cultural attachment to firearms, which is mirrored in the country's relatively liberal regulatory framework. Up until 1997, the Swiss cantons had regulated the acquisition and possession of firearms, but had already done so in a very permissive way. The first national Swiss gun law integrated the diverse cantonal laws, but did not alter their consistently permissive approach.

In addition to the pronounced Swiss gun culture, the design of the country's political institutions makes major policy change very hard to accomplish, since many institutional veto players can block reform efforts (Tsebelis 2002). Not only is the government traditionally composed of an oversized coalition cabinet, there are also two parliamentary chambers which can veto reform proposals. In addition, the popular referendum ensures that the population can vote down unpopular reform initiatives. Accordingly, the Swiss political system involves enormous consensus requirements, which often results in protracted searches for compromise.

Taken together, the cultural and political institutions of Switzerland are configured in a way that makes major policy change hard to achieve. Not only the cultural barriers to change are very high, also the politico-institutional hurdles complicate reform efforts. This combination of a strong gun culture with a political system with many veto players is strongly reminiscent of the situation in the United States, where attempts to change the federal law on firearms have been similarly unsuccessful. Accordingly, the relevant structural variables do not provide a very fertile ground for advocates of policy change in the area of gun control. In addition, also the other factors that could have helped to facilitate reform efforts were not configured in a favourable way at the point in time when policy change became a theoretical possibility. This point in time occurred in 2001, when the country experienced its most severe rampage shooting.

7.6.1 *Zug: the elusiveness of policy change in Switzerland*

The shooting in the cantonal parliament in the Swiss town of Zug took place on 27 September 2001. On the morning of that day, Friedrich Leibacher, a Swiss citizen who had nourished hatred against local politicians, entered the parliament armed with a pump-action shotgun, a semi-automatic rifle and a semi-automatic handgun (Cukier and Sidel 2006: 12). The perpetrator killed 14 politicians, wounded 14 others and committed suicide. All weapons, including the additional revolver Leibacher did not use, had been acquired legally. The shooting sparked a heated national public debate over a range of policy issues (Hurka and Nebel 2013), among them gun control. As the previous chapter has demonstrated, the politicization of the event followed both a bottom-up and a top-down path. On the one hand, the sheer imagery and magnitude of the event made ignorance an infeasible option,

When laws bite the bullet   145

especially against the background of the strong news coverage accompanying the event. On the other hand, the Swiss political system included two parties that had a long history of advocating for stronger firearm regulations and took the event as an opportunity to push for reforms (the *Green Party of Switzerland*, GPS, and the *Social Democratic Party of Switzerland*, SP). Eventually, however, the political debate did not culminate in any gun-related legislative action.

This lack of a political reaction is curious given the fact that when the Zug shooting occurred, a revision of the Swiss gun law had already been on the political agenda. The Defence Committees of the Swiss National Assembly had asked the Federal Council (*Bundesrat*) to draft a proposal for stricter gun control measures (Sicherheitspolitische Kommission 2000). In March 2001, the Federal Council delegated this task to an expert commission in the Department of Justice and Police. Despite the pending expert deliberations, members of the GPS and the SP renewed their demand for a tighter gun law, suggesting that the Zug shooting was a direct consequence of the lax Swiss firearm regime. In its response to those requests, the Federal Council referred to the pending expert deliberations and stated its commitment to engage in the public consultation process as soon as possible (Swiss Federal Council 2001). However, it took another year until the expert commission presented its proposal, which identified a range of loopholes in the existing gun law. The ensuing consultation process ended in December 2004 with an overwhelming rejection by the majority of the contributing stakeholders, which were, for the most part, gun owner organizations. In 2005, it was realized that Switzerland would have to adapt its gun regulations in the face of the imminent entry into the Schengen zone anyway and the revision of the gun law was postponed. Frustrated by the slowly proceeding reform efforts and motivated by the widely publicized shooting of the Swiss skier Corinne Rey-Bellet, a popular initiative formed in 2007, demanding far-reaching reforms of the Swiss gun laws. The initiative was opposed both by the majority of the Federal Council and the Federal Assembly. In the popular referendum on 13 February 2011, almost a decade after the Zug shooting, the initiative was rejected by 56.3 per cent of the Swiss population. Thus, all attempts of meaningful policy change in the wake of the Zug shooting failed and later adjustments were mainly driven by external pressure of the looming entry into the Schengen zone. How can this absence of any policy reaction after the Zug incident be explained?

Zug's perceived causal complexity

The policy implications of the rampage shooting in Zug were contested and causal attributions were spread widely. Among those causal attributions, the perpetrator's comparably easy access to firearms was only one causal story among many. The most dominant issue in the public discourse, however, was the security of public buildings, not the easy availability of guns (Hurka and Nebel 2013: 398). In the context of this discussion, the relatively liberal Swiss tradition of providing open public access to administrative buildings was questioned and

146   *When laws bite the bullet*

new security measures like video surveillance, metal detectors or increased police presence were discussed as possible reactions to the rampage shooting. Such measures were also implemented in some parts of the country, which remained the only political consequence of the Zug shooting (Baumann 2002). Thus, the debate surrounding public security clearly overshadowed the debate over gun control. Shortly after the shooting, Jo Lang, a local green politician, even complained that the security debate 'would dominate too much' (Merki 2001). In consequence, it proved difficult for advocates of stricter gun control to focus the debate and public attention on their policy area. As Hurka and Nebel (2013: 398, italics in original) observed:

> The focus on security matters in the aftermath of the Zug shooting deflected attention from the gun issue, and many of the gun-related statements made after the Zug shooting argued that the event did *not* highlight gun availability as a social problem.

More specifically, such arguments were primarily made in defence of the Swiss tradition of a militia system (Tagesanzeiger 2001). Thus, the public debate following the Zug massacre was not only dispersed among different frames, it also became apparent rather quickly that the reform opponents in the area of gun control would not back down.

The cohesion of reform opponents after Zug

The Swiss government, the Federal Council, has traditionally been composed of all major Swiss political parties apportioned by the magic formula, which complicates the determination of the Council's policy preferences. On the question of gun control, however, the Swiss party system is clearly split along a left-right divide. As in many other European democracies, the SP and the GPS have always been the most vocal proponents of tighter gun control in Switzerland. However, unlike the SP, which controls two seats in the seven-member Federal Council, the GPS has never been represented in the Swiss government. All other Swiss political parties are either conservative (the *Christian Democratic People's Party of Switzerland*, CVP, and the *Swiss People's Party*, SVP) or liberal (the *Free Democratic Party of Switzerland*, FDP). All of those latter parties generally oppose tighter firearm regulations, only small factions of the CVP have occasionally supported tighter gun control measures. Those divisions materialized very clearly after the rampage shooting in Zug. While the progressive position was articulated with motions tabled by the SP and the GPS respectively (Hollenstein 2001; Schwaab 2001), the SVP emerged as the most vocal opponent of tighter gun control measures in the public discourse (Hurka and Nebel 2013). Most importantly, however, both camps were highly cohesive in their positions, which contributed to a deadlock of the political negotiations. In consequence, a majority of the parties represented in the Federal Council proved to be critical of too many restrictions and anxious to protect the Swiss shooting tradition.

Societal demand for policy change after Zug

Finally, efforts of social mobilization on the gun issue were completely absent in the wake of the Zug shooting. Unlike in Great Britain after the Dunblane shooting (see section 7.1.1), there was no broad media campaign for stricter gun control and no social movement formed in response to the massacre. In the public consultation process on a revision of the Swiss gun laws, the vast majority of the participants were shooting clubs, gun collectors, and the powerful gun lobby organization *pro Tell*. Jointly, they voiced vocal concerns about the allegedly imminent 'disarmament of the law-abiding citizen' (Federal Department of Justice and Police 2004: 7). Yet, at the time of the Zug shooting, no organized social movement for tighter gun laws did exist and none came into being as a result of the massacre. As the results of the weapons initiative of 2011 suggest, such a broad social mobilization against guns is elusive in a country in which guns belong to the narrative of the nation and thereby form a considerable part of its identity.

Thus, both structural and proximate conditions impeded reform efforts after the Zug shooting. Not only cultural and politico-institutional barriers prevented substantive policy change, but also the conservative pre-dispositions of the Swiss government and the absence of any social mobilization led to the stability of the Swiss policy arrangements. Moreover, it proved to be difficult for change advocates to focus public and political attention on the issue of gun control as the matter was overshadowed of concerns about the security of public buildings.

7.7 Belgium

Over the course of the past decades, Belgium has become known for its relatively permissive approach of regulating handguns. Evidence from the International Crime Victims Survey (ICVS) suggests that while 11.4 per cent of Belgian households possessed firearms in 2004 and 2005, 5.2 per cent were in possession of a handgun (van Dijk *et al.* 2007: 279). While the former figure is neither particularly high nor particularly low in an international comparison, the latter figure is comparable to the ownership rates of Austria (5.6 per cent) and Finland (6.3 per cent). Yet, more recent studies show that the rate of gun ownership has declined sharply following the introduction of a new gun law in 2006 (Duquet and Van Alstein 2012: 16). It is noteworthy, however, that the main purpose for firearm ownership in Belgium is neither sports shooting nor hunting as in most other European countries. Instead, Belgians primarily possess firearms for the purpose of self-protection, as a recent Eurobarometer survey suggests (Flash Eurobarometer No. 383 2013: 11). The relatively easy availability of firearms in Belgium can be attributed to the fact that despite several attempts, the country never managed to fundamentally reform its outdated gun law of 1933[11] until the year 2006. While Belgium had to bring its legislation in line with the European Union's Firearms Directive[12] in the early 1990s, several very liberal elements could be maintained. Most importantly, many weapon types could still

148　*When laws bite the bullet*

be obtained legally over the counter without providing proof of a genuine need for the gun. For instance, a valid photo ID was sufficient in order to purchase hunting rifles and neither background checks about the customer's criminal history nor information about his mental state were required. Also waiting periods were not legally prescribed. It was precisely these policy measures that became the subject of intense political debate when a rampage shooting in Antwerp exposed the loopholes of the Belgian gun law.

In addition to the Belgian gun culture, which can be judged as comparably pronounced in the European context, also the design of the Belgian political institutions make the country a least likely case for policy change. In fact, the long period of policy stability between 1933 and 2006 in the area of gun control can certainly be attributed to the highly fragmented Belgian party system and the country's federal structure which both imply that negotiation and compromise are central components of Belgian politics. In the context of an external shock, such political hurdles for a decisive political reaction should prove difficult to overcome. Despite those obstacles, however, Belgium reacted quickly and decisively to an event that put the Belgian approach of regulating firearms into question. This event occurred in the town of Antwerp in the year of 2006.

7.7.1 Antwerp: breaking the resistance

On 11 May 2006, Hans van Themsche (18 years old), shot at three people in the city of Antwerp shortly after acquiring the murder weapon, a hunting rifle, legally in a gun store. As noted above, unlike in most other European countries, the purchase of the weapon was possible without a license and only a valid photo-ID had to be provided. The perpetrator killed two of his victims, a woman of Malian descent and a two-year-old girl, another woman of Turkish origin was severely wounded (Expatica News 2006b). After the incident, it became known quickly that the perpetrator had been associated with the extreme right party *Vlaams Belang* and that the shooting was racially motivated. Other than many other rampage killers, van Themsche could be arrested by the police and was sentenced to lifetime imprisonment roughly one year after the rampage (New York Times 2007). It only took one week until the Belgian parliament passed a reformed gun law, which included a range of comparably far-reaching provisions. For example, all weapons were subjected to authorization, a waiting period was made mandatory in order to prevent impulse purchases, the validity of possession licenses was limited to five years and a license renewal now required the provision of medical certificate and the successful completion of a safe handling test, and the validity of carriage licenses was limited to three years. Taken together, those reform steps were quite comprehensive and fundamentally changed the Belgian gun control system. How can this comparably swift and strong political reaction be explained?

Antwerp's perceived causal complexity

In Belgian society, it did not take long until it became clear that the Antwerp shooting would lead to a political reaction. In fact 'the emotion aroused by this racist crime focused the political debate on the easy availability of weapons and calmed the usual energetic resistance by the weapons lobby' (Berkol, 2006, original in French, author's translation). The fact that the public debate focused on the gun issue very quickly was not only a result of the blatant policy failure indicated by the Antwerp shooting. In fact, the gun control issue had been on the agenda for years, but repeated attempts to reform Belgium's outdated regulatory framework had failed due to a strong network of pro-gun interest groups and affiliated lawmakers (Berkol 2006). After an initial reform attempt had failed in 2002, the public and political debate stalled. Some observers attribute the failure of this first reform effort to the fact that the event that had triggered the political debate was not accompanied with sufficient media coverage and that accordingly, not enough pressure could be built up (Berkol 2006). However, despite those unsuccessful reform efforts, the gun issue never left the political agenda completely. Instead, a reform remained one of the central objectives especially of the leftist political parties in Belgium. When the Antwerp shooting occurred, those proponents of a reformed Belgian gun law found it comparably easy to rekindle the political debate, especially in the context of the now much stronger attention of the media.

Although the attention of the public, the media and the responsible political actors was firmly put on the issue of gun control, it should not be forgotten that the shooting had a second dimension that was activated especially by a few reform-averse actors. This second dimension concerned the shooting's racist background and the extent to which this racist motivation of the perpetrator can be interpreted as an indicator of rising xenophobia in Belgium. When it transpired that part of the shooter's family had been members of the xenophobic and right-wing party *Vlaams Belang*, the party immediately became the subject of massive public criticism. Accordingly, the legislators of the *Vlaams Belang* did not participate in the political debates on gun control to a significant extent and quietly acquiesced to a reform they arguably would have opposed strongly under normal circumstances. Thus, the xenophobia debate quickly turned into a debate about the *Vlaams Belang*, but this part of the discourse was clearly less pronounced than the debate over the Belgian gun control system. The fact that a gun control narrative for the Antwerp shooting was readily available and could therefore be activated easily by interested political actors, streamlined the public and political debate on the question of how similar policy failures could be prevented in the future. However, a real debate did not even take place, because the Belgian executive already had a policy solution at their disposal, which could now be realized without much resistance.

150 *When laws bite the bullet*

The cohesion of reform opponents after Antwerp

When Hans van Themsche committed his rampage in 2006, Belgium was governed by a four-party coalition cabinet led by the *Flemish Liberals and Democrats* (VLD) and Prime Minister Guy Verhofstadt. The other parties were the *Liberal Reformist Party* (MR) and the two socialist parties from Wallonia and Flanders respectively. Within the governmental coalition, the socialists had earned a reputation of being in favour of stricter gun control in Belgium, whereas the liberal parties, in particular the MR, had acted as the brakemen. However, in the wake of the Antwerp shooting, no real opposition against the envisioned overhaul of the Belgian gun laws emerged. Instead, all major political actors quickly subscribed to the view that fundamental changes would be in order and the gun law reform passed with only two parliamentarians opposing the reform, mainly criticizing the speed by which the project was pushed through parliament (Expatica News 2006a). Accordingly, reform opponents were essentially muted for two reasons: first, as noted above, the *Vlaams Belang* became subject of intense public criticism and did not dare to openly oppose the reform. Second, the government did not have to start from scratch and could simply accelerate a political process that had already been going on for several years. Due to the clear policy failures demonstrated by the Antwerp shooting, gun control quickly became subject to political controversy and before an opposition could even start to coordinate, the law was already passed.

Societal demand for policy change after Antwerp

Finally, with regard to societal actors, the shooting in Antwerp led to similar reactions as in many other cases. Shock and grief dominated the days after the shooting. However, it quickly became evident that societal pressure would not even be required for a major policy change to occur. The quick political reaction following the shooting essentially made sustained public pressure superfluous. In this respect, the Antwerp shooting resembles closely the two school shootings in Germany, where a rapid policy change occurred before potential public pressure could even be organized and coordinated. In Belgium, public anger was primarily directed at the political party *Vlaams Belang* and its racist ideology for fuelling xenophobic tendencies among Belgian youth (Anderson 2006). The issue of gun control, however, was not a major focus of this movement. As outlined above, since the need for a fundamental reform was largely uncontested among Belgian policy makers sustained societal demand for policy change was deemed unnecessary and the public targeted its anger to the *Vlaams Belang*, instead.

In sum, the Belgian case serves as an illustrative example of the Kingdonian notion of policy change. For a long time, policy solutions to the easy availability of firearms in Belgium had been debated without any legislative consequences. Public attention was low, because problem pressure seemed low or was not mediatized. This changed in 2006, when existing policy solutions could be

When laws bite the bullet 151

attached to an increase in perceived problem pressure, which came about in the form of a major focusing event. Accordingly, the Antwerp case is clearly comparable to the shootings in Erfurt (section 7.2.2), Kauhajoki (section 7.3.2) and Nanterre (section 7.4.1). In all three cases, a reform of the countries' respective gun laws had already been on the agenda before the shootings occurred. Under such circumstances, the time it takes to find a policy solution can be saved and the already existing policy solution can be passed quickly and without much resistance.

7.8 Comparative assessment

The case studies presented in this chapter convey several interesting insights into the factors that drive and impede gun-related policy change in the aftermath of rampage shootings. In this concluding section, the empirical evidence is drawn together in an attempt to evaluate the validity of the theoretical expectations developed in Chapter 4. The following sub-sections therefore compare the cases studied in order to detect systematic cross-case patterns. In general, this discussion is structured along the lines of the theoretical expectations, but we will find that we must consider the interaction between the theoretical arguments in order to acquire a good understanding of the causal configurations that facilitate or impede the political processes following rampage shootings. In order to enable the reader to acquire a general overview of the cases, Table 7.1 summarizes the empirical evidence for all case studies. The assessments made in this table are based on the qualitative evaluations made in the case studies and the labels 'high', 'rather high', 'low', and 'rather low' should be understood as relative ratings of the cases, not as set calibrations as they would have to be performed in a QCA study. In addition to the evaluation of the theoretical expectations, the case studies have also revealed a range of conclusions which had not been foreseen at the outset. Those conclusions will also be discussed in this section.

7.8.1 The role of perceived event complexity for policy change dynamics

The case studies provided mixed support to theoretical expectation 5, which postulated that the scope of the policy reforms carried out in response to focusing events should be related to the perceived complexity of the event. In fact, the pattern that emerges if we assess the empirical evidence presented above in a comparative manner is rather inconclusive as far as the validity of this expectation is concerned. Reforms have been adopted after highly complex events that provoked a multitude of causal stories (e.g. Erfurt, Winnenden, Kauhajoki and Antwerp) and after events that focused political attention narrowly on gun control (e.g. Dunblane). In contrast, policies have remained stable after events that primarily challenged the status quo in the area of gun control (e.g. Cumbria, Lörrach and Mauterndorf) and after more complex events (e.g. Jokela and Bad Reichenhall). Accordingly, based on the empirical evidence, it is difficult to

Table 7.1 Summary of the case studies

Case	Event complexity	Cohesion of reform opponents	Societal demand	Institutional hurdles: socio-cultural	Institutional hurdles: political	Policy change
Dunblane	*Rather low* Gun control as the major focus of the political discourse	*Low* Early defections within the Conservative Party	*Very high* Strong media pressure and the 'Snowdrop Campaign'	*Low*	*Low*	*Significant* Handgun ban
Cumbria	*Rather low* Gun control as the major focus of the political discourse	*High* Clear rejection of change demands by Conservatives and Prime Minister Cameron	*Low* No pressure group, quickly receding media attention			*None*
Bad Reichenhall	*Rather high* Alternative causal stories on media violence and the perpetrator's social background	*Not relevant* No coalition of reform opponents present	*Low* No pressure group, quickly receding media attention	*Medium*	*Rather high*	*None*
Erfurt	*High* Alternative causal stories on media violence, the education system and school security	*Low* Early defections within the ranks of the Christian Democratic Union (CDU)	*Rather low* Some general appeals ('Erfurter Appell'), but no organized movement			*Substantial* Among other changes: stronger age requirements, prohibition of pump-guns with pistol grips

Winnenden	*High* Alternative causal stories on media violence, mental health and school security	*Low* Early defections within the ranks of the Christian Democratic Union (CDU)	*Rather high* Organized movements and signature collections (Keine Mordwaffen als Sportwaffen!, Aktionsbündnis Winnenden)	*Medium*	*Rather high*	*Incremental* More enforcement rights for the police in order to ensure safe storage
Lörrach	*Low* Focus almost exclusively put on gun control	*High* No defections within the government coalition	*Low* No further activities, quickly decreasing media attention			*None*
Jokela	*High* Alternative causal stories on mental health, bullying, school security, media violence, etc.	*Low* Early concessions by the Centre Party and the National Coalition Party	*Low* No strong movement emerging, divided public and media	*High*	*Rather high*	*None*
Kauhajoki	*Medium* Alternative causal stories as after Jokela, but with a much stronger focus on gun control	*Low* Divided coalition of status quo advocates	*Rather high* Unified pressure by the media, signature collections in the public			*Substantial* Stronger age requirements, mental health checks

continued

Table 7.1 Continued

Case	Event complexity	Cohesion of reform opponents	Societal demand	Institutional hurdles: socio-cultural	Institutional hurdles: political	Policy change
Nanterre	*Rather high* Dynamic aftermath (perpetrator suicide in custody, additional events), alternative causal stories	*Not relevant* No coalition of reform opponents present	*Low* No perceived need to push gun control, due to quick political reaction	*Medium*	*Rather high*	*Incremental* Mental health checks
Mauterndorf	*Low* Clear focus on gun control with only few exceptions	*High* Cohesive opposition by the governmental Austrian People's Party (ÖVP)	*Rather high* Formation of the 'Waffen weg!' initiative	*High*	*Rather high*	*None*
Zug	*High* Major focus not on gun control, but on security measures for public buildings	*High* Cohesive opposition by several important political actors	*Low* No public pressure and quickly receding media attention	*High*	*High*	*None*
Antwerp	*Rather high* Major alternative causal story on racist motivation of the shooter	*Not relevant* Quick agreement on the necessity of gun law reforms	*Rather low* Public protest primarily focused on racism, not on gun control	*High*	*Rather high*	*Substantial* Authorization required for all firearms, mandatory waiting period, duration of licenses limited, mandatory mental health certificate and safe handling tests

When laws bite the bullet 155

argue that perceived event complexity exerts an independent effect on the occurrence and scope of policy reforms after potential focusing events. Since a clearcut relationship does not exist across the cases analysed above, the general empirical validity of theoretical expectation 5 must be questioned. In some of the cases, the qualitative empirical evidence suggests that a relationship exists, but the extent to which this is the case hardly allows for generalizations.

Thus, the empirical evidence generally suggests that there is no systematic variance between cases as regards their perceived causal complexity and the occurrence of policy change in their aftermath. This implies that the expected strategy of deflecting the public discourse during causally complex events to other causal stories was either not pursued by advocates of the gun political status quo, or it did not work well enough to contain the dynamics of policy change. The case studies illustrated that both happened to varying extents in the examined cases. In addition, the fact that few competing causal explanations for a rampage shooting exist next to the gun control story does not necessarily imply that policy change materializes. On the contrary, events that were exclusively framed as policy failures in the area of gun control never resulted in legislative changes, with the notable exception of the Dunblane case. Accordingly, the case studies suggest that the cross-case patterns with regard to the relationship between an event's perceived causal complexity and the occurrence of policy change in the area of gun control are highly unsystematic, if we try to evaluate theoretical expectation 5 individually. Are the patterns we can identify any clearer if we shift our focus to the remaining theoretical expectations?

7.8.2 The role of reform opponents – does cohesion matter?

In general, the case studies suggest that the cohesion of reform opponents is much more important for the occurrence of policy change than the event's perceived causal complexity (theoretical expectation 7). As mentioned above, some events did not entail policy change even though gun control emerged as the only meaningful causal story in the event's aftermath (e.g. Cumbria, Lörrach, Mauterndorf). In all of these cases, opponents to policy change managed to keep their ranks closed in the immediate aftermath of the shootings. Yet, as the Zug shooting demonstrates, policy change is equally elusive if multiple causal stories emerge and the status quo coalition is cohesive. Given these configurations, we may conclude that an event's perceived causal complexity appears much less important than the dedication of the reform opponents in defending the status quo if we are interested in explaining policy stability in the wake of rampage shootings.

An interesting picture also emerges if we compare cases that entailed policy change. In the direct aftermath of the shootings in Erfurt, Winnenden, Kauhajoki, Nanterre and Antwerp, politicians from all across the political spectrum embraced the idea of stricter gun legislation (of course, to varying degrees). Thus, if reform opponents do not manage to speak with one voice and if critical actors decide to switch sides early on in the political debate, reform dynamics

156　*When laws bite the bullet*

take up speed and become increasingly difficult to contain for a fragmented status quo coalition. However, the extent to which these early concessions are made strategically or sincerely is extremely difficult to gauge. In some cases, the qualitative discussion of the cases suggests that early concessions by reform opponents are made in order to take pressure out of the political debate and prevent changes of a larger magnitude. In other instances, we found that individual political actors we would have expected to act as status quo advocates based on their partisan affiliation, had already differed significantly from the rest of their party as far as the regulation of firearms is concerned before the shooting (e.g. the Conservative MP David Mellor after Dunblane or Finnish Prime Minister Vanhanen after the school shootings in Finland). Yet, even if the status quo coalition is divided, policy change does not always take place in the short run. Two cases illustrate this exceptional pattern. First, after the shooting in Jokela, a divided group of status quo advocates managed to delay the political process, until the next shooting in Kauhajoki reinforced the reform movement. Second, early concessions by reform opponents did not usher into quick legislative changes after the Bad Reichenhall shooting. Accordingly, while the cohesion of reform opponents seems to explain many instances of policy change and stability after politicized rampage shootings, we still cannot account for all of the observed variation. This changes if we compare the cases with regard to the varying degrees of pressure exerted by societal actors.

7.8.3 Pressure from below – a recipe for policy change?

One major reason for the lack of policy change after the shootings in Jokela and Bad Reichenhall cited above can be found in the comparably low mobilization for policy change on the societal level (theoretical expectation 6). In both cases, the political debate that started in response to the shootings quickly ebbed away without direct legislative consequences. Accordingly, policy stability in the aftermath of rampage shootings is often a result of the fact that societal groups either do not want to mobilize, or are unable to do so. The relevance of this pattern becomes obvious if we look at additional cases. After the Cumbria shooting, the mobilization that had followed the Dunblane massacre 14 years earlier was entirely absent. To a certain extent, this may be attributable to the fact that the major battles had already been won and the shotguns used in the Cumbria massacre were not considered as dangerous by the British society as handguns (see also the section on additional insights below for this argument). After the Lörrach shooting, no broad social movement developed arguably due to the fact that the chances of success were minimal in the context of a highly cohesive government opposing any legislative changes. Finally, in the wake of the Jokela shooting, the emergence of a social movement against guns was inhibited by the fact that broad segments of Finnish society perceived the shooting as a one-off incident and attributed blame to other causal stories – a pattern that changed when the second shooting in Kauhajoki challenged this perception. Thus, if societal pressure for change does not emerge as a direct consequence of a shooting or if such pressure cannot be sustained over a longer period of time, even the odds for incremental policy change are low.

Yet, the absence of social mobilization is not always motivated by the inability of societal policy entrepreneurs to take advantage of changes in public opinion. Sometimes, the mobilization of societal actors is rendered extremely difficult if all political actors quickly agree on incremental reforms, i.e. if the cohesion of reform opponents is low. This was the case after Erfurt and Nanterre, when almost all involved political actors made their commitment to support policy change public very quickly after the respective incidents. This suggests that status quo advocates face a very difficult decision after rampage shootings. In some instances, they can prevent policy change altogether if they remain highly cohesive. If such cohesion proves impossible to sustain, however, early concessions to accept incremental reforms can take the wind out of the sails of the pressure groups which aim to mobilize society in order to achieve more fundamental reforms. Yet, as the examples discussed in the previous section demonstrate, such a strategy can prove to be very risky. After the school shootings in Erfurt and Winnenden, it worked perfectly well for those actors who aimed to contain policy change, when the concessions made satisfied the feeling of German society that something should be done. In Dunblane, in contrast, early concessions by Conservatives only fuelled the mobilization of societal actors, because these concessions were broadly conceived as inappropriately small.

In sum, the case studies demonstrate that the final theoretical expectation on the extent to which actors on the societal level get involved into the decision-making process bears most explanatory power for the extent to which states change their gun policies in the aftermath of rampage shootings. While societal actors may not always be able to perfectly control the emergence of a political debate over gun control, i.e. the politicization process, they can be crucially important when it comes to the breaking of the issue attention cycle that typically haunts the political processes following potential focusing events (Downs 1972). If societal actors manage to organize quickly, they may not directly affect political decisions, but they can at least keep the gun control issue on the political agenda and thereby increase the chances for policy change to occur. The empirical evidence presented in this book underscores the general validity of this claim, with exceptions proving the rule.

7.8.4 Love for guns and high institutional hurdles – insurmountable obstacles?

How do structural variables condition the impact of rampage shootings on gun policies? In theoretical expectations 8a and 8b, it was argued that both political and socio-cultural institutions within an affected country could be important pre-conditions for policy change and stability after focusing events. On the one hand, the extent to which decision-makers face political constraints was expected to matter for their capacity and willingness to push for reforms (theoretical

158 *When laws bite the bullet*

expectation 8a). On the other hand, the degree of the affected nation's cultural attachment towards guns was presented as another institutional component which might facilitate or impede policy reforms (theoretical expectation 8b).

As far as socio-cultural institutions are concerned, one might have had reason to expect that also the extent to which gun control gets politicized after rampage shootings could vary systematically between different gun cultures. However, we may safely conclude that this is not systematically the case. The case studies clearly suggest that gun policies become the subject of political debate regardless of the affected country's gun culture. In other words, the extent to which gun control gets politicized after a rampage shooting is not directly related to the extent to which the affected country's population is endowed with firearms. In some countries, political debates on gun control developed despite (or maybe because of) the easy availability of firearms (e.g. Switzerland, Finland, and Austria). In other countries, gun control became the subject of political debates despite (or because of) the fact that guns are comparably rare (e.g. Great Britain). However, as far as policy change is concerned, we have observed that the more encompassing reforms have taken place in the latter types of countries.

In particular, states in which a relatively large part of the population is in the possession of firearms either absorb external pressures towards stricter rules for gun ownership (like in Austria or Switzerland) or react with incremental adjustments when focusing events put the status quo under pressure repeatedly and within a short period of time (e.g. Finland). Thus, while those states are no less likely to debate political reforms after rampage shootings, it appears that they are much less likely to actually adopt them quickly. In other countries, in which gun ownership is less widespread, more encompassing reforms have been possible (e.g. Great Britain). There are, however, exceptions to this observation, which suggests that the story is somewhat more complicated. For example, Germany and Belgium have reacted with several policy changes despite the fact that their populations are comparably well equipped with firearms. While the availability of firearms in the countries does not match the figures of Switzerland, Austria and Finland, it would still be hard to argue that gun cultures in Germany and Belgium are comparable to the British gun culture. Thus, what additional factors can help to explain varying reform developments?

In the political science literature, different designs of political institutions are often presented as the central variable explaining varying cross-national policy outputs. The case studies presented in this chapter corroborate this argument, albeit only to a certain extent. We have seen the most encompassing policy change in a state that gives the reigning government the largest leeway to pursue reforms (Great Britain after Dunblane). This example demonstrates that a government that dominates the legislature can react quickly and decisively to external pressures. In most other European countries, consensus requirements are much higher than in Great Britain and accordingly, the adopted policy reforms have been less comprehensive. Nevertheless, policy change has taken place in many of those countries as well. Accordingly, the evidence presented in this book suggests that the consensus requirements imposed by a country's political system are rather related to the scope of the instituted policy reforms, than to their adoption in general. To a certain extent, a final evaluation of the role of political institutions is complicated by the fact that the cross-national variance is somewhat limited within Western Europe. Specifically, Great Britain remains the only country in Western Europe that has a classical Westminster model in place.

If we take a look at the interplay of cultural and political institutions, it becomes apparent that the two essentially provide the ground for policy change and stability, but they are neither necessary nor sufficient for different policy reactions on their own. For example, in Switzerland and Austria, the combination of strong cultural barriers and high consensus requirements made rapid policy reactions elusive. The investigation of these two cases clearly revealed that quick political reactions are extremely difficult to achieve if many players are able to veto reforms and if gun ownership is widespread within the population. In contrast, however, Belgium also features high levels of gun ownership and high consensus requirements, but ultimately showed a relatively strong and quick legislative reaction when the status quo came under pressure. Likewise, Finland first followed the Austrian and Swiss path after Jokela, but eventually changed course after another shooting in Kauhajoki. Accordingly, while we may conclude that institutional arrangements have a role to play in the political processing of rampage shootings, we cannot fully evaluate their relevance without taking into account factors operating at a lower level of abstraction. More precisely, in order to understand the variant policy impacts of rampage shootings, it is tantamount to consider both variant characteristics of the individual events and the activities of the involved political and societal actors. In this sense, the case studies demonstrated that different institutional environments tend to go hand in hand with different types of political reactions, but there are several cases which deviate from this overall pattern. As especially the evaluations on the theoretical expectations on the cohesion of reform opponents and varying degrees of societal mobilization have shown, we cannot understand the political developments in some institutional settings without paying attention to the actions taken by political and societal actors.

7.8.5 Additional insights

In addition to the findings discussed above, the case studies have also conveyed several extra insights which had not been anticipated at the outset. Two of these insights are particularly interesting and will be discussed in the remainder of this concluding section. First, the extent to which policy change occurred in the area of gun control was often critically determined by the issue's agenda status before the occurrence of the event. Second, the precise type of the murder weapon seems to be an important variable that should be evaluated more thoroughly by future studies.

160   *When laws bite the bullet*

The relevance of the a priori agenda status of gun control

The case studies jointly point to the conclusion that firearm-related policy change after rampage shootings occurs if the issue had already been on the political agenda before the occurrence of the shooting. In such situations, rampage shootings function as a catalyst for the political discourse and re-ignite public sentiment. Most importantly, the hurdles for policy change are now lower because the debate does not have to start from scratch. Instead, readymade policy solutions are available and only need to be taken out of the drawer. If this is the case, the political process can be accelerated, because the positions of all involved actors are already known. Several examples in this chapter support this argument empirically. For instance, the quick political reaction after the Erfurt shooting was critically influenced by the fact that the government had already been undertaking a major reform effort before the shooting. This reform effort had been launched after another rampage shooting – Bad Reichenhall – which had occurred three years earlier. In contrast to Erfurt, Bad Reichenhall had not led to a quick political reaction because the gun issue had not been on the political agenda. Similarly, the quick political reaction after the Antwerp shooting was strongly influenced by the fact that the Belgian government had repeatedly tried to update the country's outdated gun laws in the years before the shooting. Also in the Nanterre case, the gun control issue had been on the agenda before the shooting occurred. Of course, the most prominent example in this context is the Kauhajoki shooting, which hit Finland less than a year after the Jokela shooting. Due to this close temporal proximity, a political process that was in danger of getting stalled could be continued. In sum, it therefore seems reasonable to conclude that the agenda status of gun control prior to the shooting represents a highly important variable if we want to account for varying degrees of policy change.

Yet, this explanation as well is not without exceptions. Gun control has been a part of the political agenda in Switzerland for many years, but even the Zug shooting did not tilt the balance towards the reform proponents. Similarly, Austria had just finalized a major gun policy reform when the Mauterndorf case renewed public interest in the matter. As we have learned, however, the case nevertheless did not evoke a policy reaction. If we expanded the geographical focus to the United States, we would find a multitude of states which have been debating gun control for decades without adopting reforms despite repeated rampage shootings. Thus, while the agenda status of gun control seems to be of relevance in some cases, it is of lesser importance in others. The Swiss, Austrian and US examples cited here suggest that the extent to which a previously existing political debate over gun control facilitates policy change after a rampage shooting may strongly depend on the socio-cultural institutions of the affected country.

When laws bite the bullet 161

The relevance of the precise firearm type

When conceptualizing rampage shootings as the unit of analysis in section 2.1, it was stipulated that the shooting must have been carried out with a firearm, but no further distinction was made between different subtypes of firearms. Instead, a broad definition of firearms as any 'weapon from which a shot is discharged by gunpowder' (Merriam Webster Dictionary 2014) was used in order make clear that the book is not concerned with other types of rampage violence (e.g. acts committed with knives or vehicles). While this delineation was generally useful for the purposes of the empirical inquiry, it becomes apparent in retrospect that a more precise distinction between different types of firearms delivers additional insights. Specifically, it appears that the type of weapon used is strongly related to the scope of the ensuing reform efforts. While rampage shootings that were carried out with shotguns and/or (hunting) rifles hardly ever led to any political consequences, shootings that involved handguns had a much higher impact on gun control arrangements. Some shootings that were carried out with hunting rifles did not even spark a political debate over gun control, even if they resulted in a high number of fatalities (e.g. the shooting in Solliès-Pont/Cuers, France). The most prominent exception to this general rule is the shooting in Antwerp, which had high policy repercussions despite the fact that it was carried out with a hunting rifle. A comparison of the cases reveals, however, that the involvement of at least one handgun is strongly related to the development of the further political process. As soon as handguns are involved, gun control invariably gets politicized, although policies are not always changed. In any case, however, the chance that policy change eventually occurs is much higher if at least one of the murder weapons is a handgun. This is arguably due to the fact that handguns are often conceived of as more dangerous types of firearms than shotguns and rifles, because they can be concealed more easily. In addition, handguns are typically less available for the general population and accordingly, changing the rules governing their acquisition are not as consequential for the broad population. In contrast, hunting rifles and shotguns are more widely available in most European countries and therefore, related policy changes affect more people.

Notes

* Sections 7.1 Great Britain, 7.1.1 Dunblane: policy change under public pressure, 7.2 Germany, 7.2.2 Erfurt: policy change after negotiation and compromise, 7.6. Switzerland, 7.6.1 Zug: the elusiveness of policy change in Switzerland, of this chapter have been reproduced with the permission of Oxford University Press: Extracts from pp. 195–203 Ch. 10 'Handguns: On Target Towards Authority?' by Steffen Hurka from 'On the Road to Permissiveness? Change and Convergence of Moral Regulation in Europe' edited by Knill, Christoph, Adam, Christian & Hurka, Steffen (2015). Free permission: Author's own material.

1 A first step towards a national consolidation of the fragmented German gun rules had already been taken in 1968, but this law only affected gun dealers and producers, not the individual customer.

162 *When laws bite the bullet*

2 Some readers will notice that the school shooting in Emsdetten (2006) is not part of this discussion. This is due to the fact that the shooting did not meet all of the attributes of a rampage shooting, as it has been defined for the purposes of this book. Specifically, the shooting did not result in any fatalities other than the perpetrator.
3 Personal email communication with Atte Oksanen (University of Tampere) on 6 January 2014.
4 The plan to raise the minimum age was revived, however, after the second shooting in Kauhajoki.
5 The perpetrator had announced his plans online.
6 In the meantime, another rampage shooting in a shopping mall in Espoo on 31 December 2009 brought gun control back to the public spotlight. This time, however, it quickly became evident that the perpetrator's weapon had been illegal.
7 Décret-loi du 18 avril 1939 fixant le régime des matériels de guerre, armes, et munitions.
8 Loi n° 2003–239 du 18 mars 2003 pour la sécurité intérieure, Articles 80–85.
9 WaffG, §17 (1), 1 March 1967, BGBl. 121/1967.
10 In the most recent wave of the ICVS, Switzerland was overtaken by Finland (van Dijk *et al.* 2007: 279).
11 Loi relative à la fabrication, au commerce et au port des armes et au commerce des munitions.
12 Council Directive 91/477/EEC of 18 June 1991 on control of the acquisition and possession of weapons.

References

Albert, M.-D. (2002). Le président de la République lie le drame des Hauts-de-Seine au problème général de l'insécurité, *Le Figaro*, 28 March 2002.
Anderson, J. W. (2006). Belgians Seek Roots of Racist Crimes; String of Attacks on Foreigners Feeds Fears About Political Appeal of Intolerance, *Washington Post*, 20 May 2006.
Arzt, I. (2010). Vorsicht vor Reflexen, *die tageszeitung*, 22 September 2010.
Baber, M. (1997). *Prohibiting Handguns: the Firearms (Amendment) Bill [Bill 3 of 1997–98]*. London: House of Commons Library, Home Affairs Section.
Baumann, M. (2002). Der Fall Leibacher und seine Folgen – Die Sicherheitseinrichtungen in öffentlichen Gebäuden, *Neue Zürcher Zeitung*, 19 March 2002.
Bell, D. S. and Criddle, B. (2002). Presidentialism Restored: The French Elections of April–May and June 2002. *Parliamentary Affairs* 55(4), 643–663.
Berkol, I. (2006). Une nouvelle loi sur les armes en Belgique. Retrieved 10 July 2014 from www.grip.org/sites/grip.org/files/NOTES_ANALYSE/2006/NA_2006-05-29_FR_I-BERKOL.pdf.
Bistum Erfurt. (2002). Erfurter Appell. Retrieved 3 May 2014 from www.bistum-erfurt.de/front_content.php?client=2&lang=3&idcat=1840&idart=8560.
Broome, G., Butler-Manuel, A., Budd, J., Carter, P. G. and Warlow, T. A. (1988). The Hungerford Shooting Incident. *Injury* 19(5), 313–317.
Bundesverfassungsgericht. (2013). Verfassungsbeschwerden gegen das Waffengesetz erfolglos. Retrieved 2 May 2014 from www.bundesverfassungsgericht.de/pressemitteilungen/bvg13-008.html.
Campbell, D. (1996). Massacre Revives Anti-gun Group, *Guardian*, 15 July 1996.
Carter, H. (2011). Cumbrian Shootings Inquest Hears Details of Shooting Rampage, *Guardian*, 2 March 2011.

When laws bite the bullet 163

Casciani, D. (2010). Gun Control and Ownership Laws in the UK. Retrieved 26 October 2013 from www.bbc.co.uk/news/10220974.

Ceaux, P. (2002). Les enquêtes sur la mort de Richard Durn concluent à l'absence de fautes graves; La mère du tueur de Nanterre veut porter plainte, *Le Monde*, 9 April 2002.

Champion, G. (2006). Dunblane 10 Years On: School Security. Retrieved 3 April 2014 from http://news.bbc.co.uk/2/hi/uk_news/4798290.stm.

Cukier, W. and Sidel, V. W. (2006). *The Global Gun Epidemic – From Saturday Night Specials to AK-47s*. Westport: Praeger Security International.

Cullen, L. W. D. (1996). *The Public Inquiry into the Shooting at Dunblane Primary School on 13 March 1996*. London: Her Majesty's Stationary Office.

Davies, C., Carter, H., Carrell, S. and Travis, A. (2010). Front: Police Believe Grudges May Have Ignited Killing Spree: Tax Worries, Family Trouble and Row with Colleagues All Advanced as Theories. PM and Home Secretary Rule Out 'Kneejerk' Rush to Tighten Gun Regulations, *Guardian*, 4 June 2010.

de La Chesnais, E. and Hofstein, C. (2013). La chasse, deuxième sport en France après le foot. Retrieved 11 July 2014 from www.lefigaro.fr/actualite-france/2013/09/08/01016-20130908ARTFIG00024-la-chasse-deuxieme-sport-en-france-apres-le-foot.php?page=&pagination=1.

Deutsche Presse Agentur. (1999). Ein Hakenkreuz als Wandschmuck. Retrieved 25 April 2014 from www.welt.de/print-welt/article589212/Ein-Hakenkreuz-als-Wandschmuck.html.

Deutscher Bundestag. (2002). Plenarprotokoll 14/234: Deutscher Bundestag, Stenografischer Bericht. Retrieved 21 November 2016 from http://dip21.bundestag.de/dip21/btp/14/14234.pdf.

Deutscher Bundestag. (2009). Plenarprotokoll 16/210: Deutscher Bundestag, Stenografischer Bericht 210. Sitzung. Retrieved 2 May 2014 from http://dip21.bundestag.de/dip21/btp/16/16210.pdf.

Deutscher Bundestag. (2010). Antrag der Abgeordneten Wolfgang Wieland, Volker Beck (Köln), Kai Gehring, Ingrid Hönlinger, Memet Kilic, Jerzy Montag, Dr. Konstantin von Notz, Josef Philip Winkler und der Fraktion BÜNDNIS 90/DIE GRÜNEN: Mehr öffentliche Sicherheit durch weniger private Waffen. Retrieved 3 May 2014 from http://dipbt.bundestag.de/dip21/btd/17/021/1702130.pdf.

Deutscher Bundestag. (2013). Öffentliche Liste über die Registrierung von Verbänden und deren Vertretern. Retrieved 21 November 2016 from www.bundestag.de/parlament/lobbyliste.

Die Welt. (2010). Waffenrecht verschärfen?, *Die Welt*, 22 September 2010.

Downs, A. (1972). Up and Down with Ecology: The Issue Attention Cycle. *Public Interest* 28(1), 38–50.

Duquet, N. and Van Alstein, M. (2012). Gun Ownership in Belgium. Retrieved 11 April 2014 from www.vlaamsvredesinstituut.eu/sites/vlaamsvredesinstituut.eu/files/files/20120919_gun_ownership.pdf.

Ellerbrock, D. (2011). Gun Violence and Control in Germany 1880–1911: Scandalizing Gun Violence and Changing Perceptions as Preconditions for Firearm Control. In W. Heitmeyer, H.-G. Haupt, S. Malthaner and A. Kirschner (eds), *Control of Violence: Historical and International Perspectives on Violence in Modern Societies* (pp. 185–212). New York: Springer.

Expatica News. (2006a). MPs Give Green Light to New Gun Control Laws. Retrieved 10 July 2014 from www.expatica.com/be/news/local_news/mps-give-green-light-to-tighter-gun-control-laws-30144.html.

164 *When laws bite the bullet*

Expatica News. (2006b). Racist Shooting Rampage Shocks Antwerp. Retrieved 11 April 2014 from www.expatica.com/be/news/local_news/racist-shooting-rampage-shocks-antwerp-29955.html.

FAZ.NET. (2009a). Debatte nach dem Amoklauf: Schulen zu Festungen? Retrieved 2 May 2014 from www.faz.net/aktuell/politik/inland/debatte-nach-dem-amoklauf-schulen-zu-festungen-1925453.html.

FAZ.NET. (2009b). Verwirrung um psychotherapeutische Behandlung. Retrieved 2 May 2014 from www.faz.net/aktuell/gesellschaft/kriminalitaet/amoklaeufer-von-winnenden-verwirrung-um-psychotherapeutische-behandlung-1919963.html.

Federal Department of Justice and Police. (2004). Zusammenfassung der Ergebnisse des Vernehmlassungsverfahrens über den Vorentwurf zum Bundesgesetz über Waffen, Waffenzubehör und Munition. Retrieved 10 October 2014 from www.admin.ch/ch/d/gg/pc/documents/3/Ergebnisse_d.pdf.

Feikert-Ahalt, C. (2013). Firearms-Control Legislation and Policy: Great Britain. Retrieved 26 October 2013 from www.loc.gov/law/help/firearms-control/greatbritain.php.

Finkenzeller, R. (1999). Warum schießt ein Lehrling auf Menschen, die er zufällig sieht? Ratlosigkeit über das Tatmotiv nach dem Amoklauf in Bad Reichenhall. *Frankfurter Allgemeine Zeitung*, 3 November 1999.

Finland Ministry of Justice. (2009). Jokela School Shooting on 7 November 2007 – Report of the Investigation Commission (Translation of the original Finnish report). Retrieved 31 May 2013 from http://oikeusministerio.fi/sv/index/julkaisut/julkaisuarkisto/200901jokelaschoolshootingon7november20078211reportoftheinvestigationcommission.html.

Finland Ministry of Justice. (2010). Kauhajoki School Shooting on 23 September 2008 – Report of the Investigation Commission (Translation of the Finnish original report). Retrieved 18 May 2014 from www.oikeusministerio.fi/sv/index/julkaisut/julkaisuarkisto/392010kauhajokischoolshootingon23september2008-reportoftheinvestigationcommission.html.

Flash Eurobarometer No. 383. (2013). Firearms in the European Union. Retrieved 23 November 2013 from http://ec.europa.eu/public_opinion/flash/fl_383_en.pdf.

Frankfurter Allgemeine Sonntagszeitung. (1999). "Waffengesetz verschärfen", *Frankfurter Allgemeine Sonntagszeitung*, 7 November 1999.

Frankfurter Allgemeine Zeitung. (1999a). Jugendlicher ersticht Lehrerin vor den Augen der Mitschüler, *Frankfurter Allgemeine Zeitung*, 10 November 1999.

Frankfurter Allgemeine Zeitung. (1999b). Verschärfung des Waffenrechts gefordert, *Frankfurter Allgemeine Zeitung*, 13 November 1999.

Frankfurter Allgemeine Zeitung. (2009a). Bundestag verschärft Waffenrecht, *Frankfurter Allgemeine Zeitung*, 20 June 2009.

Frankfurter Allgemeine Zeitung. (2009b). Der Hergang, *Frankfurter Allgemeine Zeitung*, 12 March 2009.

Frankfurter Allgemeine Zeitung. (2009c). Kein 'Kniefall' vor der Waffenlobby, *Frankfurter Allgemeine Zeitung*, 13 May 2009.

Frankfurter Allgemeine Zeitung. (2009d). Schäuble lehnt schärferes Waffenrecht ab, *Frankfurter Allgemeine Zeitung*, 13 March 2009.

Frankfurter Allgemeine Zeitung. (2010). Neues Waffenrecht "ausreichend", *Frankfurter Allgemeine Zeitung*, 23 September 2010.

Ganghof, S. and Bräuninger, T. (2006). Government Status and Legislative Behaviour: Partisan Veto Players in Australia, Denmark, Finland and Germany. *Party Politics* 12(4), 521–539.

When laws bite the bullet 165

Grabherr, S., Johner, S., Dilitz, C., Buck, U., Killias, M., Mangin, P. and Plattner, T. (2010). Homicide-Suicide Cases in Switzerland and their Impact on the Swiss Weapon Law. *The American Journal of Forensic Medicine and Pathology* 31(4), 335–349.

Halbrook, S. P. (2003). Citizens in Arms: The Swiss Experience. *Texas Review of Law & Politics* 8(1), 141–174.

Hallikainen, V. (1995). The Social Wilderness in the Minds and Culture of the Finnish People. *International Journal of Wilderness* 1(1), 35–40.

Helsingin Sanomat International Edition. (2008a). Medical Association: Responsibility for Firearms Licences Should Remain with Police. Retrieved 24 May 2014 from www. hs.fi/english/article/Medical+Association+Responsibility+for+firearms+licences+should +remain+with+police/1135239879859.

Helsingin Sanomat International Edition. (2008b). Only a Few Shooting Ranges Available for Helsinki's Thousands of Handguns. Retrieved 24 May 2014 from www.hs.fi/ english/article/Only+a+few+shooting+ranges+available+for+Helsinkis+thousands+of+ handguns/1135240381932.

Helsingin Sanomat International Edition. (2008c). Prime Minister Open to Ban on Private Possession of Handguns. Retrieved 24 May 2014 from www.hs.fi/english/article/Prime +Minister+open+to+ban+on+private+possession+of+handguns/1135239698332.

Helsingin Sanomat International Edition. (2010). Handgun Ban Divides Parliamentary Group Leaders. Retrieved 24 May 2014 from www.hs.fi/english/article/Handgun+ban+ divides+Parliamentary+group+leaders/1135253050307.

Hollenstein, P. (2001). Streichung des Rechtes auf Waffenerwerb, Waffenbesitz und Waffentragen. Retrieved 10 October 2014 from www.parlament.ch/d/suche/seiten/ geschaefte.aspx?gesch_id=20013619.

Hurka, S. and Nebel, K. (2013). Framing and Policy Change after Shooting Rampages: A Comparative Analysis of Discourse Networks. *Journal of European Public Policy* 20(3), 390–406.

IWÖ. (2002). Waffen und Waffenrecht in Österreich: Eine Kurzinformation. Retrieved 10 October 2013 from www.iwoe.at/img/Information%20fuer%20Journalisten.pdf.

Käppner, J. (2010). Waffen in Privathaushalten sind Zeitbomben, *Süddeutsche Zeitung*, 22 September 2010.

Karp, A. (2003). Dunblane and the International Politics of Gun Control. In S. S. Nagel (ed.), *Policymaking and Peace – A Multinational Anthology* (pp. 193–211). Lanham: Lexington Books.

Karp, A. (2007). Completing the Count: Civilian Firearms. In S. A. Survey (ed.), *Small Arms Survey 2007: Guns and the City* (pp. 39–71). Cambridge: Cambridge University Press.

Keine Mordwaffen als Sportwaffen! (2009a). Gründung der Initiative/Schulverweigerung. Retrieved 2 May 2014 from www.sportmordwaffen.de/gruendunginitiative.html.

Keine Mordwaffen als Sportwaffen! (2009b). Unterschriften-Übergabe im Bundestag. Retrieved 2 May 2014 from www.sportmordwaffen.de/unterschriftenuebergabe.html.

Kingdon, J. W. (1984). *Agendas, Alternatives, and Public Policies*. Boston: Little, Brown.

Kingdon, J. W. (2003). *Agendas, Alternatives, and Public Policies* (2nd edn). New York: Longman.

Kister, K. (2002). Menschen töten, Waffen auch, *Süddeutsche Zeitung*, 30 April 2002.

Kopel, D. B. (1992). *The Samurai, the Mountie, and the Cowboy: Should America Adopt the Gun Controls of Other Democracies?* Buffalo: Prometheus Books.

Krach, W. (1999). Der Martin war immer nett, *DER SPIEGEL 45/1999*, 8 November 1999.

166   *When laws bite the bullet*

Langman, P. (2012). Two Finnish School Shooters. Retrieved 18 May 2014 from http:// schoolshooters.info/PL/Articles_files/Two%20Finnish%20School%20Shooters.pdf.

Le Monde. (2002a). La carabine utilisée par le tireur est une arme en vente libre, *Le Monde*, 16 July 2002.

Le Monde. (2002b). Le Tueur de Nanterre s'est suicidé, *Le Monde*, 29 March 002.

Leuffen, D. (2009). Does Cohabitation Matter? French European Policy-Making in the Context of Divided Government. *West European Politics* 32(6), 1140–1160.

Liem, M., Ganpat, S., Granath, S., Hagstedt, J., Kivivuori, J., Lehti, M. and Nieuwbeerta, P. (2013). Homicide in Finland, the Netherlands, and Sweden: First Findings From the European Homicide Monitor. *Homicide Studies* 17(1), 75–95.

Lijphart, A. (1999). *Patterns of Democracy: Government Forms and Performance in Thirty-Six Countries*. New Haven and London: Yale University Press.

Lijphart, A. (2012). *Patterns of Democracy: Government Forms and Performance in Thirty-Six Countries* (2nd edn). New Haven and London: Yale University Press.

Lilly, J. R. (2001). Constructing a 'Dangerous Gun Culture' in Britain – New Gun Control Laws, 1997. In J. Best (ed.), *How Claims Spread: Cross-National Diffusion of Social Problems* (pp. 69–88). New York: De Gruyter.

Lindström, K., Räsänen, P., Oksanen, A. and Nurmi, J. (2011). Politiikkaprosessi ja aselainsäädännön uudistaminen Jokelan ja Kauhajoen koulusurmien jälkeen. In J. Saari and M. Niemelä (eds), *Politiikan polut ja hyvinvointiyhteiskunnan muutos* (pp. 254–271). Helsinki: Kela.

Malcolm, J. L. (2002). *Guns and Violence: The English Experience*. Cambridge: Harvard University Press.

Merki, M. (2001). Mehr Sicherheit heisst weniger Freiheit – Offene Verwaltung in Zug einschränken?, *Neue Zürcher Zeitung*, 29 September 2001.

Merriam Webster Dictionary. (2014). Firearm. Retrieved 27 February 2014 from www. merriam-webster.com/dictionary/firearm.

Morris, N. (2010). PM Rules out 'Knee-jerk' Reaction; The Politics, *The Independent*, 4 June 2010.

Morris, N. (2011). May Accused of Delaying Overhaul of Gun Laws over Delay in Tightening Gun Laws, *The Independent*, 2 August 2011.

Morris, N. (2012). MPs call for stricter checks on firearms, *The Independent*, 4 January 2012.

Nationalrat. (1997). Stenographisches Protokoll: 107. Sitzung des Nationalrates der Republik Österreich, XX. Gesetzgebungsperiode. Retrieved 10 April 2014 from www. parlament.gv.at/PAKT/VHG/XX/NRSITZ/NRSITZ_00107/fname_114203.pdf.

New York Times. (2007). Belgian Man Sentenced to Life in Prison for Racially Motivated Attack. Retrieved 11 April 2014 from www.nytimes.com/2007/10/11/world/ europe/11iht-belgium.4.7856486.html.

Oberösterreichische Nachrichten. (1997). Schock und Trauer nach dem Amoklauf, *Oberösterreichische Nachrichten*, 22 November 1997.

Oberösterreichische Nachrichten. (1998). Waffenbesitz: Vier von sechs Österreichern plädieren für ein Verbot, *Oberösterreichische Nachrichten*, 22 January 1998.

Oksanen, A., Nurmi, J., Vuori, M. and Räsänen, P. (2013). Jokela: The Social Roots of a School Shooting Tragedy in Finland. In N. Böckler, T. Seeger, P. Sitzer and W. Heitmeyer (eds), *School Shootings: International Research, Case Studies, and Concepts for Prevention* (pp. 189–215). New York: Springer.

Oksanen, A., Räsänen, P., Nurmi, J. and Lindström, K. (2010). 'This Can't Happen Here!' Community Reactions to School Shootings in Finland. *Research on Finnish Society* 3(1), 19–27.

Parker, S. (2011). Balancing Act: Regulation of Civilian Firearm Possession. In Small Arms Survey (ed.), *Small Arms Survey 2011: States of Security*. Cambridge: Cambridge University Press.

Parlamentskorrespondenz 810. (1997). Innenausschuss diskutiert Verschärfung des Waffengesetzes. Retrieved 10 April 2014 from www.parlament.gv.at/PAKT/PR/JAHR_1997/PK0810/index.shtml.

Pilger, J. (1996). The Dunblanes that Are Never News. Retrieved 11 April 2013 from www.greenleft.org.au/node/11868.

Raittila, P., Koljonen, K. and Väliverronen, J. (2010). *Journalism and School Shootings in Finland 2007–2008*. Tampere: Tampere University Press.

Reuters.com. (2007). Finland to Toughen Gun Rules after School Shooting. Retrieved 11 May 2014 from www.reuters.com/article/2007/11/09/us-finland-shooting-policy-idUSL0958215520071109.

Riding, A. (2002). Gunman Who Fired at French Leader Is in Mental Hospital, *New York Times*, 16 July 2002.

Rowe, M. (1997). Snowdrop Withers but Battle to Curb Guns Lives On, *Independent*, 2 May 1997.

Salzburg24.at. (2007). Amoklauf von Mauterndorf jährt sich zum zehnten Mal. Retrieved 2 August 2013 from www.salzburg24.at/amoklauf-von-mauterndorf-jaehrt-sich-zum-zehnten-mal/news-20071114-01161438.

Scheithauer, H. and Bondü, R. (2011). *Amoklauf und School Shooting. Bedeutung, Hintergründe und Prävention*. Göttingen: Vandenhoeck & Ruprecht.

Schwaab, J. J. (2001). 01.3606 – Motion: Kontrolle der Schusswaffen. Retrieved 10 October 2014 from www.parlament.ch/d/suche/seiten/geschaefte.aspx?gesch_id=20013606.

Siaroff, A. (2003). Varieties of Parliamentarism in the Advanced Industrial Democracies. *International Political Science Review* 24(4), 445–464.

Sicherheitspolitische Kommission. (2000). Waffengesetz. Änderung. Retrieved 10 October 2014 from www.parlament.ch/d/suche/seiten/geschaefte.aspx?gesch_id=20003603.

Soldt, R. (2010). 39 Minuten Ausnahmezustand, *Frankfurter Allgemeine Zeitung*, 21.09.2010.

Soldt, R. and Eppelsheim, P. (2009). Und niemand weiß, warum, *Frankfurter Allgemeine Zeitung*, 12 March 2009.

Squires, P. (2000). *Gun Culture or Gun Control? Firearms, Violence and Society*. London: Routledge.

Stoisits, T., Petrovic, M. and Colleagues. (1998). Entschließungsantrag betreffend Novelle zum Waffengesetz (656/AE XX.GP). Retrieved 11 April 2014 from www.parlament.gv.at/PAKT/VHG/XX/A/A_00656/fname_124994.pdf.

Swiss Federal Council. (2001). Stellungnahme des Bundesrates vom 21.11.2001. Retrieved 10 October 2014 from www.parlament.ch/d/suche/Seiten/geschaefte.aspx?gesch_id=20013619.

Tabermann, J. (2011). Moralpanik eller förnuftslogik – i Jokela-fallets diskursiva efterdyningar. *Faculty of Social Sciences, Department of Social Studies*. Retrieved 15 February 2011 from https://helda.helsinki.fi/handle/10138/24880.

Tagesanzeiger. (2001). Ruf nach einem schärferen Waffengesetz wird lauter, *Tagesanzeiger*, 1 October 2001.

Tanner, J. (2007). Finland Defends Gun Laws. Retrieved 17 May 2014 from www.washingtonpost.com/wp-dyn/content/article/2007/11/09/AR2007110901224_pf.html.

168 *When laws bite the bullet*

Tedmanson, S. (2008). Finland to Review Gun Laws after 'YouTube' Gunman Massacre. Retrieved 12 May 2013 from www.thetimes.co.uk/tto/news/world/europe/article2597907.ece.

The Times. (1996). After Dunblane, *The Times*, 15 March 1996.

Thomson, S., Stancich, L. and Dickson, L. (1998). Gun Control and Snowdrop. *Parliamentary Affairs* 51(3), 329–344.

Travis, A. (2010). The Loopholes in Britain's Gun Laws. Retrieved 26 October 2013 from www.theguardian.com/uk/2010/jun/03/cumbria-gun-laws-licensing.

Tsebelis, G. (2002). *Veto Players: How Political Institutions Work*. Princeton: Princeton University Press.

Väliverronen, J., Koljonen, K. and Raittila, P. (2012). Vital Explanations or Harmful Gossip? Finnish Journalists' Reflections on Reporting the Interpretations of Two School Shootings. In G. W. Muschert and J. Sumiala (eds), *School Shootings: Mediatized Violence in a Global Age (Studies in Media and Communications, Volume 7)* (pp. 161–180). Bingley: Emerald Books.

van Dijk, J., van Kesteren, J. and Smit, P. (2007). Criminal Victimisation in International Perspective – Key Findings from the 2004–2005 ICVS and EU ICS. Retrieved 11 September 2013 from www.unicri.it/services/library_documentation/publications/icvs/publications/ICVS2004_05report.pdf.

Waffen weg! (1998). UnterstützerInnen. Retrieved 11 April 2014 from http://gue.members.cablelink.at/promoter.htm.

Waffen weg! (1999). Info. Retrieved 10 April 2014 from http://gue.members.cablelink.at/info.htm.

Wainwright, M. (2010). Police Had no Grounds to Ban Killer's Guns, Says Report, *Guardian*, 3 November 2010.

Webster, D. (1989). 'Whodunnit? America Did': Rambo and Post-Hungerford Rhetoric. *Cultural Studies* 3(2), 173–193.

Williams, A. (2012). Hungerford Massacre: Reluctant Remembrance 25 Years On. Retrieved 3 April 2013 from www.bbc.co.uk/news/uk-england-berkshire-19208380.

YLE.fi. (2007). Finland Drops Objections to EU Firearms Directive. Retrieved 17 May 2014 from http://yle.fi/uutiset/finland_drops_objections_to_eu_firearms_directive/5808785.

YLE.fi. (2010). No Ban on Semiautomatic Weapons, Despite Recommendation. Retrieved 24 May 2014 from http://yle.fi/uutiset/no_ban_on_semiautomatic_weapons_despite_recommendation/1777018.

YLE.fi. (2011). Parties at Odds over Gun Law Reform. Retrieved 17 May 2014 from http://yle.fi/uutiset/parties_at_odds_over_gun_law_reform/5396349.

Zeit Online. (2010). Amoklauf entfacht Debatte über das Waffenrecht. Retrieved 3 May 2014 from www.zeit.de/politik/deutschland/2010-09/loerrach-waffenrecht-verbot.

8 Conclusion

Rampage shootings are phenomena that have spread across the globe since the end of the 1980s. While the large majority of these events still occurs in the United States of America, other countries have also increasingly been haunted by acts of rampage violence committed with legally acquired firearms during the past decades. Unfortunately, the scientific analysis of rampage violence has not kept up with this empirical development within the discipline of political science. While rampage shootings have been subject to academic inquires in many neighbouring disciplines, such as psychology (e.g. Verlinden *et al.* 2000), criminology (e.g. Levin and Madfis 2009) and sociology (e.g. Harding *et al.* 2002), the varying impacts of rampage shootings on gun policies have not been analysed systematically and in a comparative manner, yet. The little research that exists not only displays a strong geographical bias towards the United States, which represents an extreme outlier case as far as gun control arrangements are concerned, but also focuses primarily on school shootings only (Schildkraut and Cox Hernandez 2014). While some intriguing insights into the dynamics of rampage shootings have been gained in this research, the narrow empirical focus has hindered scientific progress towards a more comprehensive understanding of the varying political consequences of potential focusing events in general and rampage shootings in particular. In particular, this line of research could not answer the question of why sufficiently similar events often have quite diverse political consequences. This is the research question this book addressed.

By focusing on Western Europe, this book challenges some conventional wisdom resulting from the repeated failure of policy makers in the United States to draw lessons from policy failures in the area of gun policy. In particular, this conventional wisdom suggests that even after the most devastating focusing events, public and political attention will fade before meaningful legislative action can be taken (Downs 1972). As an empirical manifestation of this pattern, existing research has shown that the public typically embraces stricter gun control in the immediate aftermath of rampage shootings to a larger extent than before, but this spike in public opinion invariably disappears after a short period of time has passed (Birkland and Lawrence 2009). This pattern is typical for the political aftermath of rampage shootings in the United States, as the most recent gruesome shootings in Aurora (2012), Newtown (2012), San Bernardino (2015)

170   *Conclusion*

and Orlando (2016) impressively demonstrated. At least on the national level, all attempts to strengthen gun control after these shootings failed. For most people in the rest of the world, the repeated failure of the United States to introduce even the most common-sense measures such as universal background checks, is stunning. However, the dominant focus on rampage shootings in the United States by researchers, the media and the public in general obstructs our view on the fact that rampage violence is not an exclusively American phenomenon. While events that are comparable in scope to the shootings cited above are rare outside of the United States, they have occurred (Lankford 2016) and they have resulted in much more variant political consequences than the ones in the United States. Therefore, this book argued that if we want to learn more about the circumstances under which rampage violence actually impacts upon political processes, we must shift our focus towards other countries.

By providing the first systematic cross-national comparison of the varying political processes triggered by rampage shootings in Western Europe, this book contributes to the research program on the factors driving politicization and policy change. Specifically, the book systematically analysed the politicization processes triggered by 17 rampage shootings which have occurred in Western Europe between 1990 and 2010. This part of the book addressed the question of why rampage shootings are sometimes immediately identified as a policy failure resulting from dysfunctional gun control measures, while they pass by without a political debate at other times. Moreover, the cases which led to a political debate over gun control were studied in greater detail in case studies in order to understand why some political debates led to changes in the affected country's regulatory frameworks for firearms, while other debates petered out without any legislative consequences. This concluding chapter summarizes the lessons we can draw from this empirical inquiry and outlines avenues for future research.

Building on various theories of policy change, the book developed a range of theoretical expectations on factors deemed to be responsible for the politicization of gun control as the central policy failure after a rampage shooting and the factors that might facilitate or impede reform efforts once politicization has occurred. In so doing, the book deliberately left room for plausible interactions between the theoretical arguments. With regard to politicization, it was argued that the extent to which political actors are willing to engage in a political debate over gun control might depend on four factors: the event's severity in terms of damage done, the event's severity as perceived and portrayed by the news media, the existence of a partisan cleavage on the gun issue, and the event's timing in the electoral calendar.

Given the medium number of cases, the theoretical approach and the straightforward possibility to translate the discussed theoretical concepts into set-theoretic language, the first research question on politicization was addressed methodologically by the application of fuzzy set Qualitative Comparative Analysis (Ragin 2000). The analysis led to a range of intriguing insights into the patterns of politicization (and its absence) after rampage shootings. It was found

Conclusion 171

that there are essentially two paths that link the occurrence of a rampage shooting to the politicization of gun control. The paths were labelled the 'top down' path and the 'bottom up' path respectively. Events which follow the first logic get politicized if a party that owns gun control is represented in the affected country's national parliament and if national elections are not imminent. Contrary to the conventional wisdom that policymaking typically try to exploit crises to their electoral benefit, it seems like the calculations made by political actors in this regard are somewhat more nuanced. If elections are temporally proximate, political actors apparently rather refrain from politicizing rampage shootings (especially those of a comparably small magnitude) in order to avoid blame for trying to score political points during times of national grief. In contrast, if elections are far away, green parties find it easier to challenge the policy status quo. Yet, sometimes the decision of whether or not a political debate is in order is not completely in the hands of politicians. This occurs if events become politicized 'bottom-up'. If an event is particularly severe in terms of its number of fatalities and if the news media simultaneously devote a disproportional amount of attention to the event, policy makers are hardly left with a choice. In such a scenario, the event is simply too powerful to be absorbed by the political system. Yet, it is important to note that the argument only holds if both high objective severity and high media attention are present. If an event is objectively severe but ignored by the media, politicization does not necessarily occur, as the shooting in Solliès-Pont/Cuers demonstrates.

Which factors are responsible for the occurrence of policy change and policy stability in the aftermath of rampage shootings? In the second empirical part, this question was addressed by means of 12 comparative case studies on the events that led to a political debate. Chapter 7 put the analytical focus on a range of theoretical arguments designed to address this puzzle, yet not all of these arguments eventually proved helpful in order to explain cross-national variance in policy making. First, it was argued that the extent to which states change their gun laws in response to rampage shootings should be related to the number of causal stories that can be attached to the event. According to this logic, the more causal stories compete for public and political attention, the more difficult it will become for advocates favouring policy change in the area of gun control to focus the political debate in their favour. If multiple causal stories can be reasonably activated in order to explain the occurrence of a given rampage shooting, the less likely the broad acceptance of the gun control story should become and the chances for a deadlock of the political process increase. Second, it was argued that while a rampage shooting typically reinforces and solidifies the coalition of reform proponents in the area of gun control, the critical question for policy change should be whether or not the coalition of reform opponents can remain cohesive in its resistance to policy change. Specifically, it was argued that the more important political actors defect from their coalition of reform opponents, the more difficult it will become for the reform opponents to prevent or contain reform dynamics. Third, the theoretical part of the book argued that it takes sustained societal demand for policy change after a focusing event in order to break

172 *Conclusion*

the 'issue attention cycle' (Downs 1972) and keep gun control on the agenda for a sufficient period of time for policy change to occur. If the public turns its attention away from the event and its policy implications quickly, political attention will also eventually fade and the prospects for policy change diminish. Finally, the theory chapter put forward two institutional arguments on policy change and stability. On the one hand, it was argued that rapid political reactions should be more likely if the affected country's political system features low requirements for consensus building and places much power into the hands of the executive (Lijphart 2012; Siaroff 2003). On the other hand, it was argued that institutional hurdles are not necessarily only of a political nature. It may as well be the case that the socio-cultural background relevant for the affected policy area could play a decisive role for the output of the political processes following focusing events. In other words, it was expected that policy change after a focusing event should be particularly difficult to attain if the arrangements governing the challenged policy program is strongly enshrined in the cultural legacy of the affected nation. In order to evaluate these propositions empirically, the second empirical part of the book featured 12 case studies on the politicized events, analysing the political process in light of the theoretical expectations outlined above.

The case studies lent empirical support to some, but not all of the theoretical expectations, and they did so to varying extents. As regards the role of the events' perceived causal complexity, the case studies provided a very unsystematic picture. In fact, the empirical evidence broadly suggests that the factor is not decisive for the way focusing events are processed politically and their outcomes in terms of policy change. Both events of high and low causal complexity led to high and low levels of policy change, which implies that we must shift our focus to other factors. One of these factors is the way various political actors position themselves in the immediate aftermath of a rampage shooting. The case studies suggest that the extent to which reform opponents manage to keep their ranks closed and avoid defections in the immediate aftermath of a rampage shooting is strongly related to the way the further political process unfolds. In several instances, actors who we would have expected to defend the status quo in the area of gun policy quickly switched sides in response to a rampage shooting. The extent to which this was done strategically or sincerely varies between the individual cases. In some instances, early concessions took the wind out of the sails of the reform movement and incremental adjustments were made. In other instances, early concessions only fuelled the activity of the reform movement if these concessions were considered too small. Thus, the way political actors position themselves within the first few days after a rampage shooting is critically important for the further political process. What is even more important, however, are the developments triggered by a focusing event on the societal level. If societal actors do not manage to rally the media and the public behind their policy goals and demand policy change in a sustained manner, the gun control issue often fades from public conscience very quickly and policy arrangements remain stable. If, on the other hand, societal mobilization occurs, the odds for policy change increase. While this rule is not without exceptions,

Conclusion 173

the argument on the importance of broad societal mobilization for the occurrence of policy change after rampage shootings seems to bear the most explanatory power. As far as institutional factors are concerned, it was found that the interplay of political and socio-cultural hurdles for policy change can only explain the outcomes of a part of the analysed cases. These structural conditions sometimes led to a political deadlock if they were configured unfavourably, and sometimes facilitated the political process if the decision hurdles they implied were rather low. However, we found several exceptions to this rule, suggesting that while institutional environments broadly structure the capacity of political actors to change the regulatory status quo, the dedication of these actors and the extent to which society demands policy change in a sustained manner are crucial explanatory factors if we want to account for deviant cases. Therefore, in order to understand the complex political processes triggered by potential focusing events, it is indispensable to evaluate the interplay of actors within their specific institutional environments.

Finally, the empirical evidence presented in this book clearly supports the finding by other scholars that 'even in the wake of destabilizing crisis episodes, incremental rather than radical change is the name of the game in pluralistic polities' (Boin *et al*. 2009: 100). With the exception of the shooting in Dunblane, no shooting that occurred in Europe ever led to large-scale prohibitive measures in the area of gun control. If at all, policy changes focused on personal restrictions for gun owners or procedural rules for the storage of firearms (see also Hurka (2015)). Although the prohibition of certain weapon types was considered by policy makers in some instances, corresponding reform efforts were either abandoned or diluted during the political process. To a certain extent, the reasons for this general pattern probably lie in the relatively high consensus requirements inherent in most Western European political systems. While the most encompassing policy change to date occurred in a political system that places enormous power into the hands of the government (Great Britain), incremental policy changes have taken place where the executive faces more constraints during the legislative process. Yet, a more thorough test of this argument is complicated by relatively little cross-national variance in Western Europe as far as executive dominance is concerned.

On a general level, the book contributes to the ongoing debate over the relevance of (potential) focusing events for the progress of public policy (Birkland 1997, 1998; Boin *et al*. 2009; Jensen 2011; Kingdon 2003). Most importantly, the book puts forward the argument that in trying to understand the progress of public policies, we should not conceptualize potential focusing events as components of the 'error term', i.e. unpredictable and random aberrations of an otherwise linear process. Instead, we should conceive of potential focusing events within a given policy area as shocks that challenge the established policy order and study the political processes triggered by these events in a comparative manner (Emmenegger 2010). We may never be able to foresee the occurrence of certain types of focusing events, but we may be able to arrive at an understanding of the scope conditions relevant for their political processing once they have

174 *Conclusion*

occurred. This book is an attempt to contribute to this line of inquiry, focusing on a specific class of events and a specific policy area. Future studies may want to build on the insights gained in this book and expand the empirical focus both to other types of events and areas of public policy. In general, the factors that drive the politicization of policy failures and ensuing reform dynamics in other policy areas may be very similar to the ones identified in this book. Yet, while it is conceivable that potential focusing events occur in (re-)distributive policy areas, they are most likely to occur in areas of regulatory policy. In particular, policy areas that regulate individual human conduct are arguably most prone to the types of events discussed in this book. For instance, parallel to the patterns unravelled above, the extent to which moral shocks influence political debates within areas of social regulatory (or morality) policy (Knill *et al.* 2015; Tatalovich and Daynes 2011) may depend on the affected country's partisan cleavages and the timing of the shock in the electoral cycle. Whenever some deviant human behaviour can be construed as the consequence of a policy failure and becomes the subject of sudden increases of public attention, potential focusing events can become real focusing events and change the course of public policies. The list of relevant examples is long and includes diverse events such as the discovery of child pornography on the hard drive of a prominent politician or revelations about the illegal provision of euthanasia by a physician.[1] These random examples of deviant human behaviour imply a certain potential for politicization and policy change, but the extent to which the latter actually materialize in different contexts is hardly understood. In this sense, this book sought to lay a foundation for a more systematic inquiry into the processes governing political reactions to focusing events.

Yet, in order to understand the policy impact of focusing events, we may not narrow our analytical focus down to events that actually had an impact. While the temptation to pursue such a strategy is understandable, it involves substantial analytical pitfalls. Most importantly, we may run the danger of attributing an inflated amount of explanatory power to focusing events if we ignore *potential* focusing events, i.e. events that fulfil all requirements of a focusing event, but eventually did not entail any political consequences. Put bluntly, we are much better at explaining things that happened than things that did not happen. While the identification of these 'non-events' is a difficult endeavour, this book has hopefully demonstrated that doing so nonetheless is worth the effort. We must start to compare sufficiently similar events with varying impact on public policies systematically in order to avoid the trap of confirmation bias. In the long run, it should not satisfy the research community to resort to the identification of an external shock if existing theories fail to provide a good understanding of the political process. In other words, it is almost always possible to identify an external shock in retrospect and hold it responsible for a certain political development (Capano 2009; Nohrstedt and Weible 2010). If we do so, however, we quickly lose sight of the many comparable instances which did not change the course in the respective policy area, although such change would have been equally possible. Accordingly, future research should resist the temptation of solely arguing

Conclusion 175

that focusing events matter, but instead try to find out which events matter under which circumstances and for which political outcomes.

Thus, the research community should continue to explore the varying political consequences of deviant human behaviour, a phenomenon which has so far primarily been studied in neighbouring academic disciplines, such as psychology and criminology. While the findings provided by these studies have greatly enhanced our understanding of the causes of deviant human behaviour, comparative political science can add substantially to the big picture by explaining its societal and political consequences. In so doing, we may be able to better understand the conditions which structure political responses to sudden and disruptive crisis episodes.

Note

1 Both examples have actually occurred in Germany within the past years and led to varying degrees of politicization and policy change. While Germany recently changed its definition of child pornography in response to the first incident, the appropriateness of German euthanasia regulations also triggered public and political debates in the wake of the latter event.

References

Birkland, T. A. (1997). *After Disaster – Agenda Setting, Public Policy, and Focusing Events*. Washington, D.C.: Georgetown University Press.

Birkland, T. A. (1998). Focusing Events, Mobilization, and Agenda Setting. *Journal of Public Policy* 18(1), 53–74.

Birkland, T. A. and Lawrence, R. G. (2009). Media Framing and Policy Change After Columbine. *American Behavioral Scientist* 52(10), 1405–1425.

Boin, A., t'Hart, P. and McConnell, A. (2009). Crisis Exploitation: Political and Policy Impacts of Framing Contests. *Journal of European Public Policy* 16(1), 81–106.

Capano, G. (2009). Understanding Policy Change as an Epistemological and Theoretical Problem. *Journal of Comparative Policy Analysis: Research and Practice* 11(1), 7–31.

Downs, A. (1972). Up and Down with Ecology: The Issue Attention Cycle. *Public Interest* 28(1), 38–50.

Emmenegger, P. (2010). Non-Events in Macro-Comparative Social Research: Why We Should Care and How We Can Analyze Them. *COMPASSS Working Paper Series 2010–60.*

Harding, D. J., Fox, C. and Mehta, J. D. (2002). Studying Rare Events Through Qualitative Case Studies: Lessons from a Study of Rampage School Shootings. *Sociological Methods & Research* 31(2), 174–217.

Hurka, S. (2015). Handguns: on Target towards Authority? In C. Knill, C. Adam and S. Hurka (eds), *On the Road to Permissiveness? Change and Convergence of Moral Regulation in Europe*. Oxford: Oxford University Press.

Jensen, C. (2011). Focusing Events, Policy Dictators and the Dynamics of Reform. *Policy Studies* 32(2), 143–158.

Kingdon, J. W. (2003). *Agendas, Alternatives, and Public Policies* (2nd edn). New York: Longman.

176 Conclusion

Knill, C., Adam, C. and Hurka, S. (eds). (2015). *On the Road to Permissiveness? Change and Convergence of Moral Regulation in Europe*. Oxford: Oxford University Press.

Lankford, A. (2016). Public Mass Shooters and Firearms: A Cross-National Study of 171 Countries. *Violence and Victims* 31(2), 187–199.

Levin, J. and Madfis, E. (2009). Mass Murder at School and Cumulative Strain: A Sequential Model. *American Behavioral Scientist* 52(9), 1227–1245.

Lijphart, A. (2012). *Patterns of Democracy: Government Forms and Performance in Thirty-Six Countries* (2nd edn). New Haven and London: Yale University Press.

Nohrstedt, D. and Weible, C. M. (2010). The Logic of Policy Change after Crisis: Proximity and Subsystem Interaction. *Risk, Hazards & Crisis in Public Policy* 1(2), 1–32.

Ragin, C. C. (2000). *Fuzzy-Set Social Science*. Chicago: University of Chicago Press.

Schildkraut, J. and Cox Hernandez, T. (2014). Laws that Bit the Bullet: A Review of Legislative Responses to School Shootings. *American Journal of Criminal Justice* 39(2), 358–374.

Siaroff, A. (2003). Varieties of Parliamentarianism in the Advanced Industrial Democracies. *International Political Science Review* 24(4), 445–464.

Tatalovich, R. and Daynes, B. W. (eds). (2011). *Moral Controversies in American Politics* (4th edn). Armonk: M. E. Sharpe.

Verlinden, S., Hersen, M. and Thomas, J. (2000). Risk Factors in School Shootings. *Clinical Psychology Review* 20(1), 3–56.

Appendix A
Non-selected cases

In order to be fully transparent about the case selection (or identification) procedure, it is broadly considered best practice to justify the non-selection of cases (Schneider and Wagemann 2010: 5). Table A.1 lists all cases which fulfil all but one of the scope conditions specified in the book and are accordingly not considered in the comparative analysis. Only rampages shootings which were carried out with firearms are listed.

Table A.1 Non-selected cases

Country	Event	Date	Reason for exclusion
Finland	Espoo	31 December 2009	Illegally acquired weapon
Germany/France	Dillingen/Sierck-les-Bains	16 May 1999	Illegally acquired weapon
Germany	Freising	19 February 2002	Illegally acquired weapons
Spain	Puerto Hurraco	26 August 1990	Illegal weapons
Sweden	Falun	11 June 1994	Non-civilian perpetrator
Sweden	Stockholm	4 December 1994	Illegal weapon
Switzerland	Rivera, Massagno & Origlio	4 March 1992	Sub-national legislative authority

Appendix B
Robustness checks for the analysis of politicization

In this appendix, the intermediate solution terms we obtain by changing the thresholds for set membership within the individual conditions are presented. The reader is asked to bear in mind that different thresholds should, in fact, have a certain impact on the results. If coding instructions are changed in for a statistical analysis, the data change and accordingly, the results change as well. The critical yardstick in the evaluation of the robustness checks should therefore be whether or not the initially obtained solution term is changed in its substance or whether it only becomes more complex or parsimonious when different thresholds are introduced.

To keep the complexity of this appendix within reasonable bounds, I constrain myself to the reporting of the intermediate solutions and keep the simplifying assumptions identical to the ones I made in the book. Moreover, the robustness checks below only change one threshold at a time and keep the calibration of the remaining sets constant. Finally, only the 0.5-threshold is changed, since this threshold determines the qualitative distinction between the cases ('difference in kind'), while the thresholds of full membership or full non-membership determine quantitative distinctions ('differences in degree'). In a nutshell, the results of the robustness checks show that the two paths towards politicization identified in the book remain stable if we change the setting of the 0.5-thresholds within reasonable bounds. In some cases, we obtain an additional path, consisting of the combination of high media attention and the parliamentary representation of a green party as a sufficient causal combination for politicization.

Table A.2 Results for varying 0.5-thresholds in the DEATH set

	Intermediate solutions	Raw coverage	Unique coverage	Consistency
DEATH: reported results				
Full membership: 14	~E*G	0.56	0.32	0.95
0.5-threshold: 7	+			
Non-membership: 3	D*M	0.59	0.34	0.97
	Consistency cut-off: 0.85			
	Solution coverage: 0.90			
	Solution consistency: 0.97			
DEATH: alternative results				
Full membership: 14	~E*G**D**	0.30	0.04	0.92
0.5-threshold: 5	+			
Non-membership: 3	D*M	0.62	0.16	0.97
	+			
	M*G	0.63	0.18	0.93
	Consistency cut-off: 0.79			
	Solution coverage: 0.83			
	Solution consistency: 0.97			
Full membership: 14	~E*G	0.56	0.14	0.95
0.5-threshold: 9	+			
Non-membership: 3	D*M	0.53	0.15	0.97
	+			
	M*G	0.63	0.04	0.97
	Consistency cut-off: 0.84			
	Solution coverage: 0.92			
	Solution consistency: 0.97			
Full membership: 14	~E*G	0.56	0.14	0.95
0.5-threshold: 11	+			
Non-membership: 3	D*M	0.48	0.14	0.96
	+			
	M*G	0.63	0.05	0.97
	Consistency cut-off: 0.85			
	Solution coverage: 0.91			
	Solution consistency: 0.97			

Note
Changes printed in bold. Simplifying assumptions: G→P; D→P; M→P; E→P.

Table A.3 Results for varying 0.5-thresholds in the MEDIA set

	Intermediate solutions	Raw coverage	Unique coverage	Consistency
MEDIA: reported results				
Full membership: 63	~E*G	0.56	0.32	0.95
0.5-threshold: 21	+			
Non-membership: 7	D*M	0.59	0.34	0.97
	Consistency cut-off: 0.85			
	Solution coverage: 0.90			
	Solution consistency: 0.97			
MEDIA: alternative results				
Full membership: 63	~E*G	0.56	0.31	0.95
0.5-threshold: 15	+			
Non-membership: 7	D*M	0.60	0.34	0.96
	Consistency cut-off: 0.84			
	Solution coverage: 0.90			
	Solution consistency: 0.97			
Full membership: 63	~E*G	0.56	0.32	0.95
0.5-threshold: 30	+			
Non-membership: 7	D*M	0.58	0.34	0.97
	Consistency cut-off: 0.87			
	Solution coverage: 0.90			
	Solution consistency: 0.97			
Full membership: 63	~E*G	0.56	0.33	0.95
0.5-threshold: 40	+			
Non-membership: 7	D*M	0.58	0.34	0.95
	Consistency cut-off: 0.90			
	Solution coverage: 0.90			
	Solution consistency: 0.97			

Note
Simplifying assumptions: G→P; D→P; M→P; E→P.

Table A.4 Results for varying 0.5-thresholds in the GREEN set

	Intermediate solutions	Raw coverage	Unique coverage	Consistency
GREEN: reported results				
Full membership: 5	~E*G	0.56	0.32	0.95
0.5-threshold: 1	+			
Non-membership: 0	D*M	0.59	0.34	0.97
	Consistency cut-off: 0.85			
	Solution coverage: 0.90			
	Solution consistency: 0.97			
GREEN: alternative results				
(Crisp set)	~E*G	0.56	0.32	0.97
	+			
	D*M	0.59	0.35	0.97
	Consistency cut-off: 0.92			
	Solution coverage: 0.91			
	Solution consistency: 0.98			

Note
Simplifying assumptions: G→P; D→P; M→P; E→P.

Table A.5 Results for varying 0.5-thresholds in the ELECTIONS set

	Intermediate solutions	Raw coverage	Unique coverage	Consistency
ELECTIONS: reported Results				
Full membership: 100	~E*G	0.56	0.32	0.95
0.5-threshold: 365	+			
Non-membership: 730	D*M	0.59	0.34	0.97
	Consistency cut-off: 0.85			
	Solution coverage: 0.90			
	Solution consistency: 0.97			
ELECTIONS: alternative results				
Full membership: 100	~E*G	0.59	0.33	0.93
0.5-threshold: 250	+			
Non-membership: 730	D*M	0.59	0.33	0.97
	Consistency cut-off: 0.78			
	Solution coverage: 0.91			
	Solution consistency: 0.95			
Full membership: 100	~E*G	0.53	0.13	0.96
0.5-threshold: 500	+			
Non-membership: 730	D*M	0.59	0.15	0.97
	+			
	M*G	0.63	0.04	0.97
	Consistency cut-off: 0.85			
	Solution coverage: 0.92			
	Solution consistency: 0.97			
Full membership: 100	~E*G	0.52	0.13	0.96
0.5-threshold: 600	+			
Non-membership: 730	D*M	0.59	0.15	0.97
	+			
	M*G	0.63	0.05	0.97
	Consistency cut-off: 0.85			
	Solution coverage: 0.92			
	Solution consistency: 0.97			

Note
Changes printed in bold. Simplifying assumptions: $G \rightarrow P$; $D \rightarrow P$; $M \rightarrow P$; $E \rightarrow P$.

Index

Numbers in *italics* denote tables.

Addington, Lynn A. 29–30
Advocacy Coalition Framework (ACF) 9, 24, 32
Aho, Pekka 133
Aktionsbündnis Winnenden (Germany) 124
Albert, Marie-Douce 139
Albright, Elizabeth A. 31
Altheide, David L. 2
Anderson, Craig A. 27
Anderson, John W. 150
Arzt, Ingo 127
Assemblée Nationale (France) 136, 138
Austria 65, 113, 116, 135, 139–43, 147, 158–60
Austrian Freedom Party (Austria) 141–2
Austrian People's Party (Austria) 140–2
Auvinen, Pekka-Eric 66, 129; *see also* rampage shootings: Jokela

Baber, Mary 111
Baumgartner, Frank 16, 20
Bélanger, Éric 45
Belgium 32, 47, 62, 65, 90, 147–51, 158–9
Bell, David S. 138
Berkol, Ilhan 149
Bill of Rights 109
Bird, Derrick 66, 113; *see also* rampage shootings: Cumbria
Birkland, Thomas A. 2, 9, 16, 20, 29, 42–3, 48, 50, 63, 169, 173
Böckler, N. 27
Boin, Arjen 9–10, 19, 25, 33, 47, 49, 173
Bondü, Rebecca 119
Bosbach, Wolfgang 126
Brändström, Annika 11, 31, 33, 47
Bricknell, Samantha 61
Bruce, John M. 23, 61

Budge, Ian 80
Bundestag (Germany) 88, 119–21, 123–5, 127
Bundesrat (Germany) 88, 116, 120–1
Bundesrat (Switzerland) 145
Bundesverfassungsgericht (Germany) 123–4
Bündnis 90/Die Grünen (Germany) 88, 117, 120, 122, 124–5, 127
Burns, Ronald 29, 43

Cameron, David 81, 114
Campbell, Duncan 112
Canada 27, 30, 53
Capano, Giliberto 12, 175
Caren, Neal 69
Carter, Helen 113
Casciani, Dominic 113
Ceaux, Pascal 137
Centre Party (Finland) 130
Champion, Gail 111
Chirac, Jacques 136–8
Christian Democratic People's Party (Switzerland) 146
Christian Democratic Union/Christian Social Union (Germany) 121, 123–4, 126
Chyi, Hsiang I. 29, 48
Clegg, Nick 114
Cohen, Michael, D. 16, 19
Cohen, Stanley 29, 43
Columbine massacre 2, 64, 118
consensus democracy 116, 127–8, 140, 144, 159, 172–3
Conservative Party (UK) 112–14, 142
consistency score 72–3
Cortell, Andrew P. 42

184 *Index*

coverage score 73–4
Cronqvist, Lasse 69
Cukier, Wendy 111, 144
Cullen, Lord W. Douglas 110–13

Daily Telegraph, The 111
Davies, Caroline 114
de La Chesnais, Eric 136
Denmark 32, 65
Deutscher Jagdverband (Germany) 116
Deutscher Schützenbund (Germany) 116
Die Linke (Germany) 124; *see also Party of Democratic Socialism* (Germany)
de Vries, Michiel S. 31, 33
Donohue, John 4
Döring, Holger 80
Downs, Anthony 50–1, 119, 157, 169, 172; *see also* issue attention cycle
Duquet, Nils 147
Durn, Richard 65–6, 137; *see also* rampage shootings: Nanterre
Dutroux, Marc 32

Eldredge, Niles 20
Ellerbrock, Dagmar 116
Emmenegger, Patrick 22, 59, 174
Engeli, Isabelle 44
European Union (EU) 4, 62, 128, 140, 147
event severity: objective 42; perceived 43–4

Farley, Joshua 31
Feikert-Ahalt, Clare 113
Ferguson, Christopher J. 27
Finkenzeller, Roswin 117
Finland 62, 65, 128–36, 139, 147, 156, 158–60
firearm availability 28, 54–5, 109, 116, 128, 136, 143, 147, 158
Firearms Act of 1920 (UK) 109
Firearms Act of 1968 (UK) 109
Firearms (Amendment) Act of 1988 (UK) 110
Fleming, Anthony K. 2, 30, 53
Flemish Liberals and Democrats (Belgium) 150
Forum Waffenrecht 116, 119
Fox, James A. 30
framing 16–17, 19, 25–6, 28–9, 33, 48–9
France 65, 87, 135–9, 161
Frankfurter Allgemeine Zeitung (Germany) 127
Free Democratic Party (Germany) 121, 126
Free Democratic Party (Switzerland) 146

Frymer, Benjamin 29
fuzzy set Qualitative Comparative Analysis (fsQCA) 3–5, 67–76, 79–106

Gamson, William A. 50
Ganghof, Steffen 128
Gautsch, Johann 66, 140–1; *see also* rampage shootings: Mauterndorf
Geddes, Barbara 22, 59
Germany 21, 27–8, 33, 62–5, 81, 87, 89, 113, 115–28, 130, 136, 150, 158
Giugni, Marco 50
Godwin, Marcia L. 30
Goertz, Gary 74
Grabherr, Silke 144
Great Britain 28, 33, 50, 54, 62, 65, 91, 109–16, 121–2, 124, 132, 147, 158–9
Green League (Finland) 130, 134
Green Party (Austria) 81, 91, 141–2
Green Party (Switzerland) 145–6
Grofman, Bernard 68
Guardian, The 111, 115
gun control: party positions on **46**; *Gun Control Network* 115
gun culture 54
gun ownership *see* firearm availability
Gundel, Stephan 25

Haider-Markel, Donald P. 2, 44
Halbrook, Stephen P. 143
Hall, Peter A. 54
Hallikainen, Ville 128
Hamilton, Thomas 66, 110; *see also* rampage shootings: Dunblane
Harding, David J. 1, 29, 169
Harter, Susan 27
Hawdon, James 29, 43
Helsingin Sanomat (Finland) 131
Hepburn, Lisa M. 28, 54
Hofstadter, Richard 54
Holkeri, Harri 134
Hollande, François 138
Hollenstein, Pia 146
Holmlund, Anne 130, 132–3
House of Commons (UK) 116
Howard, John 61
Hungerford shooting 53–4, 62, 110, 113

Immergut, Ellen M. 52–3
incrementalism 17–18
Independent, The 111, 115
Interessengemeinschaft Liberales Waffenrecht in Österreich (IWÖ) (Austria) 139, 143

Index   185

International Crime Victims Survey
(ICVS) 109, 116, 128, 139, 143, 147
INUS conditions 71, 97, 102
issue attention cycle 50–1, 115, 119–20,
122, 125, 139, 157, 172; *see also*
Downs, Anthony
issue ownership 44–5
Italy 62, 65

Japan 2, 28
Jensen, Carsten 31–2, 173
John, Peter 21
Jones, Bryan D. 16, 20
Joslyn, Mark R. 2, 44
Jospin, Lionel 136, 138

Käppner, Joachim 127
Karp, Aaron 2, 110, 112–13, 115, 139
Keeler, John T.S. 42
Keine Mordwaffen als Sportwaffen!
(Germany) 124–5
Kennedy, John F. 30
Kiilakoski, Tomi 27
Kingdon, John W. 18–19
Kiss, Paul 142
Kister, Kurt 119
Kitschelt, Herbert P. 50
Klima, Viktor 142
Klingemann, Hans-Dieter 80
Knill, Christoph 12, 23, 174
Kopel, David B. 144
Koschyk, Hartmut 119
Krach, Wolfgang 118
Kretschmer, Tim 27, 66, 87, 122; *see also*
rampage shootings: Winnenden
Krug, Etienne G. 28

Labour Party (UK) 91, 102, 112–13
Lamprecht, Günter 117
Lang, Jo 146
Langman, Peter 131
Lankford, Adam 2, 28, 170
Lawrence, Regina G. 2, 29, 43, 48, 169
Leary, Mark R. 27
Leibacher, Friedrich 1, 27, 65–6, 144; *see
also* rampage shootings: Zug
Lépine, Marc 27
Leuffen, Dirk 136
Levin, Jack 1, 27, 169
Liberal Democrats (UK) 81, 112, 114
Liberal Reformist Party (Belgium) 150
Liem, Marieke 128
Lijphart, Arend 52–3, 109, 128, 140, 172
Lilly, J. Robert 54, 109

Lindblom, Charles E. 17
Lindström, Kauri 81, 83, 132
Lodge, Martin 31, 33, 42
Lott, John R. 4, 13
Lowi, Theodore J. 22

Mackie, John L. 71
Maesschalck, Jeroen 31–2
Mahoney, James 54, 72
Major, John 112
majoritarian democracy 53, 116
Malcolm, Joyce L. 111
March, James G. 54
Marx, Axel 67
mass media *see* media
May, Peter J. 20
media: attention towards gun laws in
Germany *63*; as drivers of moral panics
43–4
Mellor, David 112, 156
Merkel, Angela 123
Merki, Martin 146
Mintrom, Michael 19
Mooney, Christopher Z. 23
moral panic 29, 43
Morris, Nigel 114–15
Mucciaroni, Gary 19
multiple streams approach (MSA) 18–20
Muschert, Glenn W. 10, 27–30, 48

Nathanson, Constance A. 54
National Coalition Party (Finland) 130
Nationalrat (Austria) 141–2
necessity 70
Newman, Katherine 10, 27–8
Nohrstedt, Daniel 8, 21, 24–5, 31–2, 42,
175

Oksanen, Atte 27, 83, 129, 132–3
Open Society Institute 61
Overview of cases *66*

Park, Sung-Yeon 29
Parker, Susan 1, 110
partisan cleavage 44–8
Party of Democratic Socialism (Germany)
121; *see also Die Linke* (Germany)
Pavlovian politics 33, 42
Pearston, Ann 113
Peters, Rebecca 2
Petrocik, John R. 54
Peyerl, Martin 65–6, 117; *see also*
rampage shootings: Bad Reichenhall
Pierson, Paul 8, 54

186 Index

Pilger, John 112
policy change: conceptualization 12–3; direction of 12–3; theoretical expectations on 48–55
politicization: conceptualization 11–2; necessary conditions for 89–92; sufficient conditions for 98–102; summary of the findings on (non)-politicization 103; theoretical expectations on 41–8
Prindle, David F. 21
problem definition 19, 49
prolegal e.V. 116
pro Tell (Switzerland) 147
punctuated equilibrium framework (PEF) 20–1, 32, 64

Radmacher, Sabine 65–6, 125; *see also* rampage shootings: Lörrach
Raffarin, Jean-Pierre 138
Ragin, Charles C. 3, 64–7, 73–3, 85
Raittila, Pentti 129
rampage shooting: Aarhus 65, 81, 89, 95; Antwerp 148–51; Bad Reichenhall 117–19; Bogogno 89, 95; conceptualization 8–11; Cumbria 113–15; Dunblane 110–13; Erfurt 119–22; Euskirchen 64–5, 88–9, 94–5, 117; Jokela 129–31; Kauhajoki 131–5; Lörrach 125–8; Mauterndorf 140–3; Nanterre 137–9; Solliès-Pont/Cuers 81, 87–9, 95, 97, 105, 161, 171; Tours 85, 89; Winnenden 122–5; Zug 144–7
Reagan, Ronald 30
Rehn, Elisabeth 134
Rey-Bellet, Corinne 145
Riding, Alan 137
Rihoux, Benoît 67
Rochefort, David A. 48–9
Roth, Claudia 125
Rowe, Mark 115
Ryan, Michael 110

Saari, Matti Juhani 66, 131; *see also* rampage shootings: Kauhajoki
Sabatier, Paul A. 8–9
Sarkozy, Nicolas 138
Sartori, Giovanni 8
Savage, Jenna 27, 30
Scharpf, Fritz W. 52
Schäuble, Wolfgang 124
Scheithauer, Herbert 119
Schildkraut, Jaclyn 3, 21, 29–30, 54, 169
Schily, Otto 117, 121

Schlögl, Karl 141
Schneider, Carsten Q. 3, 59, 67–8, 70–1, 73, 82–3, 85
Schröder, Gerhard 120
Schwaab, Jean J. 146
scope conditions 59–63
set calibration 82–6
Siaroff, Alan 52–3, 109, 128, 140, 172
Simon, Herbert A. 17
Skaaning, Svend-Erik 73, 83
Snowdrop Campaign 50, 112–13, 115, 124
Social Democratic Party (Austria) 140–2
Social Democratic Party (Germany) 88–9, 91, 117, 120–2, 124
Social Democratic Party (Switzerland) 145–6
societal mobilization 50–1
Soldt, Rüdiger 122, 125
Spitzer, Robert J. 13, 23, 54, 61
Squires, Peter 54, 82, 110, 113
Steinhäuser, Robert 66, 119; *see also* rampage shootings: Erfurt
Stoisits, Terezija 141–2
Stone, Deborah A. 26, 48–9
Süddeutsche Zeitung (Germany) 127
sufficiency 70–1
SUIN conditions 71–2
Supp, Barbara 87
Swedish People's Party (Finland) 130
Swiss People's Party (Switzerland) 146
Sweden 32
Switzerland 1, 65, 116, 128, 135, 140, 143–7, 158–60

Tabermann, Johannes 131
tageszeitung (Germany) 127
Tanner, Jari 131
Tatalovich, Robert 23, 174
Tedmanson, Sophie 129
Thelen, Kathleen 54
Times, The 110–11
theoretical expectations: policy change and stability 48–55; politicization 41–8; summary of **55**
Thomson, Stuart 2, 110, 112
Travis, Alan 113
True, James L. 30
Truscheit, Karin 89
Tsebelis, George 52, 144

United Kingdom *see* Great Britain
United States of America 2, 13, 17, 26, 28, 30–1, 33, 35, 50, 53–4, 60–1, 135–6, 144, 160, 160–70

Väliverronen, Jari 131, 134
van Dijk, Jan 109, 116, 128, 136, 139, 143, 147
Vanhanen, Matti 130, 133, 156
van Themsche, Hans 1, 66, 148; *see also* rampage shootings: Antwerp
Verhofstadt, Guy 150
Verlinden, Stephanie 1, 28, 169
Vink, Maarten P. 70
Vizzard, William J. 18
Vlaams Belang (Belgium) 148–50
Vogel, Bernhard 124
Voss, Martin 42

Waffen weg! 143
Wagemann, Claudius 3, 60, 67, 70–1, 73, 82–3, 85

Wainwright, Martin 113
Walgrave, Stefaan 31–3, 47, 50
Walker, Henry A. 60
Webster, Duncan 110
Weible, Christopher M. 8–9, 21, 24–5, 175
Westminster model 109, 159; *see also* majoritarian democracy
Wieland, Wolfgang 125
Williams, Adam 110
Williams, Russell A. 31–2
Wilson, Harry L. 61
Wilson, James Q. 23–4
Wittneben, Bettina B.F. 42
Wood, Robert S. 31
Worrall, John L. 42

Ybarra, Michele L. 27

Taylor & Francis eBooks

Helping you to choose the right eBooks for your Library

Add Routledge titles to your library's digital collection today. Taylor and Francis ebooks contains over 50,000 titles in the Humanities, Social Sciences, Behavioural Sciences, Built Environment and Law.

Choose from a range of subject packages or create your own!

Benefits for you
- Free MARC records
- COUNTER-compliant usage statistics
- Flexible purchase and pricing options
- All titles DRM-free.

REQUEST YOUR FREE INSTITUTIONAL TRIAL TODAY

Free Trials Available
We offer free trials to qualifying academic, corporate and government customers.

Benefits for your user
- Off-site, anytime access via Athens or referring URL
- Print or copy pages or chapters
- Full content search
- Bookmark, highlight and annotate text
- Access to thousands of pages of quality research at the click of a button.

eCollections – Choose from over 30 subject eCollections, including:

Archaeology	Language Learning
Architecture	Law
Asian Studies	Literature
Business & Management	Media & Communication
Classical Studies	Middle East Studies
Construction	Music
Creative & Media Arts	Philosophy
Criminology & Criminal Justice	Planning
Economics	Politics
Education	Psychology & Mental Health
Energy	Religion
Engineering	Security
English Language & Linguistics	Social Work
Environment & Sustainability	Sociology
Geography	Sport
Health Studies	Theatre & Performance
History	Tourism, Hospitality & Events

For more information, pricing enquiries or to order a free trial, please contact your local sales team:
www.tandfebooks.com/page/sales

The home of Routledge books

www.tandfebooks.com